SOAKING THE MIDDLE CLASS

Suburban Inequality and Recovery from Disaster

Anna Rhodes and
Max Besbris

Russell Sage Foundation
New York

The Russell Sage Foundation

Library of Congress Control Number: 2022934194

Soaking the Middle Class is about many families recovered from Hurricane Harvey. The book focuses on households in Friendswood, Texas, a middle-class suburb of Houston, because places like Friendswood are becoming more vulnerable to climate-related disasters. How does this vulnerability play out? Presumably a middle-class, well-resourced community like Friendswood would be able to recover quickly. But as middle-class places have become more vulnerable, they have also become more unequal, with more households facing financial precarity and downward mobility. How households in places like Friendswood recover is therefore increasingly central to understanding stratification in the United States. As the authors show, the recovery process amplifies existing inequalities instead of reducing them, encourages staying in risky places instead of fostering mobility away from them, and ultimately increases divisions between neighbors, making middle-class suburbs like Friendswood less cohesive and less resilient.

ISBN 9780871547163 (paperback) | ISBN 9781610449168 (ebook)

The paper used in this publication meets the minimum requirements of American National Standard for Information Sciences—Permanence of Paper for Printed Library Materials. ANSI Z39.48-1992.

Text design by Suzanne Nichols.

RUSSELL SAGE FOUNDATION
112 East 64th Street, New York, New York 10065
10 9 8 7 6 5 4 3 2 1

Contents |

Illustrations |

About the Authors |

ANNA RHODES is assistant professor of sociology at Rice University.

MAX BESBRIS is assistant professor of sociology at the University of Wisconsin–Madison.

Acknowledgments |

FIRST AND FOREMOST, we'd like to thank all of the people in Friendswood who graciously shared their time and stories with us. To write this book, we asked our respondents to talk about personal and often quite distressing experiences. Their incredible openness made this project possible. This book is for them.

For critical and helpful comments on various parts of the manuscript, we thank Jennifer Bouek, Christina Cross, Kelley Fong, Anna Glass, Hope Harvey, Eric Klinenberg, Elizabeth Korver-Glenn, Casey Stockstill, the Rice University Qualitative Methods working group, and our reviewers. Each offered comments that pushed this book forward in important ways. For research assistance, thank you to Jean Aroom, Galo Falchettore, Marbella Eboni Hill, Bethany Lewis, Maximilien Chong Lee Shin, Katie Winograd, and the students in our undergraduate qualitative analysis class.

A very big thank-you to Jim Elliott, who not only provided support and feedback at multiple stages of the project but also helped organize a book workshop where we received extremely helpful suggestions from Dominic Boyer, Rachel Kimbro, Kathleen Tierney, and Mary Waters.

Thank you to Suzanne Nichols for her support and editorial guidance. Through thoughtful, organized, and fast feedback, she shepherded this book to completion, and it is better in many ways because of her.

This project was generously supported by the Rice University Social Sciences Research Institute and by the Russell Sage Foundation. RSF also invited Max to be a Visiting Scholar to work on the book, and the time proved invaluable.

Some of the data presented in chapter 3 were originally published in Anna Rhodes and Max Besbris, "Best Laid Plans: How the Middle Class Make Residential Decisions Post-Disaster," *Social Problems* (July 17, 2021), DOI: https://doi.org/10.1093/socpro/spab026.

We'd also like to thank our families for their love and support.

Finally, writing a book with someone else is a gratifying experience. While academia often prizes independent scholarship, this book was possible only because we did it together. We are thankful for the indelible research partnership generated by *Soaking the Middle Class*.

Introduction | Soaking the Middle Class

A FEW YEARS before Hurricane Harvey in 2017, Erin and Paul, a couple in their forties with young children, bought a two-story brick home in Friendswood, Texas, a suburb southeast of Houston. They chose Friendswood because it was close to family and provided an easy commute to Paul's office. Once they moved in, they described their new house as their "forever home" and planned to stay long-term.

Erin and Paul rarely thought about how close they lived to Clear Creek, a small river that runs through Friendswood and drains into Galveston Bay, until it overran its banks during Harvey and flooded their home with eighteen inches of water. Facing costly repairs, and with no flood insurance, they received help from more informal sources that proved vital to their recovery. Days after Harvey, when the floodwaters finally receded, friends, family, coworkers, and a large group of volunteers from their church all showed up to help Erin and Paul sort through their soaked belongings and remove wet drywall, insulation, and ruined flooring. Friends donated appliances and sold them building materials at deeply discounted rates, and a group of skilled volunteers from their church helped refinish their walls—work that would have cost tens of thousands of dollars.

Yet even with significant help and about $11,000 in direct aid from the Federal Emergency Management Agency (FEMA), Erin and Paul were unable to cover the full cost of repairing their home. So they applied for a loan from the Small Business Administration (SBA) and were approved to receive more than $100,000. Cognizant that the loan would be an added financial burden, they tried to keep costs down and avoided hiring a contractor. But doing most of the repairs themselves and hiring workers ad hoc for the more technically difficult jobs slowed the pace of recovery. Two years after the storm, their house remained unfinished, but they had to start paying back the loan.

Paul's work had also been affected by Harvey, and their household income was now less than it had been before the flood. Erin described

1

their financial circumstances two years after Hurricane Harvey, saying, "it's just tight." They were budgeting carefully and had made some tough choices to save money, including spending less on their children's education. While their family had largely returned to their pre-flood routines, Erin and Paul knew they would be dealing with the financial ramifications of Harvey for years to come.

Josie and Parker, a couple in their fifties, lived in a one-story ranch home with a large backyard that gradually slopes down to Clear Creek. They loved being able to watch birds and animals in the creek bed from their back porch, but they also knew that the creek posed a significant risk. Indeed, their house flooded twice before Hurricane Harvey—once in 1979 during Tropical Storm Claudette, and then again during Tropical Storm Allison in 2001.

The couple lived mostly on Parker's salary from his job as a construction company shift supervisor. Before Hurricane Harvey, they were having to budget carefully because they were paying down a fairly large home equity loan on the house. Even when they were extremely thrifty, they sometimes had to delay payment on different bills in order to make ends meet. So, despite the risk, Josie and Parker felt that they could not afford flood insurance. During Harvey, their home took on fifty-two inches of water.

Josie and Parker relied mostly on their family for help in the aftermath of the storm. A handful of close relatives showed up to remove their wet belongings and strip the walls down to the bare studs so that the house could dry out. Josie and Parker received $32,000 from FEMA, but they were denied an SBA loan. The FEMA assistance was not nearly enough to cover the cost of their home repairs, so Parker took all of the funds out of his 401(k) retirement account to help make up the difference. Josie was thankful that they both had some construction knowledge and could save money by doing nearly all of the work themselves. But this meant progress was slow. They lived paycheck to paycheck and bought rebuilding supplies only when they could afford them.

Two years after Hurricane Harvey, they still had several major repairs to complete, including work on their kitchen and floor installations. Parker worried about their finances. He said that they had "no money to fall back on" should another shock occur—a health care emergency, the loss of his job, another flood. Even though home prices in their neighborhood rebounded relatively quickly after Harvey, Josie and Parker were not in a position to benefit since they had not completed their repairs. With no savings and an unfinished house, Josie and Parker felt stuck. Hurricane Harvey had made their lives far more precarious and their future more uncertain.

Gina and Derek, a retired couple in their seventies, lived not far from Josie and Parker, but they were in a very different position from their neighbors after their home flooded with eight inches of water during Harvey. Two years later, they were in fact better off financially than they had been before the storm.

Gina and Derek owned a large two-story home, which they purchased in the late 1980s. When they moved to Friendswood, they looked for a home that had not flooded during Tropical Storm Claudette in 1979, figuring that if a property stayed dry then, it "was considered to be safe forever." They also had flood insurance. For years, Gina and Derek had no flooding problems as they raised their children, volunteered with their church and the local schools, and attended many of Friendswood's annual parades and civic events. They loved the "close-knit community" and, after living there for nearly thirty years, had a strong set of nearby social ties. They had also paid off their home in full and were looking forward to enjoying the space in their retirement for projects, gardening, and visits from their grandchildren.

As Gina and Derek navigated the long process of recovering from Hurricane Harvey, having flood insurance made all the difference. They received a payout of $180,000, which enabled them to purchase supplies and pay for a contractor to complete most of the repairs. Since Derek was retired, he also had the time to do some of the repair work himself. In the end, they spent less than their insurance payout on repairs and replacing belongings. As Derek said, "We made money on the deal." Not only did they have insurance money left over, but they also ended up with a beautifully refinished home that Derek told us looked better than when they first purchased it. Just two years after the flood, with their repairs completed, they were certain that they could sell their house for more than its pre-flood value. Although the recovery process had not been easy by any stretch, Hurricane Harvey actually improved Gina and Derek's finances.

Soaking the Middle Class is about how Gina and Derek, Josie and Parker, Erin and Paul, and many other families like them recovered from Hurricane Harvey. The book focuses on households in Friendswood, Texas, a middle-class suburb of Houston, because places like Friendswood are becoming more vulnerable to climate-related disasters. How does this vulnerability play out? Presumably a middle-class, well-resourced community like Friendswood would be able to recover quickly. But as middle-class places have become more vulnerable, they have also become more unequal, with more households facing financial precarity and downward mobility. How households in places like Friendswood recover from disaster is therefore increasingly central to understanding stratification in the United States. As we will show, the recovery process amplifies existing inequalities instead of reducing them, encourages people to stay in risky places rather than move away from them, and ultimately increases divisions between neighbors, making middle-class suburbs like Friendswood less cohesive and less resilient.

CLIMATE CHANGE: A GROWING THREAT TO MIDDLE-CLASS PLACES

In 2017, three of the five costliest storms since the 1980s hit the United States within a matter of months. Hurricane Harvey, Hurricane Irma, and Hurricane Maria each caused tens of billions of dollars in damage. Hurricane Harvey was the biggest of them all. The National Oceanic and Atmospheric Administration (NOAA) conservatively estimated that Harvey caused $125 billion worth of direct damage, which made it second only to Hurricane Katrina as the costliest hurricane in U.S. history.[1]

The *Texas Tribune* described Harvey as "a climate change harbinger . . . a sign of things to come as the earth warms."[2] And in 2021 the United Nations' Intergovernmental Panel on Climate Change (IPCC)—a body with 195 member nations created to provide policymakers with regular scientific assessments—confirmed that "many changes in the climate system become larger in direct relation to increasing global warming." Among the changes to the environment outlined in the report, the IPCC included "heavy precipitation" and the "proportion of intense tropical cyclones."[3] Researchers have consistently documented the escalating severity and scope of climate-related disasters as global temperatures continue to rise.[4] Specifically, as a result of warming in the Atlantic, hurricanes and tropical storms are wetter (producing more rainfall) and slower (more likely to hover in place instead of moving quickly across a particular trajectory).[5]

As a wet, slow-moving cyclone, Harvey was incredibly devastating in the Houston metropolitan region not because of especially powerful winds or storm surge but because it stalled in place for days, pouring trillions of gallons of rainwater into bayous, streams, and floodplains.[6] This extreme rainfall—over sixty inches in parts of the region—remains the highest total of any storm in the United States since reliable record-keeping began in the late nineteenth century. The immense amount of water led to historic flooding. As the climate continues to change, more storms will look like Harvey and flooding across the United States (and the world) is only expected to get worse.[7] Communities that were previously safe will take on more and more water.[8]

The growing vulnerability of communities, however, is not driven simply by the changing scope and intensity of disasters. Indeed, vulnerability also has "social roots," produced by society's interaction with the environment.[9] In other words, viewing disasters solely as "natural" limits our understanding of all the factors contributing to their devastating effects. The scholar Dennis Mileti titled his classic book *Disasters by Design* to emphasize that the decisions made at multiple levels—individual, community, societal—create the conditions for damage and loss from disasters.[10] The consequences of Harvey in the Houston metro region are a prime example. Much of the city and surrounding suburbs are built on drained marshland; according to one *Houston Chronicle* article, "there shouldn't even be a city here."[11] Houston has also grown rapidly in recent decades: in 1960 the metropolitan-area population was just over one million, and by 2017 it was slightly under six million.[12] Hurricane Harvey was so devastating and costly because massive amounts of development in a region extremely prone to flooding put more people and structures at risk. More than thirty thousand people were displaced by the floodwaters, and the storm damaged more than two hundred thousand homes and businesses.[13]

Broadly, poor and non-White households and places are disproportionately affected by disasters as a result of various forces, including environmental racism and residential segregation, that have caused poor communities and communities of color to be more frequently situated in vulnerable locations.[14] Although this was true of Harvey as well, the storm's scope and slow movement across the region caused so much rain that households spanning Houston's social geography—from ritzy waterfront properties to homes in modest subdivisions, from middle-class suburbs to poor inner-city neighborhoods—found themselves underwater.[15] As the scale and severity of climate-related disasters continue to increase, the geographic scope of their impact will also grow, affecting more middle-class and affluent places and raising broader questions about how different kinds of communities deal with fallout after major ecological shocks.[16] Put another way: climate change is altering the physical risks of middle-class communities, but we know little about how these communities are responding.[17] And so, in this book, we analyze how residents of Friendswood, Texas—a White, middle-class, suburban town outside of Houston— navigated recovery in the wake of Hurricane Harvey.

CONCEPTUALIZING THE MIDDLE CLASS

Understanding middle-class recovery after disaster first requires defining the middle class, but as the sociologist Mary Pattillo has noted, the middle class is "a notoriously elusive category."[18] Here we review three ways in which scholars tend to conceptualize the middle class. First is a largely structural approach in which middle-class status is defined by attributes like income and relative economic position; middle-class people are neither wealthy nor poor. A second approach highlights the importance of culture, arguing that the middle class is defined by distinct behaviors, consumption habits, and dispositions. And finally, various scholars have shown that place and class are deeply intertwined. American cities are highly spatially stratified, and so middle-class status can also be determined by neighborhood of residence. In other words, some places are middle-class, and living in them grants residents middle-class status.

The first structural approach to defining class is perhaps the most common. It uses socioeconomic factors such as income, occupation, and education to determine class position. The Pew Research Center defines middle-income Americans as those "whose annual household income is two-thirds to double the national median."[19] In 2017, the year Hurricane Harvey hit, the median household income in the United States was $61,372.[20] So according to Pew's definition, middle-class households made between $40,914 and $122,744 for the year. Although income-based definitions can create seemingly clear boundaries for membership in the middle class, the best method for setting these boundaries remains a point of debate. Different approaches produce varying assessments of class status.[21] Furthermore, some scholars have sought to differentiate subgroups within the middle class itself, creating categories like upper-middle and lower-middle class.[22] For example, Brookings Institution scholar Richard Reeves describes the upper-middle class as households in the top fifth of the income distribution excluding the top 1 percent.[23]

The inclusion of additional factors like education and occupation further nuances the structural determination of class membership, though they sometimes yield more stable applications since the income of an individual or household can fluctuate.[24] More recently, scholars and politicians concerned with inequality have pushed for greater consideration of household wealth in determining class status, in part because wealth can be protective against downward mobility. Indeed, in the context of an emergency or unexpected event like a climate-related disaster, wealth can help households maintain their financial stability. And so, in *Soaking the Middle Class*, we examine wealth, particularly housing value, as an important component of households' recovery, in addition to looking at incomes, occupations, and levels of education in defining Friendswood as a middle-class community.

There are also cultural meanings associated with class position. Social scientists pay attention to these shared ideas about what it *means* to be middle-class because they motivate certain behaviors.[25] For example, in the United States, being middle-class is tied to particular forms of consumption, like homeownership.[26] Membership in the middle class can also be defined by the "normative judgments" that others make about individuals' behaviors and tastes.[27] In her study of a Black middle-class community, Pattillo shows that middle-class homeowners who live in proximity to poor households often try to distinguish themselves from their less affluent neighbors by engaging in different public activities and uses of space.[28] Class status in this way can be both relational and oppositional. The sociologist Karyn Lacy similarly argues that "social identities . . . should become a standard component of our definition" of the middle class and that middle-class people have a "toolkit" they draw on to signal their social position.[29] This toolkit is developed early in life as middle-class parents teach their children to interact with institutions such as schools in particular ways that ultimately yield advantages and material benefits.[30]

Class also interacts with other identities in ways that matter for how people signal their class position. Black middle-class suburban residents, for example, consciously avoid activities and behaviors that might reify stereotypes that "to be black is to be poor."[31] Generally, a cultural approach to defining the middle class draws attention to the ways in which individuals manage their class status, how class status is signaled and perceived, and how middle-class individuals make efforts to not be perceived as poor. Indeed, as the journalist and activist Barbara Ehrenreich argues, "the fear of falling" out of the middle class—the anxiety and shame of being identified as poor or, more precisely, *not* middle-class—shapes middle-class households' consumption habits and how they spend their time.[32]

Ideas about what is appropriate behavior for the middle class may be particularly important in understanding recovery from disaster because recovery necessitates receiving help from both formal sources, like the government, and informal sources, like community groups and social networks. Notions of independence and self-sufficiency that go along with middle-classness can condition how flooded households seek aid.[33] So, in *Soaking the Middle Class* we pay close attention to when, why, and how households affected by Harvey asked for and accepted help.

While we draw on elements of structural and cultural conceptualizations of the middle class in this book, we also want to highlight the extent to which residence in middle-class communities can lead to assumed class status. Pattillo argues that "people talk about class in geographic terms, delineating a hierarchy of places rather than of incomes or occupations."[34] In other words, someone is deemed to be middle-class not simply by how much is in their bank account or by what their job title is, but also by where they live. There is a strong association, for example, between middle-class status and living in the suburbs.[35] Middle-class places afford residents access to certain kinds of institutions that affirm middle-classness. In schools, places of worship, civic groups, workplaces, and organized recreational activities, neighbors of seemingly similar class positions come together and engage in ways that perpetuate middle-class identities and lifestyles.

Importantly, place-based conceptualizations also highlight the racialized nature of middle-classness. Residential segregation is extremely pronounced in the United States, and Black middle-class households are far more likely to live near disadvantaged households and neighborhoods than are their White counterparts.[36] Middle-classness and White space are bound up to such an extent that psychologists have found that people have a difficult time conceiving of Black middle-class neighborhoods as middle-class.[37] That is, stereotypes about Black neighborhoods as places for the poor are so ingrained that even when White people are told that a Black neighborhood is middle-class, they perceive it as similar to poor Black neighborhoods. Conversely, White neighborhoods—particularly suburban ones—are assumed to be middle-class because of their racial composition.[38]

The intertwining of race, place, and class may serve, however, to obscure within-community economic differences—what the sociologist Jennifer Sherman calls a willful "class blindness."[39] In fact, the economics of being middle-class have changed dramatically over the past fifty years. Middle-class households are increasingly financially precarious as living standards have declined, debt burdens have risen, and wages have stagnated.[40] As a result of increased debt, middle-class households suffer more financial distress and poorer mental health outcomes compared to affluent households than in the past and are more likely to experience bouts of poverty.[41] Broad changes in the economy—the types of jobs available, the growing necessity of higher education for getting a good job, the assault on unions, and the neoliberal consensus of cutting social safety net programs—have reduced middle-class household financial stability and intergenerational upward economic mobility.[42] As maintaining middle-class status has become more difficult, home value has become increasingly central to ensuring a stable financial life while, at the same time, homeownership has become more expensive, taking up larger portions of middle-class households' expenditures.[43]

All of these changes have led some middle-class places, even racially homogenous ones, to become more economically diverse.[44] It took far less to buy into and remain in a middle-class neighborhood in the past than it does today. Yet the cultural and place-based nature of middle-classness may hide these economic differences, since residents of middle-class places who take part in middle-class activities are assumed to be middle-class.

Recovery from disasters requires a great deal of capital and may lay bare the reality of a more economically diverse and precarious middle class. In *Soaking the Middle Class*, our look inside a seemingly homogenous middle-class community shows that even in a well-resourced place the disaster recovery process amplifies inequality between neighbors. We reveal how climate-related disasters like Hurricane Harvey further squeeze middle-class households and communities, contributing to the hollowing out of the middle class and the stratification of America's suburbs.

VARIATION IN RECOVERY FROM DISASTER

The sociologist Kathleen Tierney describes a community's resilience in the face of disaster as its ability "to absorb the impacts of external and internal system shocks without losing the ability to function, and failing that, to cope, adapt, and recover from those shocks."[45] For many middle-class White communities, resilience is tested relatively rarely compared to poor communities of color, which are disproportionately vulnerable to disasters and often do not receive adequate help during recovery.[46]

While a lack of resources can prohibit disadvantaged places from fully recovering after a disaster, middle-class White communities generally have high levels of social capital and a strong social infrastructure. Many middle-class individuals have the skills and time necessary to comply with what past research has shown are the onerous and rigid demands of disaster aid organizations like FEMA.[47] Middle-class places also tend to have higher levels of civic engagement and well-resourced local institutions like schools, churches, and businesses that can serve as points of contact and coordination during and after a disaster.[48] As such, we would expect middle-class White communities to be highly resilient. To put it simply, a largely White middle-class place like Friendswood presents a best-case scenario for disaster recovery.

However, given the growing economic variation and precarity within middle-class neighborhoods we outlined earlier, disasters seem likely to severely strain the finances of at least some households even in middle-class places. Decades of research have shown that middle-class households are in fact downwardly mobile in the wake of sudden, inimical shocks to their finances.[49] And climate-related disasters that damage homes may be especially harmful, since households in middle-class places have most of their wealth in their houses.[50]

Insurance thus becomes a key tool for middle-class households to protect wealth. After a disaster, the uninsured cannot rely on direct government aid to fully repair their homes. While FEMA does provide some cash to affected households, these funds are limited and residents are encouraged to look to their communities for help beyond what FEMA can offer.[51] The limited assistance that FEMA can provide makes local resources, social networks, and social infrastructure critical.[52] The assumption is that a particular household without the resources to fully recover on its own is likely embedded in a wider community that can collectively support it. Friendswood is seemingly such a place, with robust and well-resourced local organizations and longtime residents who know each other well. Yet even in a community with a strong social infrastructure, the extent to which residents are connected with local institutions and organizations can vary widely. Some have connections that can provide labor, home rebuilding supplies and expertise, free childcare, emotional support, or even cash, while others are more isolated. In other words, the presence of resources within a community does not necessarily guarantee that all households have sufficient access to those resources to recover.

DISASTER POLICY AND GROWING INEQUALITY

The federal government provides billions of dollars each year to communities, households, and businesses affected by disasters. Although this aid undoubtedly speeds recovery, it also has the seemingly paradoxical effect of amplifying inequality.

Using various measures, recent studies have shown that "inequality actually increases at a steeper rate in counties that receive more FEMA aid" along the lines of race, education, and homeownership.[53] After disasters, White, college-educated homeowners with high credit scores appear to benefit the most, with many actually growing their wealth, while Black and Latino households with lower credit and fewer assets lose wealth and are more likely to experience long-term financial hardship and even foreclosure.[54] The procedures for determining eligibility and aid allocation funnel greater resources to higher-income households in White, middle-class, and affluent communities. Disaster aid, like that provided by FEMA's Individuals and Households Program, privileges the restoration of property for homeowners and leaves renters with far less. In short, the ways in which current policies distribute aid after disaster enrich already advantaged households and places.[55] Sociologists refer to this as a "Matthew effect"—named for the biblical parable of talents in the Book of Matthew—whereby those with more money or status are better positioned to increase their advantages relative to those with less.[56]

But what does this process look like in a middle-class suburb with a fair amount of wealth and a strong social infrastructure? As we show, Harvey revealed existing inequalities among middle-class households within Friendswood, Texas, and relief policies exacerbated these differences, leaving the town more unequal than before the storm.

One of the main mechanisms driving this inequality was whether or not households had flood insurance. In 1968, the creation of the National Flood Insurance Program (NFIP) expanded the role of the government in facilitating the repair of flooded properties. The NFIP, which is operated by FEMA, underwrites flood insurance for homeowners so that, in the event of a flood, they will receive a payment that can be used to repair property and replace damaged belongings.[57] The NFIP's design is based on the assumption that restoring property will help protect homeowners' housing wealth.[58] Flood insurance is a critical financial backstop for homeowners in vulnerable places, but coverage is mandated only for homeowners whose property is in an area deemed high-risk by FEMA flood maps and who have a federally backed mortgage.[59] Yet recent flooding has not been contained to high-risk areas; "From 2014 to 2018, policyholders outside of high-risk flood areas filed over 40 percent of all NFIP flood insurance claims and required one-third of federal disaster assistance for flooding."[60] Such expansive exposure to flood risk reveals that FEMA flood maps are outdated. Without up-to-date flood maps, homeowners are left with few reliable tools for assessing their risk of flooding. Those who are not mandated to have flood insurance coverage are likely to find it especially challenging to judge their vulnerability and determine their need for coverage.[61]

In fact, less than 30 percent of households that flooded during Harvey were insured—and the damage to uninsured property was two to three times higher in dollar value than the damage to insured property.[62] Other recent storms like Irma and Florence mirrored Harvey in that the vast majority of affected households were not insured. This provides further warrant for examining middle-class communities that are increasingly vulnerable to climate-related disasters: many of these households may not know their risk and will not have insurance.

More broadly, insurance uptake is correlated with education, income, and home value: more affluent homeowners are more likely to get flood insurance.[63] In communities where risk is more difficult to assess, the wealthiest households buy coverage while many of those with tighter finances do not. This variation is key in middle-class communities, which have not historically been the most vulnerable to disasters but are now finding themselves underwater owing to the effects of climate change. As the scope of climate-related disasters grows, flood maps and other tools for helping residents determine risk must keep pace. If they do not, there will certainly be an increase in the proportion of disaster-affected residents who are uninsured.

In *Soaking the Middle Class*, we demonstrate how differences in insurance coverage create more inequality as recovery progresses. Insured households are eligible for payouts of up to $250,000 for structural damage to property and an additional $100,000 for damaged belongings. After

Harvey, households without insurance who received FEMA aid through the Individuals and Households Program could collect a maximum of only $33,300.[64] In other words, the maximum insurance payout was more than ten times larger than the maximum amount of FEMA aid for the uninsured. FEMA acknowledges that the aid available to uninsured households is not enough to cover the full costs of returning a home to its pre-disaster condition. To fill the gap in repair costs, uninsured households are eligible to apply to the Small Business Administration for low-interest home repair loans of up to $200,000 for property and an additional $40,000 to replace belongings.[65] Loans are not guaranteed, however, and if they do obtain a loan, homeowners will have a lien on their property until the debt is repaid.[66] Households without insurance therefore face a tough decision: take on new debt, pay for repairs from savings and other forms of financial assistance, or sell their flood-damaged home.

For insured homeowners like Gina and Derek who live in majority-White, middle-class communities, the long-term financial consequences of a disaster may be positive. Uninsured neighbors in the same community, however, such as Josie and Parker, may be unable to afford to complete necessary repairs. Those left with depleted savings and unfinished home repairs are at risk of downward mobility and are certainly more vulnerable to future shocks. Yet this new level of post-disaster inequality within communities may not be entirely visible. Indeed, it is relatively rare to know the state of a neighbor's finances. Inequality within the community may thus be largely hidden, visible only behind residents' closed doors and in their bank accounts.

Soaking the Middle Class is about a place where residents experienced the full spectrum of outcomes after Hurricane Harvey. We look at how households in Friendswood picked up the pieces, navigated recovery, and made decisions about the future. We highlight how a disaster and the policies aimed at helping households recover from it amplified inequality *even in a well-resourced community*. Despite all the advantages of living in Friendswood, as time has passed and differences in recovery have become more pronounced across households, community resilience has become much harder to achieve.[67] Some households are more financially prepared for future shocks, while others that have not fully recovered from Harvey are all the more vulnerable.[68] Taken together, these emerging inequalities will render the community as a whole less able to bounce back after the next disaster.

OUR STUDY

Hurricane Harvey made landfall on August 25, 2017. An astounding amount of rain fell on the Houston metropolitan region for three days straight, and we watched over the news and on social media as homes and businesses began to take on water. As scholars of residential decision-making, we both kept asking the same question in the aftermath of the storm: How do households in a middle-class community, whose primary source of wealth is likely in a home that has flooded, make the choice either to rebuild and return or to sell and move?

To answer this question we turned to FEMA's early reports of flooding across the Houston metropolitan area, looking for communities with a moderate median income where a considerable number of homes flooded. Then we drove to see these neighborhoods for ourselves. In some neighborhoods, FEMA's initial reports appeared to be incorrect—little flood damage was visible. We drove through other middle-class neighborhoods that had clearly suffered flood damage, but the moderate median income was a result of expensive single-family homes in proximity to more affordable multifamily apartments. We focused on identifying an area where most residents lived in single-family homes, since presumably all affected households experienced the flood in similar ways and faced the same types of recovery decisions. Moreover, in studying a relatively advantaged community—one where households would ostensibly have the resources to recover—we would be able to see what exactly it takes to get people back on their feet after a devastating climate disaster.

When we drove into Friendswood, we knew that we had found a place that fit the bill. Nearly all of the flooded properties were single-family houses. Residents were working hard to clear out their flooded homes, and there were piles of debris and wet belongings several feet high in the front yards of many houses.

Friendswood

Friendswood was originally founded in 1895 as a Quaker settlement.[69] Since early in its history, Friendswood has known the devastating effects of major storms. In 1900 the Galveston hurricane, which is still the deadliest storm in U.S. history, destroyed Friendswood's church and schoolhouse, and many residents' homes were badly damaged. The community rebuilt, and Friendswood remained a small farming town until the 1930s, when the growing oil industry started to draw more workers to the area.

Friendswood is located inland, about halfway between Houston and Galveston (figure I.1), but several creeks and tributaries pass through the town, the largest of which is Clear Creek. Clear Creek, a placid, slow-moving river that channels runoff from the southern part of the Houston metropolitan region into Galveston Bay, was part of what drew early settlers to the area: the waterway was large enough to be navigable and could be used to transport lumber and crops. Today the Clear

Figure I.1   Map of the Houston Metropolitan Area

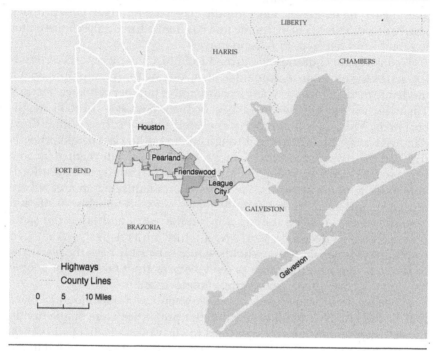

Source: U.S. Census Bureau 2017.

Creek watershed spans portions of four counties. Friendswood's location downstream from several large municipalities, including Houston, makes it highly susceptible to flooding, yet the proximity to Clear Creek did not stop the rapid development of subdivisions in Friendswood, starting in the 1960s.

In 1960 Friendswood officially incorporated, becoming the City of Friendswood, and the town increasingly served as a commuter suburb for Houston. In 1961 the National Aeronautics and Space Administration (NASA) chose a location in Clear Lake, just ten miles from Friendswood, for the Manned Spacecraft Center (now known as the Johnson Space Center). Many of NASA's new employees moved into the town, furthering local growth. Between 1950 and 1970, the population grew nearly fivefold, from fewer than one thousand residents to almost six thousand, as developers rapidly built new subdivisions in and around Friendswood. This growth has only continued, and by the time Hurricane Harvey hit

Friendswood in 2017 the community was home to nearly thirty-nine thousand people.

The City of Friendswood spans about twenty-one square miles, and most of the development that borders the creek is residential. In the aftermath of Hurricane Harvey, while nearly three thousand homes in the community were flooded, many parts of Friendswood stayed dry. In fact, about two-thirds of the houses in Friendswood did not flood. Most of the local schools and churches remained undamaged, and some served as shelters during the storm as well as places to organize volunteer efforts when the waters receded.

In 2017 the neighborhoods in Friendswood that border Clear Creek were more than 80 percent White and had median household incomes between $63,000 and $82,000—not far off from the median for the Houston metro area, which was a little more than $65,000.[70] The entire town of Friendswood—including those communities that do not border the creek—was close to 75 percent non-Hispanic White, with a slightly higher median income of $99,000. This figure reflects the fact that several of the subdivisions closest to the creek were some of the earliest developments in the late 1960s and early 1970s, when Friendswood first became increasingly attractive as a suburban destination. Compared to homes in neighborhoods that were developed more recently, these single-story ranch-style homes are typically smaller, more dated, and as a result more affordable than homes farther from the creek.

Although residents living close to Clear Creek speak about the pleasures of seeing birds and other wildlife daily, proximity to the water is not an amenity that has significantly driven up home values. In many places, waterfront properties are the most expensive, but this is not the case in Friendswood. Neither fishing nor swimming is encouraged in Clear Creek because of concerns about the quality of the water.[71] Additionally, the creek has overrun its banks and flooded nearby homes in the past. So, while Friendswood has always had many well-off households, the homes closest to the creek are not necessarily the largest, most expensive, or most sought after.

Over time Friendswood has become increasingly affluent, and as a result even residents who purchased the smaller homes along the creek are more likely to be white-collar professionals than in the past. From 1970 to 2017, in the neighborhoods bordering Clear Creek, the share of residents working in manufacturing declined from more than 18 percent to 11.5 percent, while the share of professional, educational, and health-care workers rose from 13.2 percent to more than 29 percent.[72] In 1970, when some of the subdivisions closest to Clear Creek were being completed, craftsmen and related workers were the fourth-largest occupational category in Friendswood. By 2017, however, no blue-collar occupation was in the top five. Moreover, about two-thirds of residents had some college education, and 10 percent had advanced degrees, up from only 41 percent and 8 percent, respectively, in 1970.[73] We further detail these changes and the differences in household finances within Friendswood in chapter 1 and show how they set the stage for the unequal aftereffects of Harvey.

Even as the community has grown and changed over the years, residents have consistently been attracted to Friendswood because of its "small-town feel," robust civic life, and well-regarded local schools. After its founding in the late nineteenth century, Friendswood was one of the few towns in the region to have a school building. Today Friendswood is served by two school districts. Clear Creek, a municipal boundary line dividing these two school districts, also separates Harris County and Galveston County. North of the creek, Friendswood households are residents of Harris County (which includes Houston) and are served by the Clear Creek Independent School District, which encompasses several other nearby suburbs. On the south side of the creek, Friendswood residents live in Galveston County and are served by the smaller Friendswood Independent School District. Although the districts vary in size, both have extremely good reputations, and in the 2017–2018 school year both districts received A ratings from the Texas Education Agency.[74]

Friendswood is also home to a robust group of around twenty churches as well as other civic organizations like the Rotary Club. The city regularly organizes holiday parades and other events, and families often talked about all the activities available around town for their children. In other words, even as Friendswood has grown, residents noted that it has not lost its sense of intimate community. Socioeconomically, racially, and culturally, Friendswood looks like a stereotypical middle-class suburb (though, as we discuss in chapter 1, this stereotype is less and less descriptive of the current reality in American suburbs). Residents described the community as idyllic before the storm — indeed, very few residents had anything negative to say about Friendswood.

Gathering Data after a Flood

In the first few weeks after Harvey, we volunteered at a local relief center organized by one of Friendswood's many churches. We sorted donations and helped flood-affected residents select cleaning supplies, basic toiletries, clothing, and food. The center was located in a building on Friendswood's main commercial street, and the church allowed FEMA to set up a disaster recovery center in another part of the same building. Flooded residents would walk in and wait to be seen by a FEMA representative, who would help them file or review their claims.

In those early days after the storm, the community was buzzing with recovery efforts. Residential streets were clogged with cars and trucks as volunteers helped homeowners sort through wet belongings, remove what was ruined, and take out carpet, sheetrock, and insulation—a process referred to as "mucking out." Teams of volunteers, organized by local schools, churches, and civic organizations, were working every day. The work was tiring, and the weather was hot and muggy. Volunteers drove around with coolers full of water and soft drinks, or they cooked and delivered meals, sometimes serving them warm from the backs of pickup trucks. It seemed like everyone was either helping or being helped.[75]

When we began volunteering and conducting initial observations in Friendswood, most flooded residents were still in the middle of mucking out their homes. Given the traumatic event that these residents had just survived, and the intensity of the mucking-out process in the first weeks after Hurricane Harvey, we delayed our formal interviews until six weeks after the storm. By then, most households had largely finished mucking out what was wet, but the studs inside their walls were often not yet dry enough to begin repairs. If they put up walls too quickly, mold might begin to grow.[76] So everyone was just waiting. And as they sat on their porches and in their front yards, many residents were happy to tell us their stories.[77] We met many flooded residents first by walking along the streets that bordered Clear Creek. An accurate list of all flooded households in Friendswood was not available in the immediate aftermath of Harvey, so we used multiple strategies to gather a nonrandom but heterogeneous sample of flooded households.[78] All names used throughout the book are pseudonyms, and many were chosen by our respondents themselves.

We sat on plastic chairs in homes with no walls and on back decks with uneven boards warped by floodwater. We sat on camping chairs in front yards, swatting away flies and mosquitoes that seemed to multiply exponentially around the piles of debris—some as high as six feet—that lined up along the streets. These piles contained nearly all of a house's contents—belongings collected by each resident over a lifetime. We sat in backyards surrounded by carefully laid out items (clothes, photos, important papers, family china) that people were hoping would dry in the sun so they could be salvaged. We sat in trailers parked in driveways that would serve as people's homes in the coming months. And we met flooded residents at the local coffee shop, where they could get away for a few hours from their wall-less homes and piles of belongings reminding them of the loss they had recently suffered.

Flooded residents were happy to share the information about our study and sometimes sent us down the street to knock on a flooded neighbor's door, saying, "Tell them I sent you." To ensure that we tapped into multiple social networks within the flooded neighborhoods, we also mailed letters to every home that flooded in two census tracts that border Clear Creek. This yielded several additional interview respondents who also connected us with people they knew. We volunteered with several local church and community groups and asked them to share our recruitment flyer and information with flooded residents. And one respondent posted our information in a Facebook group for residents of Friendswood whose homes flooded. These strategies helped us gather a sample of fifty-nine households.

Over a period of two years, we completed four waves of interviews.[79] All fifty-nine households were interviewed in the first wave. We stopped recruiting new households when we reached a point of saturation—that is, when we were hearing such similar narratives that further data collection was unlikely to reveal new patterns or processes. Of the original sample of fifty-nine flooded households, we interviewed thirty-eight prior to January 2018. Many of these early respondents had not yet received money through FEMA or insurance at the time of their initial interview, and so we conducted second interviews eight months after the flood with twenty-eight of these households to get updates on their finances. Around the one-year anniversary of the flood, in the fall of 2018, we contacted the full sample and conducted follow-up interviews with forty-seven of our original fifty-nine households. Then, around the second anniversary of the flood in the fall of 2019, we again contacted the full sample and interviewed forty-eight households, for a total of 182 interviews with flooded residents. We supplemented these with additional interviews with City of Friendswood and FEMA officials, as well as interviews with several local landlords and real estate agents. We also observed community events related to flooding and flood recovery efforts and attended multiple meetings held by city officials where issues related to recovery were discussed.

Out of our sample of fifty-nine households, the vast majority (over 80 percent) were White, reflecting the demographic composition of Friendswood. Our sample also included individuals ages twenty-six to seventy-six at all stages of life: single adults, families with young children who had recently purchased their first home, and older retirees who had lived in Friendswood for decades. More than 70 percent of our respondents were married, but the sample included single, divorced, and widowed individuals as well. Nearly 20 percent of our sample had an advanced degree, and more than 90 percent had at least some college. The majority were working full- or part-time, 20 percent were retired, and 20 percent were not employed; most of the unemployed respondents described themselves as stay-at-home mothers. The vast majority of our respondents also owned their flooded homes; only five out of the fifty-nine were renting when Harvey struck.[80] Respondents' homes took on between three and seventy-two inches of water; 80 percent of the sample experienced flooding of more than twelve inches. Meanwhile, only 52 percent of our respondents had flood insurance coverage (see table I.1). A year after the storm, only nine of the households had permanently moved out of their flooded house; the remaining fifty households chose to return to, reinvest in, and rebuild their properties. We detail our methods, site selection, sample, and interviews further in the methodological appendix.

SOAKING THE MIDDLE CLASS

Throughout the book, we address the themes of inequality and residential mobility in different ways. Largely, the chapters follow a chronological timeline. First, we outline the reasons why residents moved to Friendswood. These narratives often continued to animate residents' decision-making during recovery from Hurricane Harvey. We then describe the flood, how households evacuated their homes, and the damage they witnessed when they were finally able to return days later when the water receded. At this point, residents had to decide whether or not to repair their property or to move away. If they chose to stay and rebuild, they needed to marshal resources, ask friends and family for help, hire contractors, and apply for government assistance—activities that are not usually part of middle-class households' day-to-day lives. In other words, recovery is a novel, complex, and burdensome experience. We then examine the aid provided to affected households, looking at how help-seeking behaviors changed over time. As recovery wore on, we describe how various forms of inequality were exacerbated and emergent. Households with more resources before Hurricane Harvey tended to finish repairs faster, while others struggled to fully recover. Two years after the storm, everyone in Friendswood—both those who financially benefited from recovery and those facing greater financial precarity—had to assess and confront their vulnerability to future disasters.

In chapter 1, we explore residents' reasons for moving to Friendswood, and we trace how the kinds of households arriving in the community have shifted over time. As Friendswood has grown, new families are increasingly more affluent, more educated, and more likely to work in white-collar jobs. In other words, the composition of the "middle class" in Friendswood has changed. The community's residents now occupy quite heterogeneous socioeconomic positions, yet the suburban nature

Table I.1   Sample Characteristics

Variable	Percent	Mean	Range	Median
Age		50.32	26 to 76	
Sex				
Male	23.73			
Female	76.27			
Race				
White	83.05			
Hispanic	10.17			
Black	0			
Asian	0			
American Indian	1.69			
Other	5.08			
Marital status				
Single	13.56			
Married	71.19			
Divorced	6.78			
Widowed	8.47			
Number of children		2.23	0 to 6	
No children	15.25			
Income		$123,364	$10,000 to $750,000	$100,000
Education				
High school or GED	5.08			
Certificate	5.08			
Some college	23.73			
Associate's degree	8.47			
Bachelor's degree	37.29			
Professional degree	18.64			
Doctorate	1.69			
Employment status				
Full-time work	42.37			
Part-time work	8.47			
Self-employed	6.78			
Not employed	22.03			
Retired	20.34			
Monthly mortgage or rent		$1,081.25	$0 to $6,000	$950
Ownership status				
Own	91.53			
Rent	8.47			
Flood insurance				
Yes	52.54			
No	47.46			
Inches of flooding		31.46	3 to 72	

Source: Data from interviews.

and white-picket-fence feel of the town can obscure this variation. Despite these changes, households' reasons for moving to Friendswood have stayed the same. Friendswood was and still is attractive because of the highly regarded schools, affordable homes, community events and activities, and proximity to work, friends, and family. Middle-class residents moving into the suburbs are often seeking out a particular lifestyle, and residents told us that Friendswood offered a unique "small-town feel."

The same qualities that drew people to Friendswood also served to protect home values, even after Hurricane Harvey. Moreover, these qualities facilitated the formation of long-term plans for stability in Friendswood before Harvey. That is, most of the residents we spoke to had planned on living in Friendswood for many years, and these plans, as we show later in the book, motivated their decisions to stay and rebuild after the flood. However, the financial variation in residents' circumstances before the storm put them in very different starting positions as they began to recover.

In chapter 2, we turn our attention to residents' expectations before Harvey and their experiences of the storm itself. No one thought Harvey was going to flood their home, and many were unprepared—only 52 percent of our sample had flood insurance at the time of the storm. In general, residents believed that a lack of recent flooding (the last major flood events were during Tropical Storms Claudette in 1979 and Allison in 2001) meant that they were safe. Indeed, some residents had been told by their neighbors—and in some cases by their insurance agents—that the risk was low and so flood insurance was unnecessary. And without a clear sense of risk, those who were managing tight household budgets felt that flood insurance coverage was a low priority.

Relying on the past to predict the future, however, is clearly risky when climate change is quickly altering the size and scope of disasters. The floodwaters from Hurricane Harvey exceeded everyone's expectations, and residents were left scrambling to escape to local shelters. The floodwaters did not recede for days, and residents faced the challenge of finding longer-term temporary housing while they navigated the recovery process. During the search for places to stay, flooded residents' social networks became central sources of support. We describe what it was like for residents to return to their homes, see the damage, and imagine the challenges they would face in the coming months. In other words, we show just how devastating Harvey was, and what it was like for households realizing that they were in for a long process of recovery.

After returning to their properties and assessing the damage, residents had to make a decision about whether to leave Friendswood or repair their homes and return. This decision-making process is the subject of chapter 3. Middle-class households typically search for housing with an eye to long-term residence and are able to maintain a high level of stability. This chapter addresses what happens when these households are forced to make mobility decisions after exposure to a disaster and subsequent residential displacement. We show how residential mobility decisions—whether to stay and rebuild or move—were guided by households' preexisting residential plans. The majority of households decided to remain and rebuild their homes despite having the financial capacity to move and pressure from friends and family to relocate to a less vulnerable place. The households that stayed had long-term plans to remain in their homes before the flood, while the few who decided to move generally had well-defined plans to leave in the near future before the storm hit. The chapter highlights the importance of pre-storm expectations in understanding post-storm behaviors and reveals why, in general, households can be so reluctant to leave vulnerable places even if they have the financial resources to do so.

Chapter 4 turns to the long-term process of recovery from the storm as residents sought and received help once they decided to return to and rebuild their homes. This chapter highlights rapid changes over time in what we call the "local ecology of aid," or the help provided by community organizations, local institutions, and the social networks of community members. The local ecology of aid affected when and how flooded residents felt comfortable asking for help. In the immediate aftermath of the storm, it seemed to residents of Friendswood that everyone around them was either helping or being helped, and it was easy for flooded households to reach out to friends, family, and other members of the community when they needed something. But as the months went by volunteers disappeared and offers of help subsided. As the local ecology of aid changed, those in flooded households that were still in need began to feel less comfortable asking for help and thought that if they did, they would be stigmatized for not recovering more quickly. Those who, for various reasons, could not complete the majority of their repairs as fast as their neighbors found themselves in an environment where help was less and less available, even as their need persisted. In other words, help dried up before recovery was complete.

Chapter 5 delves into how patterns of inequality within Friendswood emerge over time. We revisit Erin and Paul, Josie and Parker, and Gina and Derek and look at several additional cases to examine the nuanced ways in which household finances, social networks, and residents' own construction knowledge and available time all came together to shape their recovery experience. As residents engaged with contractors, mortgage lenders, and insurance companies to complete and pay for repairs, we reveal how preexisting inequality across the community became more pronounced after Harvey. Although those without flood insurance received their FEMA aid quite quickly, the funds did not go far, and they were forced to take on debt or manage their repairs slowly, paycheck to paycheck. For many, repairing their homes in the aftermath of Hurricane Harvey would have lasting financial consequences; their financial precarity increased after they dipped into savings and retirement accounts in order to return to safe and habitable homes. In contrast, those with flood insurance and considerable pre-storm financial resources were able to treat Harvey as an opportunity: remodeling their homes to fit their tastes and sometimes even adding to their savings. Two years after the flood, Friendswood had become a patchwork: some houses were completely updated, and some still had no floors. Some households had fewer financial concerns while some were holding on by a thread.

Chapter 6 examines residents' understanding of risk as it shapes their future residential plans and their evaluations of the need for flood insurance. Even for the households that recovered quickly, Harvey was a traumatic event, and it revealed to everyone that Friendswood was vulnerable to flooding. Nevertheless, it was hard to make sense of the risk of continuing to live in a region poised to experience more climate-related disasters in the future. Many residents expressed confusion about how to assess their risk and how to evaluate the role of development, climate change, and local mitigation efforts in shaping that risk. Faced with this uncertainty, and after having navigated a long and arduous rebuilding process, most residents expressed increasingly contingent future residential plans. In other words, although they rebuilt and returned after Harvey, they said they would sell and move in the event of another flood. Their attachment to Friendswood became conditional on not having to recover again.

As climate change increases the scope and intensity of disasters, a broader set of places are vulnerable, including more middle-class communities. How will households in middle-class places respond to disasters, navigate recovery, and make choices about whether to stay or move? The residential decisions of the middle class have been, and will continue to be, highly consequential for the spatial patterning of inequality.[81] Less explored are the consequences of this growing inequality within neighborhoods and communities. How will places like Friendswood change as households within them grow further apart financially? How can we best help communities that will have increasingly different needs across households after a disaster? These questions are essential as places like Friendswood continue to get soaked.

Chapter 1 | The Changing Middle Class in Friendswood, Texas

IN *CRABGRASS FRONTIER*, a landmark study of suburbanization in America after World War II, the historian Kenneth T. Jackson wrote, "The dream of a detached house in a safe, quiet, and peaceful place has been an important part of the Anglo-American past and a potent force in the development of the suburbs."[1] Friendswood is characteristic of the type of suburban communities described by Jackson that grew rapidly in the mid-twentieth century. Less than thirty miles from downtown Houston, the town is close enough that many residents commute to the city for work. They return each evening and drive past single-family homes with manicured lawns on quiet residential streets. The community is known for its annual holiday parades, low crime rate, and well-respected public schools. Given all of these qualities, Friendswood repeatedly makes online lists like "The Best Suburbs to Raise a Family in Texas."

Much of Friendswood's growth occurred at a time when the federal government actively promoted suburban development and subsidized suburban homeownership for White families, while denying similar support to Black Americans.[2] The postwar explosion of the suburbs can be understood as a racial project using laws and regulations to *make* the suburbs — and to make them White.[3] During these years of rapid suburbanization, federally backed mortgages allowed even blue-collar White families to purchase suburban homes.[4] Put another way, the housing stock and the demographic composition of suburban communities like Friendswood are products of broader social, political, and economic forces that have made residential racial segregation a durable reality. Even as the United States has become more diverse since the 1970s, with rapid growth among Hispanic, Asian, and multiracial populations, racially isolated majority-White suburban communities have persisted. Many White suburban residents "continue to occupy a world where the vast majority of residents

24

are also White, despite the diversity explosion."[5] In Friendswood, nearly 75 percent of residents are non-Hispanic White, compared to just 37 percent throughout the Houston metropolitan area (figure 1.1). The vast majority of Friendswood residents who do identify as Hispanic or Latino also identify as White.[6]

In more recent decades, as the Houston region has grown—and grown more diverse—Friendswood's development has slowed. More than 72 percent of homes in Friendswood were constructed before 2000, in large part because the town has remained geographically small compared to nearby suburbs. Even after annexing several subdivisions in the 1980s, Friendswood encompasses just twenty-one square miles. And our respondents reported that Friendswood had retained its "small-town feel." They described children playing in the streets, regular attendance at municipal and church events, and active homeowners' associations (HOAs) that regulated the upkeep and maintenance of the housing stock.[7] When Hurricane Harvey hit, more than 83 percent of Friendswood's housing was detached single-family homes, and about 80 percent were owner-occupied with a median home value of around $256,000. For comparison, across the Houston metro, about 62 percent of housing is detached single units, and 60 percent are owner-occupied with a median home value of around $166,000.[8]

Despite being a largely White and generally advantaged place, Friendswood is somewhat socioeconomically diverse (figure 1.2). The same forces that encouraged suburbanization and segregation throughout most of the twentieth century also facilitated wealth accumulation and upward mobility for many White households. Development in Friendswood in the 1960s and 1970s attracted not only white-collar workers employed in Houston or at the Johnson Space Center but also blue-collar oil and gas industry workers, all of whom benefited from federal policies subsidizing home loans. This socioeconomic diversity has persisted, even if it is somewhat obscured by Friendswood's robust community life, large proportion of owner-occupied single-family homes, and racial homogeneity.[9]

Indeed, as the economy has shifted, what it means to be middle-class has changed. Since the 1960s, the cost of owning a house has risen faster than real earnings, so it takes more to afford residence in a place like Friendswood today than it did for past generations.[10] The households now moving in are more likely to be highly educated and to work professional jobs, and the housing stock in Friendswood reflects these changes. Houses from early periods of development are mostly single-story ranch-style homes, while those built in the 1980s or later are often two stories with brick facades and pools.

Figure 1.1   Map of Non-Hispanic White Population in Friendswood and Nearby Communities, 2019

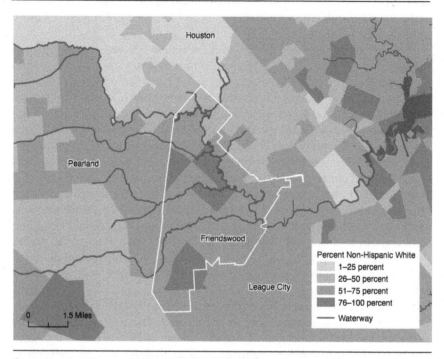

Source: American Community Survey, 2015–2019 (U.S. Census Bureau 2019b).

Today in Friendswood two neighboring households may both own their homes but have starkly different financial lives. One neighbor may be an elderly widow who lives on a fixed income from Social Security and whose husband worked a blue-collar job when they bought their home in the early 1970s with a loan from the Department of Veterans Affairs.[11] Next door the neighbors may be a young family who moved to Friendswood in the past ten years, with two parents earning high salaries from professional jobs. Both households live in a middle-class community and have access to all of the amenities that come with it, even though they are in vastly different financial positions.

When we examine the reasons residents moved to Friendswood, we find remarkable consistency across households at all income levels, occupations, and life stages regarding the town's appeal. Schools and proximity to work and other amenities were key, but residents also moved to

Figure 1.2   Map of Median Household Incomes in Friendswood
and Nearby Communities, 2019

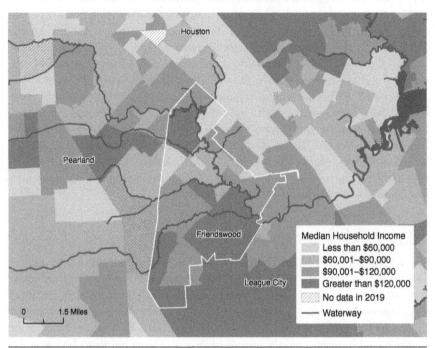

Source: American Community Survey, 2014–2018, 2015–2019 (U.S. Census Bureau 2018 and 2019a).

Friendswood because it felt familiar in terms of demographics, ambience, and geography.[12] Many of the younger residents moving into Friendswood grew up in the suburbs and were looking to raise their children in a similar environment. Residents were also attracted to the suburban ideal, which, whether stated explicitly or not, continues to offer status and material benefit through the accrual of housing value, especially in Whiter communities.[13]

Put another way, we show that moving to Friendswood is an act of social reproduction whereby families are leveraging their existing economic and racial advantages to buy into a place that will yield more advantages in the future. Buying a house in Friendswood before Hurricane Harvey was seen as a safe investment, as residents expected their home equity to increase over time. Rising housing prices create more wealth that can be passed down to the next generation. And the economic heterogeneity in Friendswood reflects how lower-middle-class and even some working-class White households are able to access highly resourced White suburbs—though doing so is more difficult now than it was for much of the twentieth century.[14]

These currents—variation across household finances within Friendswood, consistent racial homogeneity, and rising housing prices—are also essential for understanding recovery after Hurricane Harvey, which we unpack later in the book. The elderly widow on Social Security and her neighbors, the young dual-income family, faced distinct challenges after the floodwaters receded. Although living in a middle-class, majority-White suburban community may protect home values overall, in the aftermath of a devastating flood only those who are able to fully repair their homes are in a position to benefit. As more middle-class places are forced to deal with the devastating effects of climate-related disasters, this heterogeneity in households' finances will play a large role in both individual recovery and the resilience of communities more broadly.

A "SMALL-TOWN" COMMUNITY FEEL

Since 1960, when it officially incorporated with fewer than one thousand residents, the City of Friendswood has grown and changed from a farming town to a suburban bedroom community. Despite this growth, Friendswood residents assert that it feels like a small town. The center of Friendswood is nearly four miles from Interstate 45, the main highway connecting Houston to Galveston. Much of the land between I-45 and the center of town looks undeveloped, and the drive into Friendswood feels long, giving the impression that Friendswood is set apart from the surrounding suburban sprawl.[15] Friendswood's main street is marked by some local businesses and fast-food restaurants, but its most prominent buildings are the city hall and a few large churches. Banners hang over the main street advertising local events and parades, and during football season many of the businesses have their windows painted to support the local school team.

The small-town feel also derives from a tight-knit, stable community of residents who often remain for many years. The percentage of residents living in the same house year to year is consistently close to 90 percent. Some of our respondents were original homeowners who still lived in Friendswood after raising their families and were now retiring in place. People who grew up in the area moved back to town to raise their own families, seeking safe, quiet, and bucolic residential neighborhoods that would provide their kids with childhood experiences similar to those they had experienced themselves. This small-town feel has been a longtime draw for residents over the years, from those who purchased homes in the early 1970s to those who bought their homes more recently.

Claire and her husband, parents in their thirties, bought their home in Friendswood less than five years before Hurricane Harvey. Claire told us that they were looking to purchase a "forever home." The term "forever home" is common among middle-class households who, because of their economic stability, often expect long-term residential stability. These households leverage their financial resources to choose a neighborhood and a house that they expect will meet their needs for years to come. Poorer households, by comparison, are more likely to describe their housing as "temporary," since they struggle to afford quality housing and are more likely to face negative shocks (nearby violence, job loss, and so on) that can prompt mobility.[16] Claire told us that, as she and her husband searched for a "forever home," they were looking for a place with the same community feel as the town where her husband grew up.

Claire described her husband's childhood neighborhood as a place where kids "just go from door to door to door. You play outside, like, super-safe neighborhood, super-safe town actually. You know, you go outside until you come in when the streetlights come on kinda thing. So we wanted that for our family." Claire grew up in a suburb near Friendswood, and when they were planning to move and her husband asked, "What's the best school district?" Claire said she quickly responded, "Well, that's easy. It's Friendswood." When they came to look at houses, Claire told us, "we drove down the street and he was like, 'I feel like this is where I grew up.' You know, 'cause we had the cul-de-sac, there was a basketball goal in the cul-de-sac. . . . It was just a super-close-knit [neighborhood]." Both the neighborhood and the house they found met all of Claire and her husband's desires.[17] She said, "We were looking in other areas, but we wanted the yard, we wanted the cul-de-sac. We had everything we wanted, you know, kids upstairs, us downstairs, office for my husband." They quickly made an offer on the house because, Claire told us, "we knew we had to have it." After they moved in, Claire said, the neighbors regularly gathered in the cul-de-sac, just as her husband and his family used to do when he was a child. "Every evening and summer time we'd just go outside, and the kids, we would have, like, 'Hey, it's bicycle night, everybody come to our cul-de-sac.' . . . So everyone would come here and we [would make] like a little raceway around the circle."

Nick, a retired widower in his sixties, moved to Friendswood in the early 1980s with his wife and baby daughter to be close to his job. He told us, "I came for work. I worked in the oil field." While Friendswood's proximity to Houston was appealing, Nick was happy to live somewhere that felt more like a small town. He told us that even though Friendswood had grown over the years, the sense of place that initially attracted him remained:

> Friendswood does all of those little things that a small town does. They still try to do that, even though it's not a small town anymore . . . you know, put up all the Christmas decorations and celebrate Easter and the Fourth of July with parades and things like that. But that—it's a nice community, it was good to raise my daughters in. Like I said, the school systems are good.

Although work initially drew Nick and his family to Friendswood, they enjoyed the town's amenities and overall feel. Nick told us, "You couldn't ask for a better place to raise a family."

While other nearby suburbs have continued to swell in population in recent decades, Friendswood's growth has been comparatively modest. The population of nearby Pearland, Texas, for example, grew by more than 100 percent between 1990 and 2000 and by nearly 150 percent between 2000 and 2010, while Friendswood grew just 27 percent and 23 percent over the same periods. As a result, Friendswood has maintained an intimate sense of community, and the robust schedule of events reified the small-town feel Nick valued.

Carla, a married woman in her fifties, grew up in the Friendswood area and moved back when her children were young. She and her husband chose Friendswood instead of other nearby southeastern Houston suburbs because "it's quaint. It's comfortable. It's not trafficky. It's not hectic. There's parks, lots of parks, and it's just easy. There's not a lot of businesses, and I think that's the part I like about it the most is that it's really residential." Although Carla and other residents undoubtedly appreciated Friendswood's relatively low level of development, the words they used to describe it, like "quaint," "comfortable," and "residential," all carry a racialized meaning as well. In spurring suburbanization and maintaining residential racial segregation, housing policy and the real estate industry have produced distinct ideas about space: suburban subdivisions are tied to Whiteness, while denser housing is associated with Blackness.[18] However, residents typically attributed their regard for Friendswood to seemingly universal ideas about what makes somewhere a good place to live. Carla, for example, loved that Friendswood residents stay for a long time and build deep ties. She told us, "I mean, you get to know the police officers there and the firemen that work there. I mean, people stay there for a very long time. Kids come back from college and settle there, and my kids want to settle there." She went on, "I think it's just a comfortable area." Indeed, several of our other respondents grew up in Friendswood or nearby suburbs and were drawn back to the area to raise their own children.

Carrie and her husband, parents in their thirties, were already living in the southeastern Houston suburbs, but as their family grew they wanted a larger home. They chose a house in Friendswood because, Carrie told us, "schools was a big thing." Her husband grew up nearby and knew Friendswood would offer their children a "good" education.[19] Carrie told us, "It was just time to start to think about schools as well as a bigger home. So we were able to sell that house . . . and came to Friendswood. My husband . . . already kind of had history here, knew the schools were good, and it was a small town, and yeah, so that's kind of why we moved and then found this house." Not only did the community offer good schools, but it also provided a highly desirable, if less definable, quality that Carrie described as "the Friendswood feel."

FRIENDSWOOD'S MIDDLE CLASS OVER TIME

Early development in Friendswood occurred at a time when White Americans working blue-collar jobs could afford to buy into middle-class suburban enclaves. Today buying into Friendswood is more expensive.[20] Not all of the newer residents are white-collar, but less affluent households typically purchase certain kinds of homes: older houses in need of repair or ones in foreclosure. As a result, across the community there is more class heterogeneity than perhaps most residents realize. The trappings of the "small-town feel" and the racial homogeneity of the community can obscure these material differences, making residents seem more socio-economically similar than they actually are. In the aftermath of the flood, however, the variation in households' financial circumstances became incredibly consequential.

Phyllis and her husband were some of the first homeowners to move in during the building boom of the late 1960s and 1970s. Before they moved to Friendswood, Phyllis received her GED and worked as an administrative assistant. Her husband had two years of college classes but no degree, and he worked for a construction company. They were able to move to Friendswood using her husband's VA loan and putting just a dollar down on a newly built $29,000 home that, she told us, "we watched grow from a slab." After their children were born, Phyllis, who is now retired and in her seventies, stayed home while her husband commuted to work in Houston.

We asked Phyllis what Friendswood was like in the 1970s. She told us, "When we first moved in, you know, everybody was in the same situation, everybody was out putting down flags and pulling weeds and watering their lawns, and the kids were all getting to know each other, and the neighbors were all getting to know each other." She acknowledged that the town was very White back then, though she believed that it had become less so over the past forty years. Phyllis and her sister Vera, who moved in with Phyllis after they were both widowed a few years before Harvey, described the change in Friendswood:

> PHYLLIS: Well, it's become more, let me think how to put it, a more mixed neighborhood, which is, you know, everybody— we haven't had any trouble or anything with anybody, it still seems to be a nice neighborhood.
>
> INTERVIEWER: When you say "mixed," you mean income, or race, or both?
>
> PHYLLIS: I would say race maybe, because it wasn't—I don't think there were any Blacks. There may have been a few, but um, you know, now there seems to be a few more, but they're—
>
> VERA: Like, you've got Mexicans and Indians and, I mean, they're all down through here.
>
> PHYLLIS: And everybody seems, as far as I know, seems to get along well, which they should.

Phyllis and Vera perceived Friendswood as growing more racially diverse over time, though the town is still extremely White relative to the region. Furthermore, the sisters did not report any notable variation in household finances in the town despite the growth of larger and more expensive homes in nearby subdivisions and their own relatively constrained financial position compared to some of their neighbors.

At the time of the flood Phyllis was one of a few remaining original homeowners. When we first interviewed her not long after Harvey, we asked her when she and her husband had fully repaid their mortgage. "Heck, we paid it off probably, maybe twenty years ago," she told us. Owning the house helps keep Phyllis and Vera's monthly expenses down. The sisters both receive Social Security, but Phyllis is still paying off medical debt from her husband's hospital stay and treatment before he died. "It was quite a bill," she said. When we asked about her income the year of the flood, Phyllis told us, "I'm on Social Security, so let's see, it wasn't a lot." Beyond her home, Phyllis's only asset was an IRA account with less than $30,000.

After the flood, Phyllis was not surprised that the assessed value of her home went down, but she was shocked when just one year later the value increased by $30,000 even though their repairs were not complete. (As we detail further in chapter 5, a year after the storm their contractor had not even started repairs, and there was no way Phyllis could sell the home for its new assessed value.) She told us, "I thought it was funny. . . . I told Vera, I said, 'That's ridiculous. How do they judge that?' I mean, especially, I thought since the flood that it would go down, not up." The assessed home value certainly did not reflect the reality of the sisters' financial position, or even the physical condition of their house.

Elizabeth and Richard, who were both in their seventies, had also lived in Friendswood for more than thirty years. Before retiring, Richard worked as a pipefitter for an oil and gas company, and Elizabeth was a nurse. After graduating from high school, Elizabeth completed several medical certificate programs and received professional licensure through "on-the-job training." Today, she noted, "you have to literally go to school to get it. . . . I was one that—the elderly ones that got it earlier." Richard went to school through twelfth grade and then attended a technical school to train as a machinist.

Elizabeth grew up in Texas and worked for some time in the Galveston area before moving away. After she and Richard married, she wanted to return and knew that Friendswood should be their destination.

ELIZABETH: We moved straight to Friendswood. . . . I just like the community. . . . And I love this area. It was just something country. From Galveston to Houston was nothing but pasture back in those days. . . . [Friendswood] was a dot. . . . It was just a little cow town. I mean, a little farm town. It really was.

INTERVIEWER: And why was that so appealing to you?

ELIZABETH: Because I love the country. I love outside. I just thought it was just an awesome place to be. And when Richard and I decided we were coming, I said, "Let's check out Friendswood." . . . I believe Richard had looked at a couple of places. . . . He checked Clear Lake. He checked Webster. He checked other places out, and he said, "I really like Friendswood." I said, "I told you you would."

Elizabeth was thrilled with the community and the schools for their children. "These were really strong educated schools."

Richard and Elizabeth moved to Friendswood at a time when his blue-collar job and her nursing work enabled them not only to buy a home in the suburbs but to save. "We've been very blessed and lucky to always have good jobs," Richard said. "Work construction, you know, to put money back for when you're gonna need it." When Harvey struck, the couple had long since paid off their mortgage, Richard was retired, and Elizabeth was working only part-time. She fully retired before our last interview in 2019; at that point they were living off of Social Security.

Although Elizabeth and Richard had some savings, they considered their home the central element of their wealth—their financial safety net. In fact, before the storm they had planned to sell their house and move closer to their children and grandchildren. They had estimated their home to be worth $250,000 to $280,000, but after the storm the assessed value dropped to $185,000, and Elizabeth was worried about their financial future. However, two years after the storm home values across the neighborhood were rebounding and their home had been rebuilt and updated. In 2019, Elizabeth told us, "if I was to sell the house right now I would take nothing less than $250,000." This desired price represented a great deal of equity for Elizabeth and Richard. They believed that selling the house at that price would allow them to easily afford another home with cash left over. In 2021 they sold the house for around $275,000.

Over time the occupations and incomes of Friendswood residents began to change, and newer households tended to be more white-collar than the families that moved in when Elizabeth and Richard were able to buy a home. Alicia and her husband, who were in their sixties, bought a home in Friendswood during the wave of new developments in the 1980s. At the time she was working as a lawyer in Houston and her husband, who has a technical degree, worked for a communication company.

Friendswood was appealing to Alicia because it was close to her extended family and an easy commute into Houston for work. She elaborated on what drew her to the community:

> I had been actually driving in and around Friendswood all my life, because, you know, it was a known community, but it had recently kind of grown . . . it was a farming community. . . . There wasn't a whole lot of development going on, because the land was being used for rural purposes. But about in the '80s, it started changing. There was more developments, more families were selling their land, and so there was more home building going on.

Alicia wanted to raise her children in a place that would replicate many of the things she cherished most about her own childhood. She said:

> We've had a really good, stable neighborhood. And I feel very, very fortunate, because I grew up back in the day when people would open their doors and go, "Kids, get out of the house, stay gone, I'll see you at supper," you know . . . "Go hang with your friends, go do stuff, do whatever," and I realized that it's got more and more difficult for families to live in those kind of

places where you can basically just turn your kids loose, and say, "Go play, go be a kid." You know, "Go get dirty, get hurt, I don't care," but you know you still have a relative comfort level that they're just going to be doing kid stuff. And that's been the way this community—this neighborhood, I guess I should say—has been.

Even after their children had grown up and moved out, Alicia and her husband planned to stay and enjoy their retirement years in Friendswood. "My husband likes his big garage.... I've got a garden and stuff in the back, you know. I like space ... it's comfortable, and I have now turned one of my bedrooms ... into a kids' room for grandkids to spend the night."

When we first interviewed Alicia a few months after Harvey, she was worried that the storm would depress local real estate prices. However, this was not the case. She told us:

This house is worth way, way, way more than we paid for it. I mean, I was surprised.... It's interesting because I'm looking at, now, the current appraisals, which is like, are we taking the hit with Harvey that everybody's house values have now dropped like a rock? And apparently not. It's still hitting, you know, we're hitting in the high fives [$500,000s].... It was a surprise to me.

Alicia pointed to Friendswood's desirability as the reason for the sustained price increases. "People are still buying properties here in Friendswood and, you know, [are] willing to pay significant money for it ... even if they've got a history of flooding.... I think in our little economic or whatever they call it, uh, category, we're not being penalized for the fact that it was a flooded house. If it happens again, it could be different." For Alicia, the economic character of Friendswood overall protected property values even in the face of perceived risk.

Indeed, the quick rebound in Friendswood home prices shows how the housing market works to shore up wealth in privileged places. And it is not only the middle-class character of Friendswood but also its Whiteness that buffers against economic loss. Living in Friendswood, despite the destruction of the flood and the vulnerability it revealed, remains highly valued.[21]

THE REMAINING BLUE-COLLAR RESIDENTS

Even as it became increasingly expensive to buy into Friendswood, blue-collar or service-sector workers have continued to find ways to purchase homes in the area. In our sample, most blue-collar residents who had moved more recently to Friendswood bought houses that were in foreclosure or they lived in properties inherited from their parents. William, a married father in his forties, bought his home in Friendswood as a single man in his twenties. He purchased an older home, built in the 1970s, that was affordable because "it was a foreclosure. The bank owned it." He said, "I qualified for a $100,000 loan, and I was like, 'There is no way.' You know, I think I was making, shit, maybe $37,000 a year at that time, and I was a blue-collar guy. I was, you know, working in a manufacturing plant. And I was like, 'There is no way I can afford a house payment that much.'" But when he found a more affordable house in foreclosure, he said, "I was thinking, you know, it's a great school district. . . . Friendswood as a community is amazing. It's awesome. It's like a, you know, small-town type of feel . . . it's just a nice neighborhood." So William decided to buy a house.[22] After he met and married Carol, they began to slowly renovate and update their home, doing a few projects every year.

When Hurricane Harvey hit, William and Carol were both working white-collar jobs in oil and gas, but they were still careful about their finances because of the instability in their industry. They told us about the continued reverberations from the major "nosedive" in energy prices a few years before Harvey. William said, "We're going through layoffs and wondering if we're gonna have a job come the next week." Carol agreed, describing her company as "a ghost town. . . . They laid off so many people. It's worse than it was in the '80s." So, while Carol and William did not plan on remaining in Friendswood forever—they wanted to move closer to family—they were cautious about any major financial decisions like selling their house and buying a new one.

Carol and William knew that the storm would affect home values in the short term, but they expected prices to eventually rebound. "According to the lady who is a real estate friend of ours," Carol explained, Friendswood "is a unique neighborhood because it's still a starter home neighborhood and a good school district in a very nice area." William also thought that the location between Galveston and Houston and the proximity to NASA were appealing factors for many potential home buyers. Compared to what he purchased their home for, he told us, "these homes, you wouldn't believe what they go for. . . . One of them sold for, what, $170,000?" When Carol said that she "would never pay that for this, it's a small house," William interjected, "But its location. . . . And the community is strong. Real strong . . . and lovely."

Andrea and her husband, parents in their thirties, were also able to afford to move to Friendswood by purchasing a property in foreclosure. Andrea grew up in the southeast suburbs of Houston, so moving to Friendswood was a move back to a community near where she had spent her childhood. She attended some college and was primarily a stay-at-home mother who also took on some childcare jobs to supplement their household income. Her husband had an associate's degree and worked as a driver. When they began their housing search in the late 1990s, they were on a tighter budget than many other young families moving into Friendswood, and this made their search challenging. Andrea said:

> We searched for about six months, looking for that one elusive four:two [a house with four bedrooms and two bathrooms] for less than a hundred grand that was actually in a decent area, 'cause good Lord, some of the homes we walked into when we were searching, you know it looked really nice in the pictures, and then when you drove up to it you're like, "Wow, did they really need to have two toilets in their front yard next door?" (*laughs*) You know, it was just—they were not nice neighborhoods or . . . very obviously not up to code.

They got lucky when they found their current home. "It was a foreclosure," Andrea said. "The original pictures online show trash in every room." Yet the minute she saw the property she told her real estate agent that they wanted to put in an offer. She told us, "When we walked in here ten years ago and it was four bedrooms, two full baths, open-plan living kitchen. This kitchen was all open and beautiful. We were like, 'There's a pool. Cool!'" Not only did the house meet all of their needs, but it was in a neighborhood with well-regarded schools for their kids.

Over the past ten years, their house has steadily grown in value. Before the storm, Andrea said, "it had climbed up to being worth $165,000." Their home was their nest egg—it represented all of their household wealth. She described their family's financial position: "I pretty much say we're working poor, because we get by, but there's so much more we'd like to do that we just, we just can't." After Hurricane Harvey, without flood insurance coverage, they were living paycheck to paycheck and directing all they could toward home repairs. Andrea worried that after the flood they would never be able to sell their home. She knew that "we might get back up to $165,000 value in another ten years," but she and her husband "hadn't originally planned on staying that long." If they were unable to sell the house for its pre-flood value, not only would they be unable to move into a larger house as their children got older, but they would lose out on the equity they hoped to gain through homeownership.

By the second anniversary of the storm, however, Andrea was thinking that "we'd easily get $170,000," and she was more certain that, "if we actually put the money in that pool and do everything we want to do, if the housing market stayed the same, we'd probably get around $200,000-plus, easy." Andrea wasn't the only person amazed by how quickly prices rebounded; she talked about it with her neighbors, and all of them, she told us, were "really surprised." While Andrea's family's day-to-day finances were still extremely tight, rapidly increasing home prices post-flood mitigated the devastating effects of the storm on their long-term financial security.

THE AFFLUENCE OF NEWER RESIDENTS

Households like Andrea's, with moderate incomes and no bachelor's degrees, represent a shrinking portion of Friendswood residents. More and more often, new residents are similar to Brian and Linda, a lawyer and a doctor. A married couple in their thirties, Brian and Linda moved to Friendswood a few years before Hurricane Harvey. When we asked about their move, Brian told us, "We had decided we wanted to purchase the home and, and stay kind of in one spot for the foreseeable future. We had been moving around a fair amount prior to this, and we finished our education and whatnot, and we were looking to stay in one spot for longer. . . . We had saved up for a down payment." He went on: "We don't have kids yet, but we will hopefully in the future, so we were planning ahead in that regard." People in their social network recommended both of the local school districts serving the Friendswood area. Brain told us:

> We talked to somebody who, who knows about such things, and they also vouched for Clear Creek [Independent School District], and so we were, we were okay to move based on that information. . . . I wouldn't say we were exclusively not considering other places, but I kind of got a strong recommendation again, from, from a family friend who is familiar with school districts in the area, and she vouched pretty heavily for, again, Friendswood [Independent School District].

When it came to selecting a particular home, their real estate agent took Brian and Linda to an open house for a home they loved, but demand in the area was high. "Somebody beat us to that one basically," Brian said, "and then we were pretty quick to, to jump on this one." They eventually chose a property that overlooks the creek. "It's waterfront, right, so the backyard really just sort of extends down to the bank of Clear Creek," Brian said, "which was a pretty strong factor in why we like it. The house was nice, location was fairly close to Interstate 45. I mean, honestly, the backyard had a lot to do with it. It's a pretty scenic backyard." Besides the great yard, the property satisfied many of their other preferences as well, such as proximity to Linda's family, and it was in a good school district.

Even after the storm, their home, which they purchased for around $240,000, retained its value. Two years after Hurricane Harvey, Brian said, the price of his house "seems to be about the same or even a little bit higher, which I'm kinda surprised at. I wonder if it's going to dip back in a while? But just looking at house sales around here, it didn't seem to affect it too much." Given the repairs they made after Harvey, Brian hoped "that it's at least worth $260,000, $270,000, 'cause of the improvement, I would think." Like Brian, many other flooded residents were both surprised and satisfied by how quickly their home values rebounded. By the second anniversary of the storm, many expected even higher home values.

Samantha and her husband, parents in their thirties, also moved to Friendswood a few years before Hurricane Harvey. He worked in finance, she was a stay-at-home mother, and they both had a bachelor's degree. They were motivated to leave Houston and move to the suburbs primarily for their kids. Samantha told us:

> I grew up here. . . . Swore I would never come back. . . . Then, once I got pregnant with my second, we just started looking down here. . . . Especially coming from [the] inner city, you know, there's a lot more community stuff available here, more resources. . . . So, like, just the community and more space and extracurriculars. It was all for the kids really, you know, better school district. You don't have to get on the lottery and fingers crossed or pay for private school or whatever. So that's what attracted us back here. Family help and the stuff available for our children.

Samantha's personal history in Friendswood made it feel like a natural place for them to move, and they quickly narrowed their search to a neighborhood that provided easy access to the highway for her husband's drive into Houston for work. "Since my husband does commute . . . we were only looking in this neighborhood. We didn't look anywhere else in Friendswood because we wanted to be where he could jump on 45 and head up." They found a large two-story home that met all of their criteria.

Samantha and her husband bought their home in Friendswood for nearly $600,000. Two years after Harvey, she suspected that they had lost some equity, but, she said, "I feel like if we listed our house, we could probably get more than what we paid for it five years ago, especially because now it's completely updated." Since the storm, they have been carefully tracking home sales across the neighborhood and were pleasantly surprised to see a home just down the street from them sell for more than $600,000. Samantha was still worried about how much their home would ultimately sell for in the future, but she kept in mind that "a lot of people rely on the fact that Friendswood is such a great community to live in that there'll always be people who want to live here. . . . I think there's things about Friendswood that keep people here and draw people here. And I think . . . the small-town feel and the community and the schools and that kinda thing definitely plays a part."

Friendswood looks a lot like the stereotype of an American middle-class suburban community, one filled with single-family homes with green lawns and where children play in the street. Friendswood's reputation as a close-knit community with a "small-town feel" has continued to attract households looking to fulfill the middle-class dream of suburban homeownership. The community has also remained majority-White as it has grown, even at a time when the Houston region has rapidly diversified. Although it is relatively racially homogeneous, Friendswood's subdivisions do contain socioeconomic heterogeneity. As the cost of homeownership has outpaced the growth in earnings, access to middle-class suburban spaces has narrowed. In Friendswood, the financial circumstances of most newer residents are not the same as those of the residents who bought in decades ago.

Friendswood remains a largely privileged place to live. No matter when they bought, people who purchased a home in Friendswood did so assuming that it was a sound investment—particularly as changes in the overall economy have made home equity an increasingly central component of creating intergenerational wealth (and racial disparities in wealth).[23] Hurricane Harvey initially appeared to threaten that investment. In the wake of hurricanes, floods, and other disasters, housing prices do tend to go down, but these drops tend to be more severe in non-White and poorer neighborhoods.[24] When residents of Friendswood found that the value of their homes rebounded much more quickly than they anticipated after Harvey, their experience highlighted the valorization of Whiteness and the high value put on property in White places. Initially, residents anticipated that it would take five if not ten years for the market to erase their losses caused by the flood and for new buyers to forget Harvey. But prices returned to pre-flood levels within two years. After all, Friendswood was still a White, middle-class community with highly rated schools and a reputation for robust and family-centered civic life. As Samantha put it, "There'll always be people who want to live here."

Yet not all households in Friendswood were able to benefit from rising housing prices. Residents entered the recovery process with starkly different financial resources at their disposal, and as we will see in chapter 5, some less affluent households that could not complete their repairs were unable to capitalize on their equity. The process of disaster recovery amplified the pre-storm disparities between residents, even in a well-resourced, middle-class community.

Chapter 2 | "A Slow-Motion Disaster"

On Wednesday, August 23, 2017, Harvey was moving through the Gulf of Mexico as a tropical depression. Weather forecasts predicted that it would make landfall along the Texas coast as a category 3 hurricane. When the models of the storm's path began to converge, it became clear that Hurricane Harvey was likely to stall and move slowly across southeast Texas, bringing not only hurricane-force winds but also extreme rainfall.[1] Anticipating the devastating effects of this storm, the governor of Texas declared a preemptive state of disaster for thirty counties expected to be in the storm's path. By Thursday, the National Hurricane Center (NHC) had issued stark warnings in a special advisory:

> Harvey has intensified rapidly, and is forecast to be a major hurricane at landfall, bringing life-threatening storm surge, rainfall, and wind hazards to portions of the Texas coast. Preparations to protect life and property should be completed by tonight. . . . Life-threatening flooding is expected across much of the Texas coast from heavy rainfall of 12 to 20 inches, with isolated amounts as high as 30 inches, from Friday through early next week.[2]

As Harvey headed toward land, the storm's winds intensified quickly, even more than was predicted, with the eye of what was now a category 4 hurricane hitting Rockport, Texas, at 10:00 PM on Friday, August 25. The storm then slowed dramatically, its wind speeds rapidly decreasing, as it crept across southeast Texas at about five miles per hour.

Harvey weakened to a tropical storm once it hit land, and then, as the National Weather Service put it, the storm "meandered" across southeast Texas. The storm stalled for nearly four days and dropped historic amounts of rain. Analyses by the NHC concluded that "Harvey was the most significant tropical cyclone rainfall event in United States history, both in scope and peak rainfall amounts, since reliable rainfall records began around the 1880s."[3] The highest total rainfall reported from the storm was more than sixty inches, far above the initial dire predictions from the NHC. In Friendswood, between forty-seven and fifty-six inches of rain fell in a matter of days.

In this chapter we describe what Friendswood residents were expecting before Harvey hit and how their expectations differed from what happened when the storm's extreme flooding displaced so many people from their homes. These experiences of Harvey are key for understanding the recovery process. Indeed, as the sociologist Kai Erikson has shown, the intensity of collective traumatic events can prompt new kinds of decisions by individuals, who may reassess certain aspects of their lives after the shock of a disaster.[4] This may be particularly true when housing is damaged or destroyed, because homes ground daily life and are imbued with a great deal of meaning and emotion by the people who live in them.[5] By showing just how disruptive Harvey was, we can better contextualize the choices made by individual households in Friendswood in the years after.

EXPECTATIONS AND BENCHMARK STORMS

For longtime residents of Friendswood, the news of an impending hurricane does not create panic; instead, everyone simply heads to the store to stock up on water, nonperishable food items, and extra batteries. Hurricane Harvey was no different. People prepared to lose power for a week, anticipating that the worst-case scenario would involve street flooding and a few days in the uncomfortable August heat without air conditioning. No one seemed to alter their routines.

At first, the slow-moving but powerful storm was not predicted to hit the Houston metropolitan area directly, and there were no calls for evacuation.[6] Residents of Friendswood certainly did not expect the storm to flood their homes. Grace, a widow in her sixties, told us that she expected to "get quite a bit of rain, maybe lose power . . . maybe a little street flooding." She lived in a home that had been in her family "since '77 and never had a flood," and she did not expect Harvey to be any different. Grace, like most of her neighbors, went to the store for basic necessities, preparing to be stuck at home for a few days:

> Just in case we did lose power or did get some area flooding, you know, we had extra batteries and flashlights, food, things we could heat up outside over a fire, you know. . . . We did get some bottled water just in case, but other than that, I mean, we didn't take any precautions like you would if you are going to get a full-fledged hurricane. Because we didn't expect to get the hurricane. We knew that [it] was coming in further south.

Research shows that even when people have experienced hurricanes in the past, they do not necessarily prepare more if another hurricane is heading their way.[7] Friendswood residents were no exception. Charles and his wife Barbara, a retired couple in their seventies, were used to hurricane weather, and they thought the forecasts on the news were always a little exaggerated. Charles told us:

> We have lived in the Gulf Coast, and Friendswood in particular, since 1976. . . . And we have become conditioned to weather events, or threatened weather events. . . . The style of the weather forecasters, the people on TV, [is] to create hysteria to the extent that they can. . . . But what happens on our end is, you get conditioned to it. So when you keep hearing it . . . you kind of treat it with a little bit of . . . you don't ignore it, but there's not a whole lot you can do anyway, and you just don't know what's true and what's not true.

Despite experiencing several major storms, Charles and Barbara had never suffered significant damage to any of the homes they had lived in over the years. "We've had a few that have come in here, but nothing overwhelming in our case," he noted, and so they expected that Hurricane Harvey would be the same. This perspective is not necessarily surprising: those who live near areas that experience a disaster but are not significantly affected themselves have a decreased perception of risk and tend to prepare less for future disasters.[8]

Most households in Friendswood used past floods as their benchmark for understanding the likelihood of flooding and their risk more generally.[9] There had been no major flooding in Friendswood since Tropical Storm Claudette in 1979 (though there was some flooding during Tropical Storm Allison in 2001), and so none of our respondents imagined that Harvey would flood their homes. According to Angela, a married mother of three in her forties, "I was thinking, 'It's not going to hit us,' and, 'We're gonna have flooding maybe,' but I thought it would just be—we've never flooded in this area. Like even during Allison. . . . There was no flooding in this area here. . . . So I was expecting maybe the power to go out."

While many residents used Claudette as the high-level benchmark in assessing their likelihood of flooding, some also referred to Allison as a reason to believe that their homes were at relatively low risk of taking on water. Mia, a married mother in her thirties, said:

> I grew up in Houston. So I have been through a few hurricanes. None that were super-disastrous, but I did expect us to lose power. I know how hot it is during hurricane season, so I was expecting that to just be miserable. . . . We

had heard from all of our neighbors that had been through Tropical Storm Allison. None of the homes flooded in [our] area, so we were good. So that meant I was in total denial that there could be any sort of flooding.

FLOOD INSURANCE COVERAGE

In light of how long it had been since the last major flood, there was a widely shared perspective in Friendswood that flood risk was low. The general absence of worry informed some residents' decisions about flood insurance before the storm. When Harvey hit, only 52 percent of our respondents had flood insurance coverage. This coverage rate may seem low, but in fact only around 30 percent of all households across the region that flooded were insured.[10] Why do residents in vulnerable areas forgo insurance?

Only households with a federally backed mortgage who live within a one-hundred-year floodplain—an area determined to have a 1 percent chance of flooding in any given year—are required to carry flood insurance. The floodwaters from Harvey extended well beyond this boundary (figure 2.1). Many of the residents we interviewed whose houses flooded lived in the five-hundred-year floodplain, which has a one-in–five hundred (or 0.2 percent) chance of flooding in any given year. These residents were not required to maintain a flood insurance policy, and the lack of a mandate certainly contributed to the skepticism of some that they were at risk. And yet they were: a study of the Clear Creek watershed prior to Hurricane Harvey found that 50 percent of losses from earlier flooding had occurred outside the one-hundred-year floodplain.[11] Despite this past flooding, risk was often downplayed. Some residents even reported receiving advice that their risk was low enough that they could reasonably forgo flood insurance coverage—advice highlighting the lack of knowledge about risk more generally. Finally, other residents did not have flood insurance before Harvey because of constrained finances.[12] When household budgets are tight, other expenses take priority, especially when perceptions of risk are low.

John, a widower in his late fifties, told us that he did not have flood insurance because "I didn't think it would flood." He bought his home after Tropical Storm Allison in 2001, and when he asked neighbors about that storm, they told him that there was street flooding but not many homes took on water. Based on these reports, John did not think his home was at risk, and so he never purchased flood insurance. Luis, a single man in his fifties, said, "I had flood insurance the first year. . . . It was like four hundred and something dollars." When it was time to renew, he told us, "the bill went up, but I didn't think anything was gonna flood," so he

Figure 2.1   Map of Inundation from Hurricane Harvey

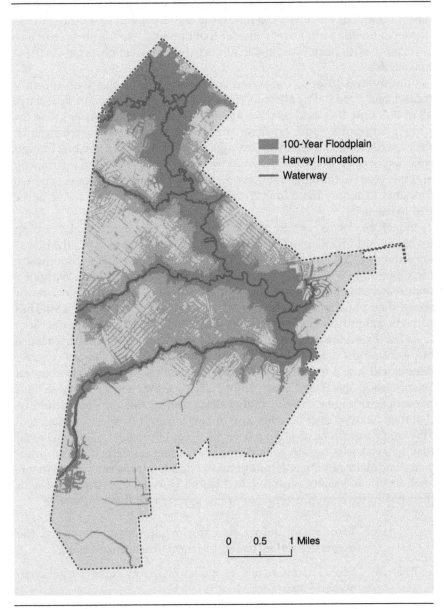

100-Year Floodplain
Harvey Inundation
Waterway

0   0.5   1 Miles

Source: FEMA 2020.

dropped his coverage. Similarly, Jennifer, a woman in her forties who lived with her boyfriend, told us, "We didn't have insurance, you know? We haven't flooded . . . we've gotten water in the street, but . . . nothing in the house, so I really didn't ever consider that flooding." In the absence of any experience with prior flooding, insurance did not seem necessary to these households.

Tammy and Joseph, a married couple in their sixties who recently retired, had lived in Friendswood for almost twenty-four years. For nearly all of that time they had paid for a flood insurance policy. After going for so long without a flood, however, and facing some financial constraints, they too decided to drop their coverage for 2017. Then Harvey hit. Tammy reflected on their decision: "Almost every year we had it [flood insurance], and this year we thought—at that point we didn't have the money, and we thought, 'What are the odds? We've had it all this time, and we've never had to use it.'"

In fact, as storms become slower and wetter, past benchmark flooding events are unreliable predictors of future risk. In other words, "the odds" are changing. Yet for people who have lived in a particular community for a long time with no flooding, this risk is difficult to assess. Without a requirement to maintain coverage, some residents chose not to purchase or renew their policies. Households with lower incomes, for whom a $400 bill could be a significant expense, were especially likely to make this decision.

Other Friendswood residents could more easily afford insurance but were advised, often by insurance agents, that it was not necessary. Aleena and Jay, a married couple in their thirties, bought their home in Friendswood less than a year before Hurricane Harvey. They chose their home specifically because it did not flood during Allison. Aleena told us that they "moved over here because out here wasn't flooded." Jay agreed: "We don't want a house that's been flooded, obviously." They believed that their risk was low, given that their new home was in the five-hundred-year floodplain, not the one-hundred-year floodplain; as such, flood insurance coverage was not required. Just before Harvey, they discussed with their insurance company whether or not to purchase flood insurance:

JAY: Two weeks before this storm happened, we called the insurance—they called us, right? Insurance called.

ALEENA: Yeah, I had to renew my policy on my mortgage, my [home-owners] insurance.

JAY: So they was like, "Hey, you guys really want flood insurance?" And we're like, "What do you think about it? You know, this house, you know, like you guys said, it's never been flooded.

Do you think [we should]?" At this point, they're like, "You're just wasting money buying flood insurance."

ALEENA: Yeah, we're in a low-risk zone. You know, low-risk, so—

JAY: What's the point of us wasting an extra four hundred bucks? Then we'll never flood.

Clearly frustrated after Harvey, they recalled that "we were willing to pay for it." Regarding their insurance agent, Aleena said, "They basically talked us out of getting it. . . . She's like, 'Well, it's a difference of four hundred bucks.' I was like, 'Okay, cool. That's not bad. Just the security, four hundred bucks. I will take it.' They're like, 'No, why would you want that? Your house has never flooded. You're just wasting money.'" Aleena and Jay took their insurance agent's advice and therefore did not have coverage during Harvey.[13]

Diane and her husband Jack, parents in their forties, reported receiving similar advice about not needing insurance because their house was not in an area where insurance was mandated. They did not realize, however, how close they lived to the one-hundred-year floodplain. Diane explained:

> Our floodplain was a five-hundred-year, and we didn't have any idea that the people across the street were one-hundred-year floodplain. And so, for instance, the one-hundred-year floodplains have to have flood insurance, their mortgage companies make them get that. . . . But because we sat on a five-hundred-year, our mortgage company did not require it.

Jack recalled asking whether they needed flood insurance and being told no, they did not. "From what I remember, they were saying that it would take a pretty big event for us to take water in our house." Of course, Harvey turned out to be "a pretty big event." Diane and Jack were left to navigate recovery without insurance.

Flood insurance policies must be renewed annually, and so maintaining coverage, even when it is mandated, takes attention and time. It also often requires coordination with mortgage banks as well as with insurance companies. Lucy, a married mother in her thirties, described the process of maintaining her flood insurance policy as "a conscious effort." She had always been insured, even though her house had never flooded before Harvey, because, she told us, "it's gotten close, from Hurricane Allison and things like that. . . . For $400 a year, it's very reasonable if you use it." But, she added, "I know people who let it lapse."

Indeed, in the aftermath of Harvey, many households were unclear about whether or not they were covered. Some were lucky and discovered that they did have an active policy, while others found out too late that they did not. Susanne and her husband, parents in their thirties, thought that they had coverage, but realized after the storm that their policy had not been updated when they refinanced their mortgage a few years earlier. Under the assumption that they had insurance, Susanne's husband even "videoed every single room" to document belongings and the state of their home in order to facilitate an insurance claim. Susanne told us, "We had refinanced a couple years before, not knowing you had to redo the insurance. . . . It didn't transfer over because we went with a different bank . . . and they didn't tell us. We'd gotten things in the mail from FEMA about flood insurance, but we just assumed, we were like, 'Oh, we already have it.'" She added: "Hindsight's 20/20. We probably should have looked a little more into it, but you know, what can you do?" Susanne and her husband were not alone in believing, incorrectly, that they had an active flood insurance policy.

Cora and her husband Michael, parents in their forties, were unclear if their policy had lapsed before Hurricane Harvey because of a late payment. After the storm, Cora told us, "there was a lot of confusion." The insurance company told her, "'Oh, you're in a lockout.' It's like a thirty-day lockout, and we were like twenty-two days in a thirty-day lockout [when Harvey hit]. But as it turns out, flood insurance is paid by escrow in our mortgage, and so that payment had already been made. . . . It had been paid in May."

Cora's close call and Susanne's missed policy update demonstrate that the onus for maintaining coverage—dealing with various bureaucracies like insurance companies and banks, knowing dates of coverage, maintaining payments, being aware of flood risk zones—is on residents. Homeowners can easily miss a payment, assume that their coverage automatically transfers to a new bank, or lose a letter from FEMA in the pile of unopened mail. For the residents of Friendswood we interviewed, the limited scope of existing insurance mandates, the cost of flood insurance, the frequent reliance on past storms as benchmarks, and advice from neighbors and other authorities that risk was low combined to lead almost half of them to be uninsured when Harvey struck. For many, the water seeping into their homes was the first unfortunate reminder that they did not have insurance.

RISING WATERS

When Harvey stalled over southeast Texas, it seemed like the rain would never stop. Lynne, a married woman in her sixties, described the disastrous downpour: "This thing was just a slow-motion disaster. I mean, it didn't all happen all at once. You know, it spread out over days." Friendswood ended up squarely in the path of Harvey. Beginning on Friday, it rained intermittently, leading some residents to hope that the storm would not be a problem at all. By Saturday night, however, the rain was coming down hard as band after band of precipitation passed over Friendswood. Residents remained hopeful into Saturday night that their homes might stay dry if only the rain would stop. But it never let up. At first, the flood-waters rose slowly, but by late Saturday night and into the early hours of Sunday morning, homes began to rapidly take on water. Tanya, a married mother in her forties, told us, "Standing in your home, watching it happen to you is incredibly sad and frustrating. You can't stop it. You can't fix it." Many residents did not know when to leave, and the decision to evacuate their homes was complicated by the fact that most properties did not begin flooding until the middle of the night on Saturday.

Caroline, a mother in her forties, told us that when she went to bed on Saturday night around midnight, water had not entered her home and the rain was relatively light, so she thought everything would be okay. "By 6:00 AM it was already too late. We woke up, and there was water in the house." With the water flooding their house as they slept, Caroline was deeply frustrated that she had lost the opportunity to try to save their belongings.

> My biggest regret over this whole situation is that it happened at night. I mean, what the fuck? I mean, if it had happened during the day and we had seen the [water] rising, do you know how much of a difference that would have made? Jesus. We could have gotten our cars out of there. We could have secured our possessions. You know, we could have spent the day moving shit into the attic, for crying out loud. You know? I mean, but by the time we knew it was happening, it was too late.

Some people did stay up Saturday night—many were watching a highly publicized boxing match between Floyd Mayweather Jr. and Conor McGregor (one of the most watched pay-per-view events ever televised). Marissa and Jason, a married couple in their thirties, stayed up to watch the fight, so they were awake when floodwater started entering their home. "I'm really thankful that they were showing that fight," Marissa said, "and that for whatever reason we were interested. . . . It was around, I guess around three in the morning when it finally started coming into our house. . . . If we weren't awake we would not have saved half of the stuff that we were able to save." Marissa had time to pack clothes, important documents, and supplies for their dog.

> I was able to grab our birth certificates, my license, our marriage certificate, our badges for jobs and stuff like that—stuff that we absolutely needed. And then a couple changes of clothes. . . . I would have been panicked if I had

not been awake . . . and I was preparing myself mentally. Like, "Okay, it's gonna come in, there's nothing we can do. . . . We're gonna flood." . . . So, it was not as bad I think as it could have been for us, or how bad it was for a lot of our neighbors who just woke up and put their feet in water and then just panicked.

Sarah told us that she and her husband Cal, parents in their forties, watched the rain fall for hours. With each rain band the water would creep farther up the yard, but after each rain band passed they got a small reprieve and the water stopped rising. Around three o'clock in the morning, thinking their home would be safe, they finally decided it was okay to get a few hours of sleep:

> Saturday we stayed up all night and all day until technically 3:00 AM Sunday morning, and we watched the water . . . it came about halfway up my yard and it stayed there. It had been there for five hours halfway up my yard. Water was flowing, we had good current, so I thought, "We're draining, we're doing good. No big deal. It hasn't moved up or down in five hours, we'll just maintain this, we'll be good to go." I talked my husband into three hours of sleep. . . . When we went to bed we prepared for . . . the possibility of maybe a couple of inches of water in the house. We put Ziploc bags on the bottom of our tables. We lifted all the chairs up. Um, I didn't grab my important documents and things like that because they were two feet off the ground, so I thought, "We're good." I mean, if we end up with a couple of inches of water, we're still safe.

When Sarah's alarm went off at six o'clock, she turned to get out of bed and found herself almost floating. "In three hours it went from the middle of my yard to the top of my king-sized mattress in my bedroom, in my entire house. I couldn't believe it. . . . It took me a minute to process. I mean, I processed water very quickly in the house, but it's not a sight you're ever prepared to see."

RESCUE AND EVACUATION

As the waters rose Saturday night and into Sunday, many residents began evacuating their homes. Others tried to wait it out, hoping the rain would abate and the water would recede. One of the greatest predictors of early evacuation from disaster areas is access to information, and since most local news reports were forecasting much lower levels of rainfall than eventually happened, few Friendswood residents were prepared to leave their homes.[14] But as the water continued to rise, people started calling 911 for rescue or tried to flag down one of the boats that were going by in their neighborhoods after the sun rose on Sunday. Others decided to pack a few things and try to make their way to safety by wading through the water or using kayaks, inflatable mattresses, or anything else that would float. Without clear guidance about when or how to safely leave, many simply made what felt like the best decision possible in the moment.

Kevin and his wife, who are both in their fifties, watched the water rise on Saturday night and eventually called 911 for rescue. The city's boats were on the other side of the creek, however, and were unable to cross the fast-moving water, which he said looked like "white water rapids." He described their wait for rescue:

> From 10:00 to 12:00, all we could do was just watch the water come in, and now at midnight I'm calling 911, Friendswood 911, and they tell me, "I can't get to you." . . . And I tried to, I tried to express to them with as much desperation as I could, "Well, the creek is coming, [it] will be here soon," and there's still nothing they could do about it. . . . I'm walking around with my hands in the air, praying, and telling God, "My faith is strong. Whatever is going to happen is going to happen, but I got faith that you can stop this flood. Stop it. Stop it. Stop it." Well, it just keeps coming, and a little after midnight the water breached the house from the front and the back, the sliding glass door, it looks like an aquarium starting to fill up . . . like we're inside the aquarium. It was really, really strange. And it went from ankle deep to waist deep inside the house in forty-five minutes.

After their drains and toilets overflowed, Kevin and his wife decided they had to leave the house in order to avoid further exposure to potentially toxic floodwater. Kevin's wife told him, "We have to get out of here," when they started to "smell lawnmower gas and oil and the sewer was starting to bubble up." He went on: "When we decided to leave the house and go outside and sit in the bed of the truck, it was already probably four feet deep in the driveway."

With no access to a rescue boat and the water still rising, Kevin and his family, together with some neighbors, decided that they needed to find their own way out. They used a neighbor's small metal boat to try to cross the fast-moving water in the street so they could wade toward the nearby elementary school that was serving as a shelter. It was a harrowing experience. Kevin loaded his grandson, daughter, and wife into the boat with their pets, while he waded alongside with the neighbors. As they tried to navigate through the fast-moving water in the street, everything went wrong almost immediately. "We launched . . . and took about three paddles," Kevin said. "The boat went sideways, and it went into the intersection, and in the intersection there's rapids this way, and there's rapids this way, and the boat just, it hit a wall of water and capsized and sent everybody into the water, and we lost our cats right [there], they were in carriers."

When the boat capsized, Kevin's neighbors got swept away by the current. "One of my neighbors, he immediately went underwater, and I never saw him again. I found out later that he survived." Kevin was also separated from his wife, whom he watched get "further and further away" in the water. He told us, "I couldn't see her anymore, and then I could only hope. I could only hope that she's thinking like I am: 'Stay afloat till you land somewhere.' . . . I can't see her anymore at all, but I can hear her. She's screaming. We're communicating by screaming." He focused on grabbing his daughter and grandson so they could hold on to the boat. "I never lost control or lost my grip on the boat, but it's capsized. And I pushed the boat to my daughter, who had grabbed [my] grandson by the neck, and I pushed the boat to them . . . and we're just at the mercy of the current. . . . And we finally crashed at the end of the street."

Thankfully, they landed in the yard of a neighbor whose home was on higher ground. After regrouping, Kevin and his family slowly made their way through the yards of houses where the water was not moving quite as fast. This was a slow and treacherous process, since it was still raining hard and it was the middle of the night. They did not make it to the elementary school serving as a shelter until morning. What was normally a two- to three-minute walk had taken them five hours.

Helen, a single retired woman in her seventies, was alone in her home during the storm. She was taken aback by the power of the floodwaters, and she struggled to decide what to do. On Sunday, with "the water going down the street looked like a raging river," the water rose high enough to enter her home. "I just panicked," she said. "I just didn't know what to do, and I piled what I could on the dining room table." Rather than wait alone in her home, she decided to go to her next-door neighbor's house, where they waited together for a rescue boat. Helen told us, "It was a couple of hours before the fire department had a boat . . . and it came down the street and got us." From the boat, she said, "everywhere I looked there was water. I mean, you just couldn't not see water."

After waking up to water in their home, Sarah and Cal waited for eight hours before getting in a rescue boat. They kept sending boats to their neighbors first. Sarah said, "We're fairly young, so we didn't feel the need to use that resource at that time when there were people in the neighborhood who are elderly, with small children . . . people that we felt needed it more than we did." But when they started to get cold, they decided it was time to go. "Our hands were starting to shake, we had very, very mild signs of hypothermia setting in. But after eight hours I thought, 'We've done our part. We've turned away rescue probably two dozen times,' and it was time to go." To get on a boat Sarah and her family moved out into their driveway. "We pulled the kids out of the attic with our dogs; we put them on top of our vehicles and we waited."[15] The rescue boat had to carefully maneuver to get to them because the water was still moving so fast. Sarah told us that "rescue could not come up our driveway because we had such a strong current coming through here." Eventually they were able to safely load into the boat, and they were brought to the local elementary school.

Elizabeth and Richard, the retired couple in their seventies, woke up to rapidly rising water inside their home. By the time they were rescued at 3:30 AM, the boat was able to float over their deck and come directly to their back door. Elizabeth told us that they evacuated quickly, with little more than "the clothes on our back." She continued:

> We had gathered up the medication that [Richard] needed and, and luckily, he had opened our safe and got all of the important insurance papers and everything like this out. And we had two little bags, like Santa Claus, on our back. And for the first time in my life, I truly experienced what it was to be misplaced. I had no place to go. And the rescuers took us over to the school, and we sat there and . . . it just, the realization hit me that, wow, this was not going to be an easy fix.

SHELTER AND SOCIAL INFRASTRUCTURE

The evacuation was unexpected and, for many, traumatic, but the majority of properties in the town did not flood. As a result, local social networks could provide aid—plenty of unaffected Friendswood residents helped once the waters receded—and Friendswood's social infrastructure, the physical spaces of engagement and interaction, remained largely intact. Social infrastructure is key to recovery after disasters, since these spaces allow flooded residents to come together and collectively express needs and share resources.[16] Most of the key institutions that made up the town's social infrastructure, including approximately twenty churches and twelve public schools, remained largely unaffected by the storm.[17] Friendswood's main commercial street, where the majority of the town's businesses and city hall sit, was far enough away from Clear Creek that few nonresidential structures flooded. Thus, local churches, schools, and businesses could provide a place for volunteers to mobilize and effectively administer support. This type of community engagement immediately after disasters can foster a broader sense of solidarity and shared experience.[18] Without social infrastructure, recovery can be difficult, since flooded households remain isolated and aid is hard to coordinate.[19]

During Harvey, most Friendswood residents who had to evacuate their homes went to neighborhood public schools or local churches that were set up as shelters. Several of these sites were makeshift and not originally part of the City of Friendswood's emergency plan. But they were dry and safe locations that residents or the police opened to create impromptu shelters when the floodwaters rose faster and more intensely than anyone anticipated.

Kathleen and Robert, parents in their thirties, told us that as people evacuated their homes to seek dry ground, they headed toward the local elementary school because it was the closest safe space. People "broke into the school" and began to set it up as a shelter. Multiple respondents reported that local volunteers and residents fleeing floodwaters forced open the doors of the school. No one expected any consequences from this break-in—particularly as the number of residents requiring shelter began to swell. This expectation arose from both a strong sense of community ownership over the space and the general privilege of middle-class White residents who know they have little to fear from breaking the rules during an emergency. By contrast, poor and non-White people affected by hurricanes and other disasters often either fear the consequences of using unoccupied buildings as temporary shelters or are prevented from doing so by authorities.[20]

The homes near the school also remained dry, and a group of volunteers organized quickly to bring necessary supplies and to help those arriving at the makeshift shelter. Kathleen said, "They announced that [the] Red Cross was supposed to be there, but they didn't know when they were coming. I don't think they knew what to do. It was kind of just, 'We have a building. Let's get people in the building. Let's start at least finding dry clothes for them or at least dry towels, blankets, whatever we [can].'" Since the roads around the school were largely impassable, local residents provided a great deal of support and resources for many hours before government and Red Cross employees arrived.

Carol and William, a married couple in their forties, made it to the elementary school with their daughter after being rescued by boat. William said, "the water was so deep [that the boat driver] was concerned that his crop on his engine was gonna hit the top of a car or mailboxes." When they arrived at the school, he said, "I think they broke into the cafeteria, 'cause all they had was like crackers and chips and stuff like that." Carol told us that neighbors from around the school "were bringing in what they could, what they had in their stock that hadn't been flooded. . . . I mean, they were all trying to chip in as best they could." In general, flooded households were extremely grateful for the outpouring of support from other Friendswood residents during the evacuation.

Frank and his wife, who were in their fifties, evacuated their home and made their way to the other side of the neighborhood, where a church had opened its doors to serve as an impromptu shelter. At first volunteers used the church's day care snacks to provide food, but as Frank told us, they "realized that they didn't have what we thought they had food-wise. . . . They said, 'No, we are a little short on food. We have got to make sure we feed the kids first, and then we are going to feed the elderly, and if there is anybody sick, we will make sure we share with them first, and then we will share whatever else there is.'" But soon thereafter, through a combination of efforts by the county, the Coast Guard, and community members, more supplies were delivered using high-water trucks and boats. Frank told us:

> Local restaurants all donated. The Chinese place. Rubin's BBQ. The Mexican place right there on the other side of the creek. And they found ways to get it across the creek. There was somebody who had a speedboat . . . and they were able to bring stuff to the church. The church was like a little island. Water all the way around it. It was crazy. . . . But, yeah, at the church the donations were coming in. . . . There was good food for everybody. And then they had a whole big truck full of clothing and hygiene items and whatnot. Everybody was able to get a toothbrush. It all just came from nowhere.

Frank stayed in the shelter for three days and said that nearly two hundred other people passed through during that time. This church and several others then continued to serve as sites for organizing recovery efforts in the weeks after Hurricane Harvey.

Harvey's immense precipitation but relatively weak winds meant that damaged homes in Friendswood were concentrated around Clear Creek. Thus, many homes were spared and local social networks remained intact, as did much of the social infrastructure that would aid in recovery in the weeks afterward. This support was essential.

TEMPORARY HOUSING

Once flooded residents were in shelters, they confronted the problem of where to go next. The floodwaters remained high for days. After all, Harvey was stalled over the region, continually dumping more water, precluding any possibility of returning home quickly. Finding a place to stay became more urgent as residents who had landed at the school-based shelters were told by FEMA and Red Cross administrators that they were going to be bused to Dallas (a four-hour drive away), where FEMA would provide them with accommodations. No one wanted to leave. Fortunately, many flooded residents had family or friends who could put them up, and those who did not immediately find somewhere to stay turned to their social networks.[21]

Karen and her husband, who were in their forties, were relieved when they finally made it to a school shelter with their children. They were grateful to be somewhere dry where they could think about what to do next. She told us, "We have a meal in our belly, we have dry clothes. . . . Our neighbors were in there, but everybody was kind of distraught." The school provided a safe place to get away from the floodwaters, but within two days, the organizers of the shelter called a meeting. Karen recalled:

> They had like a megaphone thing, and he was just as blunt as could be, but tactful. And he said, "Hey guys, look, we've taken on this as a makeshift shelter not knowing the magnitude of this. And this is probably your last meal you are going to be having here. We need to get you all out. Having said that, you can't return back to your homes." And so, I'm thinking, "Where do we go?" . . . Then the blow hit, and he said, "You have about four hours, the buses are going to pull up, and we are taking everyone to Dallas, and you get on or you get a second means to get to somewhere." And at that point I went back, I asked my neighbors, "What are you all going to do?" They said, "We have family probably."

Karen knew that going to Dallas could introduce a different set of challenges. She told us, "I don't want to go to Dallas. I am like, this is the worst thing for us. My husband's job, we can't spend two weeks out in Dallas. At the same time, you are at that surrender. I started calling family members, begging at that point." Finally, one of her family members who lives on the other side of Friendswood responded and came to get Karen, her husband, and their children.

Karen, like many other residents, did not want to leave Friendswood. Doing so would disconnect them from local social ties, and many wanted to be as close to their homes as possible so that they could view their properties immediately after the floodwaters receded. Flooded residents also knew that they would have to return to work, and that their children needed to attend school. Dallas seemed like a poor solution to these immediate problems. So, like Karen, flooded residents tapped into their social networks to find somewhere nearby to stay. Residents of Friendswood tend to have strong and resourced networks: all of our respondents found temporary shelter, and none of them went to Dallas.[22]

After Elizabeth and Richard had safely made it to the school shelter, Elizabeth called a close friend and asked if she would come get them. The floodwaters were so high across roads in the area that after about ten hours in the shelter Elizabeth and Richard decided to wade through the water to a drier area of town where her friend could pick them up. "So our little plastic bags on our back, we walked out, and we walked and we walked and we walked. Waded was the word, in the water. . . . They finally were able to come up. It was a service station that was there, and they were able to come in . . . and then we were able to get into their vehicle."

After arriving at her friend's home, Elizabeth said, "I thanked them both, said a prayer, went to the shower, and washed my hair, because the amount of sludge, the amount of water that we were wading in, it was absolutely gross. It was oily, nasty, stinky. I mean, it was horrible." After putting on borrowed, oversized clothes, she told us, "I felt like I had been fitted with a mink coat. It was so refreshing to have something clean on." But as they thought about their circumstances, the situation hit hard. Elizabeth said, "I truly know what it was like to be left. Abandoned was not the word, but just—we were displaced. We had no, no place."

Her friend was able to arrange for Elizabeth and Richard to stay in an empty commercial space. It was small, with just a few offices and a kitchen. Elizabeth and Richard took to calling it "the apartment." They set up an air mattress in one of the empty offices and used the kitchen to cook meals and store food. It was dry, safe, and, importantly, close to Friendswood. Elizabeth and Richard could easily work on their flooded home during the day, while having a place to sleep each night. Elizabeth told us, "That's where we're residing now, until we can get this place [their home] set up."

Sarah and her family spent only a few hours at the school shelter. One of her best friends lived near the school, and her home had remained dry. Though Sarah was worried that she and her family—four people and their dogs—would be a burden, her friend insisted that they come stay. With nowhere else to go, Sarah agreed.

> My best friend, bless that woman's heart . . . she absolutely demanded we come to her house. . . . I said, "Are you sure you want me to do this?" . . . You're gonna end up with nine people in your house. Nine people and six dogs in a three-bedroom house. . . . The longer I stayed here thinking about it, the more, not uncomfortable I became, but the more kind of guilty I felt about [it]. . . . I'm already displaced. Here I am putting this on another family, but she wouldn't hear of it.

After making it safely to her friend's house and getting everyone cleaned up and settled, Sarah told her friend not to go out of her way to take care of them. Over the next few days, as the roads became passable, Sarah gave her friend $60 to offset the cost of additional groceries she might buy and insisted that they would make do with the MREs (meals ready-to-eat) they had brought from their emergency supplies. Her friend had other plans.

> I said, "Don't buy extra for us, we're good with MREs, we're good with ramen noodles. Just $60 worth of stuff for us and that's it." They came back with $500 in groceries, and she cooked and cooked and cooked. She had a theme, and I kind of realized it about day two. The first day for dinner she made biscuits and gravy, then she made lasagna. . . . She was taking care of us through comfort food.

Sarah knew that staying with her friend would not be a sustainable long-term solution, so after a few days she called her father-in-law, who owned a motor home. When Sarah asked if they could borrow it, he quickly responded, "Not a problem," even though it was currently in the shop for repairs. She told us that her father-in-law "called the shop, and he said, 'You have to get a move on, on that motor home. My son's house flooded, and he needs it to live in it.'" And within two weeks of the flood, "he drove it down, we backed it in the driveway, we hooked it up, and we've been in it since." Quite a few Friendswood residents were able to borrow RVs, which provided households with a somewhat private space and the ability to remain on their property as they worked on home repairs.

Claire and her husband, parents in their thirties, evacuated their flooded home on Sunday. Getting their children safely out of the house and into the rescue boat was traumatic. Claire told us that she put "floaties on [my daughter], and they were trying to pick her up and carry her, and she was screaming, 'Mommy, Mommy, Mommy,' just super-scared. . . . I don't think I'll ever forget her screaming for me, and I was telling her, 'I'm coming, I'm just getting our stuff so we don't have to come back for, you know, for a couple of days, in case we can't come back.'" The family stayed with friends who lived nearby in an area that did not flood while they decided what to do.

Claire said that after several days, when the water began receding, "my husband's like, 'We can't stay here, like, you know. I feel like we're intruding.'" With the roads finally clear, they made the decision to stay with Claire's mother in a nearby suburb. "Basically, once we were able to get there safely, we kind of packed up and went over there." Not only did Claire's mother provide them with a roof over their heads and help with the kids, but staying with her for several months was also a key form of financial support. Claire told us, "I can't imagine trying to live somewhere else . . . trying to pay for a rental for a family of five." They gave her mother the money FEMA provided for rental assistance, which Claire believed was around $3,000. By staying with family, they avoided the substantial additional cost of renting somewhere new.

Most properties that flooded were uninhabitable after the storm. Many were one-story houses, but even two-story homes had ruined kitchens. So most residents needed a place to stay not just for a few days but for months during the repair process. The relatively well-resourced social networks of Friendswood residents provided guest bedrooms, RVs, pool houses, and rental homes—typically at no cost, though many residents, like Claire, gave friends and family the money FEMA provided for rental assistance. This housing assistance became a lifeline for many. Only two Friendswood households we spoke to decided to rent a dry home immediately after the flood; each paid about two times their normal housing costs per month for a year after Harvey. Most households, however, were unable to take on a monthly rental payment in addition to keeping up with their mortgage payment or other monthly housing costs and paying for home repairs at the same time.[23] Instead, they relied on their social networks either to remain on their property in a loaned RV or to double up with friends or relatives not far away.[24] Staying close by allowed flooded residents to swiftly return to damaged homes once the streets were passable.

THE SHOCK OF RETURN

It took three days for the waters to recede far enough for people to return to their homes to assess the damage. Mia described what her husband experienced when he went back to check on their home: "We had stuff just strewn everywhere. . . . Any and all efforts to preserve anything on the first floor were just shot. I mean, there was just no way that anything was going to be salvaged." When Victoria, a married mother in her thirties, was finally able to return to her house, she was greeted by a similarly horrible scene:

> It was a disaster. You know, couches, everything was turned upside down, you know. Just everywhere, everything, it was horrible. My husband had . . . [a] whole big pan of oil, and he put it up higher in the garage just to get it—so it wouldn't spill on everything. Well, the water went over that, and so it was, like, covering everything in the garage. Just disgusting, every single thing in the garage was filled with that. So it was really bad.

Mark, a married father in his late fifties, discovered that the floodwaters had picked up everything in his house and swirled it around. "The current was swelling around in the garage for days, and when we opened the door ... everything had been mixed like it was in a giant blender, including that giant workbench with all tools on it. Everything was capsized and then a giant pile of junk." In the house, everything on the first floor was ruined. "There was crap floating everywhere. That's when I found the cedar chest floating around. There was our big upright piano, which, you know, weighs a few hundred pounds, [it] was floating in the dining room. Couches and beds. It was just crap everywhere." The water had even carried things from other properties into their home. "We found things in the house that didn't belong to us. We said, 'Where did this come from?' Yeah. And I don't know, but we found a catfish there and all sorts of other things. . . . It was about an eighteen-inch catfish in the middle of the family room."

Caroline returned to her house before the water had fully subsided in order to gather her jewelry and secure the guns that were in her home. They could not drive all the way to the house: "We hit the floodwaters too deep for us to continue driving, so at that point we hoofed it back through the waters until we got to our street." Seeing the state of her house was distressing:

> We got to the house and, um, oh God, that was very hard. . . . The smell was unbelievable. It hadn't been looted, which was good. So we had a walk around, just in shock. Everything was ruined, and stuff was all over the house because the water had moved everything. . . . It was all piled up inside as well as outside. The back deck had come loose, tore loose from the house, and had been floating around in the yard and broke up into pieces. And yeah, it was very difficult.

That first day, "we grabbed my jewelry box, my guns. . . . The whole place was completely filled up with water so we . . . kind of went through and gathered what we could and then left, and with the intent that we would be back in a couple of days when we could actually drive down the road." They were able to return to the house a few days later with family and a few volunteers to start the process of salvaging what they could and throwing out the rest. Caroline told us:

> That was probably the worst day of my life. I got to watch everybody gather up all of my belongings to throw them to the curb like trash. Things that—just my life, you know? This is my life. This is my entire life's worth of items collected, and it didn't mean anything to any of these people, you know? They were there trying to help me, and I appreciated it, but it was very hard to watch everything I loved being thrown out onto the grass as trash.

Most residents similarly described returning to their homes as devastating. Lives had been upended, belongings destroyed, and homes made unlivable.

Most households in Friendswood did not expect Hurricane Harvey to be especially bad. The town's past experiences with flooding informed these expectations. Tropical Storm Claudette in 1979 was so far in the past that many residents assumed that the lack of flooding in the intervening years meant that they were safe. The remoteness of that event also led some residents to view flood insurance as unnecessary or to be somewhat lax about making certain that their coverage was up to date. Harvey not only revealed these expectations to be misguided but shattered the daily life of the town and its residents. As the water crept in, residents had to leave under dangerous and harrowing conditions. They had to figure out what to do next—where to go and for how long—and they had to start marshaling resources for recovery.

In chapters 4 and 5, we delve further into the recovery process—what it looked like, how much it cost, and how long it took. But before flooded residents began the long and arduous work of repairing their homes, they had to decide whether to return to Friendswood at all. How did these households make the choice to stay and rebuild or to move? We turn to this decision-making process in the next chapter.

Chapter 3 | Why Do People Return to Vulnerable Places?

SARAH AND HER husband Cal, parents in their forties, moved to Friendswood more than ten years before Hurricane Harvey, when their first child was just a toddler. Even though their daughter was quite young, schools were already the family's top priority. They considered homes in a few suburban communities southeast of Houston, focusing their search on neighborhoods that were part of the Clear Creek Independent School District (CCISD). When we asked Sarah why they were attracted to Friendswood, she said matter-of-factly, "The school district. . . . I knew pretty quick I wanted CCISD." Sarah and Cal also had to find a house that made sense financially. In Sarah's words, "We are not a poor family, we're not a rich family. We're pretty average and we're comfortable." They looked "for middle-class, well-priced [homes]. . . . We didn't want to be house-poor. . . . We were big on trying not to live in debt." They were thrilled to find an affordable home they loved in Friendswood.

After moving into their preferred school district, Sarah and Cal developed a long-term residential plan for their family that was oriented around their children's education. When we asked how long they expected to stay in Friendswood, Sarah told us, "We're not planning on leaving until my son [their second child] graduates high school." After that, they intended to "sell and retire."

For Sarah and Cal, this residential plan guided their decision-making in the immediate aftermath of Hurricane Harvey. Even when more than three and a half feet of water flooded their home, they stuck to the plan they had made before the storm. Sarah told us: "The flood doesn't mean we change our game plan. We had a plan for life before the flood. This was an interruption. Yeah, we hit a bump. You hit the bump, but you've got to keep going. It wasn't a mountain, it's a bump, it's a bump. I've just got to remove the pebble from my shoe and keep going."

Once the floodwaters receded, Sarah and Cal started rebuilding and hoped to be able to move back in quickly. Sarah told us that returning to their home "was a simple decision that was almost not even talked about. [We] never talked about leaving." This family's singular focus on remaining in their home reflects how pre-storm plans oriented decision-making after the flood. Most flooded residents chose to stay in Friendswood despite the damage from Hurricane Harvey and the vulnerability revealed by the flooding.

RESIDENTIAL PLANS GUIDE POST-DISASTER DECISIONS

In the previous chapter, we showed just how shocking Harvey was for Friendswood residents. Not only was evacuation traumatic, but the loss of so many belongings and the damage to their houses from the flood was overwhelming. Faced with this devastation, flooded homeowners had to make a decision: whether to sell their homes and move, or repair them and return.

In this chapter, we examine this decision more closely. Research on past disasters has shown that there is a clear relationship between physical damage to housing and increased residential instability.[1] That is, people whose homes are damaged during flooding and other disasters are more likely to move—and to move more often—compared to households that do not experience damage. Yet the vast majority of Friendswood residents whose houses flooded decided to return and just a small handful departed. One year after the flood, only nine households in our sample had moved, while fifty (or just over 84 percent) were repairing their homes and had either already moved back in or were planning to do so soon.

Staying is not necessarily the obvious choice. Although there is generally low residential turnover in Friendswood, many flood-affected households had the financial capacity to leave. More and more research reveals that staying and rebuilding is often a complicated process that causes higher rates of stress for those who remain compared to those who voluntarily relocate.[2] What motivates these decisions? Why do some people stay and others go?

To answer these questions, it is helpful to understand how people decide to move.[3] The type of residential decision that Friendswood residents confronted after Harvey—unplanned and under duress—is relatively uncommon among middle-class households. Compared to lower-income households, middle-class residents face fewer events that often cause people to relocate, such as job loss, eviction, or foreclosure.[4] Instead, middle-class households generally choose to move when their home or neighborhood no longer matches their preferences or needs.[5]

By leveraging their financial and social capital, middle-class households are able to intentionally search for housing that fits into a long-term plan for residential stability.[6] Put another way, middle-class households have resources that allow for unrushed, considered moves into a variety of neighborhoods and homes.

As we saw in chapter 2, households in middle-class places are not immune from residential displacement in the wake of a disaster; nevertheless, historically poorer communities have been the most vulnerable to damage from natural hazards. A toxic mix of segregationist federal and local housing policies as well as decades of environmental racism has created a landscape where the neighborhoods that are most vulnerable to disasters—and most likely to be exposed to environmental hazards like pollution—tend to be poorer and non-White.[7] Yet, with events like Hurricane Harvey increasing in intensity and scope as a result of climate change and past benchmark storms becoming less effective predictors of risk, a wider set of places—including middle-class communities—are likely to be affected. Indeed, the floodwaters from Hurricane Harvey surprised the residents of Friendswood and served as a rare type of exogenous shock that displaced many from their houses and forced an unexpected residential decision.

In our conversations with flooded residents, we found that the decision to move or stay was strongly shaped by households' expectations about their residential future before the storm—their residential plans. Like Sarah and Cal, most households had clearly defined ideas about where they would be living for the next several years, if not longer. As outlined in chapter 1, these households chose to live in Friendswood for various reasons, many of which drew them back after the flood. Yet, on a deeper level, what motivated these households' residential decisions was not simply a particular amenity (such as the high-quality schools in Friendswood), but instead their vision of stability into the future. Amenities may be factors in forming a residential plan, but once a plan is in place, residents use it as a reference for making decisions.[8]

Indeed, the past casts a long shadow into the future as individuals use their past experiences to form expectations about what might happen in both the near and long term.[9] As such, examining the plans that people make is a useful way to understand decision-making, since plans cognitively bound the range of potential actions that they think are possible. We define residential plans as a household's projected future in relation to their current residential context—that is, their expectation that they will stay indefinitely or that they will move at some point.[10] These plans guided residents toward either stability or residential mobility in the aftermath of the storm, thereby narrowing the options they considered.

Sarah and Cal's plans for their home in Friendswood extended until both of their children graduated from high school. The temporality of a household's residential plans can influence action in the present by defining the anticipated timing of mobility.[11] The households that were most open to leaving Friendswood in the wake of Hurricane Harvey had already planned to move in the short term. Thus, Harvey was somewhat temporally aligned with their preexisting plans to leave. But for most flood-affected residents, Harvey did not match their expected timeline for moving. Instead, like Sarah and Cal, most residents planned to remain in Friendswood for many years, and these long-term plans for stability oriented them toward repairing and returning to their homes. Highly durable plans can create expectations that constrict options and narrow possible responses to an unexpected event. And indeed, we broadly find that households' plans were remarkably stable in the face of the flood. Whether they planned to stay or planned to move, few households in Friendswood changed their plans after Hurricane Harvey.

MOVERS: SHORT-TERM PLANS FOR MOBILITY

Most families who moved after Hurricane Harvey had short-term plans to leave Friendswood before the flood.[12] Many were renters, for whom the logistics of moving may have been easier, but as the examples in this section show, those who left after the storm included homeowners as well. The damage to their homes caused by Harvey simply motivated them to act on their preexisting plan to move soon.

Caroline, a mother of two in her forties, was renting a house in Friendswood from a family member. Before Hurricane Harvey, Caroline and her family had planned to stay in Friendswood only one more year. "[We'd] actually been planning to move from Friendswood when my son graduated high school next summer," said Caroline. "So we had already been looking at various areas and where we wanted to go." Indeed, people often use life-course events like graduation, marriage, having a child, and retirement as prompts to move.[13] Caroline and her family knew they wanted to move out of Texas and had been discussing this plan, but they had not yet settled on a new location.

For Caroline, Harvey simply accelerated her family's planned move. When the flood displaced them from their home, they decided not to wait. Caroline told us that while they could have stayed—their landlord was a relative, after all—the house "was damaged to such a degree that it was not livable anymore. . . . We stripped it down to, you know, bare framing basically, except for the outside walls. So, I mean, we would've had to literally rebuild the entire house . . . and it would've been a monumental job that would've taken a lot of time." In the face of this intensive rebuilding task, they chose instead to leave Friendswood right away. "Our thinking was, we have to relocate regardless. Our situation has been forced . . . and since we already knew we wanted to leave Texas anyways, we were like, 'Let's just do it now. We don't have very much stuff. It'll be easy to move.'"

During their displacement, the family discussed possible destinations, including Colorado, Florida, and the Pacific Northwest. Caroline told us that their first thought was to move to Florida, but "literally the next day after we were discussing doing that, freaking [Hurricane] Irma reared her ugly little head and all the news was like, 'Heading right to Florida.'" Less than a month after Hurricane Harvey devastated Texas and Louisiana, Hurricane Irma made landfall in the Caribbean and Florida and millions of Floridians evacuated their homes. For Caroline and her family, vulnerability to hurricanes was enough to cross Florida off their list of potential places. "We did sit down and discuss it," Caroline said, "and the kids were really, 'We don't want to live somewhere where this is going to happen again.'" So, as a family, they settled on moving to the Pacific Northwest.

Notably, while most of our respondents faced pressure from friends and family to move out of their flooded and now seemingly risky homes, Caroline was pressured to stay.

> My dad had this whole illusion at first that we would temporarily just move in with them for, like, six months while we built the house back up together, and then I'd move back into the Friendswood house, and he got really mad when we were like, "No, we're leaving." You know, he thought that was a mistake. He felt we should stick around.

For Caroline's family, their preexisting plan to move out of Texas remained durable even in the face of this familial pressure, and since most of their belongings had been ruined by the floodwater, they faced few impediments to making a quick move. Within a month of the storm, they were already settling into a new home in the Pacific Northwest.

Grace, who was in her sixties when Harvey hit, had moved to Friendswood years before with her son so that she could help take care of her aging parents. "[I] took care of my dad until he passed away," she told us, "and then took care of my mom until she died." Grace continued living in her family home with her son for years, renting it from a family member who took ownership of the property after her parents' death. For Grace and her son, the house held a lot of memories.

In recent years Grace had started seeing someone new. As their relationship progressed, she and her boyfriend discussed moving in together in the near future, and their plans were accelerated when Harvey flooded her home. Grace told us, "We had talked about a more permanent arrangement, but we had talked about giving it a little more time. So this kind of upped my timeline." Grace also took the flood as a sign that it was okay to move out of her family home, even though it was hard to leave. She told us:

> I'm going to get emotional. So, I kind of stood there one day and thought about it and thought maybe this was God's way of telling me it was time to move on. That house was built in the sixties. It had never flooded in all the floods in Friendswood history; it had never had one single drop of water in it. So, you know, why now? . . . Maybe it's time to move on.

Grace and her son moved in with her boyfriend after evacuating their home and stayed there while they mucked out their flooded house and tried to salvage what they could of their belongings. She told us that she felt no pressure to make the move to her boyfriend's house long-term, but having a plan to move in together before the storm led to a discussion about making the arrangement permanent.

> He said, "You know, if you want to move back into [your] house, we will. That's totally up to you. It's your call. But, you know, I have a bigger house. It's newer. It didn't flood, didn't lose power. If it happens again." So, I said, "Okay." . . . And so now I guess [my boyfriend's house] is where we're going to stay.

Grace decided to leave her house in part because living with her boyfriend was already on the table. Although she had not yet agreed to move in with him, they had discussed the possibility, and so she already had an alternative to staying in her home after Harvey. Put another way, Grace had a clear idea about where she might move next and the flood turned this plan into action.

Kathleen and her husband Robert, parents in their thirties, were renting their home when it flooded during Hurricane Harvey, but they had plans to purchase a home in Friendswood. "We had kind of already planned to buy in the summer of next year, 2018," she told us. "Just in between school break so that we could pack everything up." They had even started looking at houses for sale in their neighborhood. As Kathleen began to explain that "we originally wanted to stay in the same school district," Robert interjected to say, "We were actually looking at a neighborhood that flooded. Originally, we had planned to stay in that area." Although they had been planning an imminent move, Robert admitted that just before Harvey hit they had decided against going through the hassle of searching for a home and moving that year. "Honestly, we planned to buy earlier this year," he said, "but really, we were lazy and didn't feel like moving. That was the truth of the matter. Like, 'We have all this stuff, and I don't feel like moving quite yet.' So we just re-upped the lease one more year."

When their home flooded and they were forced out, they simply activated their plan to buy a home. Kathleen told us, "We had been saving up money and everything. So we just kind of were like, 'Well, this is the time. So might as well just . . .' So now we know what didn't flood, so we ended up here." They prioritized remaining in Friendswood, since they had built a close-knit community. "I didn't want to move outside of this area," Robert confirmed. "We have established ourselves [here]." They looked at several homes and purchased one in a subdivision adjacent to their previous neighborhood where homes had remained dry during the storm.

Many residents who were renting a home had temporally shorter residential plans; they usually planned to move in the not-too-distant future, while homeowners more often had long-term plans to remain. This difference is not especially surprising given that homeownership requires more capital and that people purchasing a house tend to do so with an expectation that it will serve as a longer-term residence.[14] However, renters were not the only residents of Friendswood who activated short-term plans to move after Harvey; homeowners with pre-flood plans for mobility also relocated after the storm.

Tammy and Joseph, a married couple in their sixties who had recently retired, had planned on selling their home and buying an RV to travel the country. Joseph told us, "We've been threatening for years to sell the house, sell the belongings, get an RV, and head out." In the years leading up to Harvey, as they helped their young adult children establish themselves, Tammy and Joseph kept putting off the decision to sell their home. "I mean, at some point we would have," Joseph said, "but you know . . . it probably would have been [another] two or three years." Their plans were concrete enough, however, that they had already started looking at motor homes. Tammy told us, "I had been looking at this one place where we ended up buying our motorhome . . . for, gosh, probably close to eight or nine months." Since they had already taken active steps to move, she said, "Harvey just kind of accelerated everything." Joseph agreed: "I don't think any of the decisions we made were just out of frustration, which a lot of times that could happen. Because we had been kicking it around, it just accelerated everything."

Tammy and Joseph were certain that they did not want to go through the hassle of repairing their flood-damaged home, and they listed it to sell as-is. Joseph said, "We were tired of it. We'd been there twenty-four years, it needed repair work, and you know, we talked about repainting it, we just weren't that interested. . . . And that was before the flood, by the way." Their home sold quickly, and they were thrilled with the price they got, which was close to the pre-flood value minus an amount that they believed to be a fair estimate of the repair costs. In the wake of the storm, there was ample opportunity to sell flooded houses. Residents regularly received mailers and phone calls from investors offering to buy their property. Although some of these were considered lowball offers, respondents who wanted to sell their properties as-is in the aftermath of the storm were generally able to do so quickly for prices they deemed reasonable, and often for considerably more money than they expected. Tammy said, "The amount that we came up with was perfect. . . . We still had quite a bit left over for, you know, various things that we needed. So it was almost like it was, you know, God said here, 'I want y'all to go and do what you've been planning on doing for all these years.' And so it worked out great." Since they had already planned for a residential future that involved moving, it was easy to pick up and leave.

Not all Friendswood residents had the resources to enact their plans in the exact ways they envisioned. Financial constraints led some families to adjust the timeline of their plans, even as they continued to work to achieve their pre-flood residential goals. Marissa and Jason, a married couple in their thirties, moved to Friendswood to be closer to Jason's office. As Marissa explained, their pre-flood residential plan had a short timeline. "We purchased this house thinking we would only be here for a year or two and we would, you know, turn it around, rent it out, and buy a bigger home somewhere else." When Harvey hit, they did not have flood insurance coverage, and so to save money on expensive repairs they did much of the work themselves. Even in the face of unexpected, costly, and time-consuming repairs, their plan remained durable—they still intended to buy another house soon. However, rebuilding delayed their mobility timeline by nearly a year. Marissa described the situation:

> It's kind of pushed that back and . . . we're not finishing things as quickly as we probably should have. . . . So we've given ourselves a deadline, like, we're done by the end of the year, you know, no matter what, so that we can do what we wanted to do with selling or renting the house out and finding a bigger home. So I think that's probably been the hardest, just kind of throwing a wrench in our plans.

Yet their commitment to maintaining their plan paid off: when we reinterviewed Marissa and Jason around the second anniversary of the flood, they had purchased a larger home in a nearby suburb and were renting out their flooded home. Marissa reminded us that this was "what we were planning on doing before it even flooded."

Although the financial resources of households in middle-class places may allow them to form long-term plans for stability, the exogenous shock of a disaster catches them at different points in their planned residential timelines, with some closer to their anticipated move than others. The reliance on their preexisting plans to inform post-disaster decisions shows that mobility is predicated on having somewhat defined ideas about when and where to move.

STAYERS: LONG-TERM PLANS FOR STABILITY

Most households that chose to return and rebuild after the storm had plans with a much longer temporal reach. Some households viewed their current home as their "forever home," while others were mapping their long-term residential plans onto a specific life-course event that they anticipated would change their needs or preferences in the future—often retirement or a child finishing high school. Although the flood was a highly disruptive event, it typically did not alter families' plans for long-term stability. Instead, these long-term plans continued to guide decisions after the storm, and more than 84 percent of our respondents chose to return and rebuild their homes.[15]

Like many middle-class families, Erin and Paul bought their Friendswood home with a plan to stay over the long term: "When we bought, it was for this to be more of a forever home." With this goal in mind, they searched for a house that would meet a few important needs. They wanted to be close to work and family, and as their children got older they knew they would need more space. After finding the perfect house in Friendswood, Erin and Paul quickly built strong relationships with the neighbors on their street. Erin said, "To come into this small community, everybody—it was almost instantly some of our favorite people in the whole wide world. . . . The community was welcoming, and the kids all welcomed our kids. Yeah, it just immediately felt like home." These friendships only further solidified Erin and Paul's view of their Friendswood home as a place they wanted to live long-term.

During the storm, Erin and Paul's home flooded with eighteen inches of water, but this damage did not prompt them to consider moving. Instead, they quickly decided to repair their house and return. When we asked if she and Paul discussed moving after the flood, Erin told us:

No. That was never . . . my mom mentioned it, because there's two houses for sale in the front street [of our neighborhood] that did not flood. My mom is a realtor, so she is always looking up houses for sale and stuff. She threw it out there. She was like, "You guys should just sell that house, and buy one that was not flooded." But that was not an option for us. We really like the house. We love . . . our neighbors are amazing. . . . We love our yard. We love our pool, which—don't look at the pool right now. It's green. Yeah. It was never really an option.

Rather than imagining a new residential future in the aftermath of Harvey, Erin and Paul were guided by the residential plans they had established before the storm, which oriented them toward repairing and returning to their flooded property.

Chachi, a widow in her late fifties, moved to Friendswood almost fifteen years before Harvey. She and her husband looked at several suburban communities southeast of Houston, wanting to avoid the bustle of the city in favor of something quieter. In the years since they moved in, Chachi has established strong local ties that strengthened her desire to stay in Friendswood long-term. "You get to know your neighbors, you know. You become pretty much a family. The idea that [I am] able to go walk or ride a bike, or take my dog for a walk at night, and I feel safe." In fact, she described a neighboring household, a married couple, she had grown especially close with as "like my brother and sister. They're up about six houses." Chachi's husband died shortly before Hurricane Harvey, and these neighbors were a great source of support to her. During the flood, Chachi went to their house to wait out the storm, and the three of them escaped to a local shelter together.

Chachi's home flooded with four and a half feet of water, so most of her belongings were unsalvageable and the house needed a huge amount of work. Her adult children, who lived closer to Houston, encouraged her to sell and move, but Chachi was resolute about repairing and returning to her home.

> CHACHI: Well, it couldn't get worse. You know, the tiles were popping with black water. There was nothing to save, absolutely nothing. So now, it's like, "Okay, how much is this going to cost?" And my sons are going, "Mom, please, just leave. Sell the house. Take what it's worth and walk away."
>
> INTERVIEWER: Why not? Why not walk away?
>
> CHACHI: I can't. This is my home. This is my home. My husband worked very, very hard, even after he was diagnosed

with cancer, even after he was taking chemo, to make sure that that house was going to be paid for, for me. So . . . this is my house. Yes, it's a nightmare. It's been a nightmare, but stupid Harvey is not going to run me out. It's like I don't consider myself a victim anymore. I'm a survivor.

The emotional and financial investment Chachi and her husband had made in their home shaped her plan to stay. Her plan for stability remained durable, even as the repairs to her home took more than a year, during which time Chachi lived in a trailer in the driveway. She also faced several conflicts with her mortgage company concerning the dispersal of her flood insurance payment, as well as with her contractor, who, she said, consistently underestimated the timeline and cost of repairs. Despite these challenges and the pressure from her children, Chachi remained committed to her plan to stay.[16]

Staying Despite Risk

In the aftermath of Hurricane Harvey, the plans of many flood-affected households to live in Friendswood long-term remained durable, even as they acknowledged the risk that their homes could flood again. In other words, residents who decided to repair and return to their homes, in keeping with their long-term residential plans, were not necessarily denying the flood risk.

When Claire and her husband, parents in their thirties, purchased their home, they were looking for a community that would provide the same small-town feel as the area where her husband grew up. As we saw in chapter 1, they found it in Friendswood. They bought their house with a long-term plan to stay, thinking of it as their "forever home." Even after Hurricane Harvey hit, this plan did not change. "We're not going anywhere," Claire told us, even though some of their friends did not understand their decision to rebuild and return. Claire said she was asked questions like, "Why don't you just cut your losses and go somewhere else?" She told us that moving was never an option. "[We] knew we were coming back at all times. . . . We picked this house out almost four years ago, like I said, and this is our forever home . . . perfect cul-de-sac, love our neighbors, love our neighborhood, love the schools." Their long-term plans for stability remained durable even when friends and family encouraged them to move elsewhere.

For flooded residents like Claire, the desire to stay was not the result of denied risk. We address risk further in chapter 6; here it is important to note that plans to stay in Friendswood were durable despite households' understanding that the area could flood again. Claire said, "I know it's always a possibility." Even in the face of this recognized risk, she and her husband still viewed their property as their "forever home," so rather than moving, they used the repair process to remodel. In other words, the flood enabled Claire and her husband to "make [the house] the way we want it to be." There were even times over the two years after Harvey when Claire framed the flood as an opportunity: "We were wanting to remodel anyways, so, well, we're basically, have the chance to do it now. So we say 'silver lining.'" Despite believing that her home was vulnerable to future flooding, and despite pressure from friends to move, her family's long-term plan remained the same even after the disaster.

Susanne and her husband, parents in their thirties, had a clear long-term plan to remain in their home before Hurricane Harvey. When we asked: "Before the storm, did you have an idea of how long you wanted to live here, or, you know, or what the future held?" Susanne told us, "Yeah, my husband and I said, 'You know, this is kind of our forever home.' This is where we were gonna live. . . . We wanted one of our kids to buy the house. We talked about putting, like, a little apartment in here, so one of our parents can live there if we ever need to." This long-term plan guided the family's decision to return to their home after making repairs, even though they recognized the risk of future flooding in their home.

In fact, Hurricane Harvey was the second time their home had flooded. "We knew that this house had flooded, but it flooded back . . . it was '79, when everybody flooded." Despite this history of flooding and their experience with Harvey, Susanne and her family still chose to rebuild and return. However, the risk did inform some of their choices about how to rebuild. For instance, Susanne told us, "we chose tile, woodlike tile, throughout the house. If we ever flood again, we won't have to rip it out again like carpet, you know, just little things that . . . choices we made about the house, if we ever flood again."

Even though future flood risk informed some of their rebuilding choices, Susanne told us, "I really do think we'll stay here. You know, we love this lot, we love this community. Especially after this storm, just to see people come out and support [each other]. We definitely want to stay here."

THE INTERACTION OF PLANS AND HOUSEHOLD FINANCES

Although preexisting residential plans oriented households toward certain residential decisions, plans alone did not determine residential mobility or stability after Harvey. Instead, residents' plans interacted with their financial resources and structural constraints as they made their decision to stay or move. Luis, a single man in his fifties, owned a home that he shared with his adult daughter, Nicole, and his grandson. Their decision to move to Friendswood shortly before Harvey was primarily motivated by schools. After Nicole researched different school districts, Luis told us, "she said the schools are good. I said okay. So we narrowed it down to Friendswood." They were searching for a home on a relatively tight budget, so Luis was excited when they found an affordable home in Friendswood. Luis moved in with a long-term plan for stability oriented around his grandson's education.

When we asked Luis and Nicole where they thought they would be in ten years, he told us, "I'm gonna be here. Taking care, I have to raise him. . . . Yeah, it'll be ten years, he'll be graduating. . . . So I got a ten-year plan." After the storm, this plan proved durable and oriented how Luis and Nicole responded to the flood. Not wanting to change school districts, they quickly decided to repair the house and move back in. Their decision to stay, however, was also motivated by financial considerations. Since they had recently purchased the home, the mortgage on the property was still sizable; it would have been difficult to sell the house for a price that would cover both the remainder of the mortgage and the purchase of a new home. "We owe too much money not to come back," Nicole said. "If they gave us enough money to pay off the house and a down payment for another, sure. But is that really gonna happen? No. That's a lot of money . . . so we were always going to come back."

Nicole also told us, however, that even if they got an offer that would enable them to afford to purchase another home, "we still want to be around here . . . 'cause, I mean, it's just a nice community." While material constraints certainly affected post-Harvey residential decisions, plans narrowed how households envisioned the future. For Nicole, even if her family had to sell and move, they would try to remain in Friendswood and stay connected to the local community and public schools that they liked so much.

Fortie, a single mother of two, was renting a home that flooded during Hurricane Harvey. She had initially moved to Friendswood for the schools. "I had a choice between League City or Friendswood, and I, you know, did research and talked to a lot of people, and I just chose Friendswood based on . . . the programs that they provided and the help that [her son] would be needing, [so] I chose to move to Friendswood." After moving, the schools lived up to her expectations, and she was pleased with her children's educational experience. So Fortie's plan was to remain in Friendswood at least until her youngest son graduated from high school.

She was forced to find another place to live, however, when her land-lord failed to appropriately repair her rental home after the flood. She told us that her landlord "did not cut enough sheetrock, he never treated the walls for mold, he literally gave the house, with fans and the A/C on sixty [degrees], a day and a half to dry out." Unable to find an affordable rental in Friendswood, Fortie leased an apartment in a nearby suburb. Yet her plan remained unchanged: "We really want to move back into Friendswood. . . . My goal and my hope is we're able to move back to that neighborhood." After Hurricane Harvey, Fortie continued to search for housing in Friendswood, and just before the second anniversary of the storm she purchased a home in the same neighborhood she had been renting in two years earlier. Thus, for some flood-affected households, like Fortie's, even when faced with constraints, plans remained remarkably durable.

Some constraints, however, were too great to overcome in order to maintain pre-flood plans. Lena and her husband Nicholas, parents in their forties, were committed to living in Friendswood long-term. Lena told us, "We planned to stay as long as we could because of the kids, the school, and their friends." After their home flooded with nearly five feet of water during Harvey, Lena said, they still intended to stick with the plan: "We want to stay in Friendswood if possible." However, the floodwater affected their house significantly enough to result in a determination of "substan-tial damage," which meant that their home was deemed to need repairs that would cost more than 50 percent of the value of the structure (exclud-ing land value).

To bring a house with substantial damage up to code and obtain per-mits for repairs, a homeowner typically has to undertake the incredibly costly process of elevating the house. Even when a homeowner is eligible for federal and local grants, approval can take many months; that delay is an additional barrier to rebuilding and returning to the property. Lena told us, "I reached out to the city about grants support. . . . Maybe there's going to be a possibility to get some grant money to raise the house, but they don't know when." As they waited, hoping they would be eligible for some additional funds, she and her husband estimated the expense of elevating their home. Determined to stay, they "tried everything," Lena said. "So basically, we hired an architect. He did the design, and then we talked to builders and . . . the cost and everything they predicted was way more than we thought." Months later, Lena and Nicholas learned that they were not eligible to receive any aid from the city or the federal government to raise their house. Ultimately, they decided that they had to sell their flood-damaged home as-is.

Lena estimated that their home was worth around $250,000 before the flood. After Harvey she worried that they would not be able to get more than $80,000 for their property. However, less than ten months after the storm, they listed their house for $175,000, and "within six days . . . the house was sold," the final offer having been "very close" to their list price. Although financial constraints motivated the sale of their flooded home, the housing market conditions in Friendswood rebounded quickly, making it feasible to sell their property for a price that allowed them to purchase another home in Friendswood and keep their children in local schools. Lena told us that "the mortgage we took out was not more than the mortgage on our old house. So now we have a new house that never flooded."

As families navigate post-disaster residential decisions, their plans and financial constraints interact. Sometimes financial constraints are significant enough to derail their plans—Lena and Nicholas, for instance, moved despite wanting to stay. Because of the relative stability of house prices in this middle-class White community, however, they could sell their house at a price that allowed them to purchase another home in Friendswood and avoid disrupting their children's lives.

After Hurricane Harvey, residents across Friendswood were displaced from their homes and faced a decision about whether to rebuild and return or move. Before Harvey hit, households had already developed plans for what to do in the next few years or longer. By and large, Harvey did not disrupt these plans. Instead, pre-storm residential plans oriented the choice that households made between staying or moving after the storm. With more than 84 percent of the households in our sample choosing to return to their homes, two things are clear. First, households in this middle-class community typically have long-term plans for residential stability; and second, even in the face of revealed risk, these plans for residential stability remain durable, anchoring households in place.

Plans specified households' expectations for their residential future in a way that narrowed their post-disaster responses and quickly focused their efforts toward stability or mobility. Plans then interacted with financial constraints to determine households' post-disaster residential decision-making. With their resources, middle-class households can make long-term plans for stability, but when disaster strikes, each household makes its own decision about staying or moving depending in part on where they are in their planned residential timeline—some are closer to anticipated moves than others. Those with long-term plans to stay returned to their homes when possible, while those with pre-flood plans to move away soon went ahead and did so. Even residents who acknowledged the risks of staying or faced financial constraints that changed their mobility timeline continued to let their plans guide their decision-making. A devastating event like Harvey did not alter what flooded residents imagined for their future. Understanding mobility choices in the wake of a disaster thus requires taking into account not only factors like finances and property damage but also households' expectations and plans.[17]

Over the next few chapters, we explore the recovery process in Friendswood after Harvey. It was far more difficult than most residents expected. As we describe that process, we continue to trace the themes that emerged in this chapter and return to them more directly in chapter 6 and in the conclusion. The residential decisions that households were forced to make—choices that were guided by preexisting plans—reveal why households in vulnerable places like Friendswood are often drawn back after a disaster.

Chapter 4 | Help-Seeking and the Local Ecology of Aid

It took nearly three days after the rain stopped for the floodwaters to retreat in Friendswood. When residents were finally able to return to their properties, it was clear that making their homes habitable again would take a great deal of work. Recovery after a severe flood takes time, labor, money, and materials. It also requires help.

Indeed, assistance, whether from the government or from more informal sources, is key to households' recovery after a disaster.[1] But individuals generally do not treat aid from formal sources like FEMA the same way they treat help from friends, family, and the local community.[2] Government assistance rarely provides enough to enable people to fully recover, so past research has highlighted the vital importance of informal post-disaster aid, such as help from social networks.[3] We certainly found this to be true in Friendswood. But to understand when, why, and how flooded residents sought out and accepted help from nongovernment sources, we had to go beyond analyzing the breadth and depth of affected households' social networks.[4] Instead, we came to see help-seeking as a more dynamic and contextually contingent process.[5]

In the weeks and months after the storm, Friendswood residents faced a changing landscape of informal support, what we call the "local ecology of aid."[6] An ecology of aid is not simply the sum of all the help that disaster-affected households receive from their social networks, but rather the environment in which households find themselves in need. The conditions in this environment—which include local resources and informal sources of support, social network assistance, and prevailing attitudes about offering, asking for, and accepting help—are experienced collectively. And as the local ecology of aid changes, residents' feelings about asking for and receiving help also change.

Flooded residents of Friendswood were open to receiving assistance in the immediate aftermath of the storm, but as time passed they did not seek or accept help to the same extent they had immediately after Hurricane Harvey. They increasingly expressed concern about being stigmatized for receiving aid from informal sources, which prompted us to think about what, if anything, had changed in Friendswood over time.[7] Put another way, we wanted to examine the community as a whole in order to understand why households would feel comfortable with certain kinds of help at one point in time but uncomfortable with the same form of assistance later.[8] One of the benefits of following flooded households over a two-year period was that we were able to view these changes, and their consequences, in real time.

Broadly speaking, being in need in the United States is an unenviable position. People in need of assistance are often marked as undesirable or outside the norm.[9] In a culture that reveres self-sufficiency, meritocracy, and independence, asking for help is often stigmatized. However, when people consider the conditions that create individual need to be external or beyond the individual's control, they may think of receiving aid as less shameful. For example, we tend to view disasters as creating "victims," or those who are perceived as "morally blameless" for the losses they face.[10]

Nevertheless, we still expected that many in Friendswood would express complicated and potentially contradictory feelings about seeking aid from official sources like FEMA or engaging their social networks with requests for help.[11] Indeed, before the storm the residents of Friendswood tended to think of themselves as givers, not receivers, of interpersonal assistance, and only a handful reported previous experiences with direct government aid, such as Supplemental Nutrition Assistance Program benefits (food stamps), reduced or free school lunches for children, or Temporary Assistance to Needy Families (welfare).[12] Middle-class households generally lack experience interacting with organizations that may provide aid during times of financial stress, and they tend to be averse to engaging resources that are associated with helping the poor.[13] After Harvey, however, Friendswood families found themselves in the position of needing a lot of help quickly. As they navigated the process of seeking assistance, residents evaluated what was acceptable based on the prevailing sentiments of the local ecology of aid. Their help-seeking reflected the behaviors and reactions of those around them.

After evacuating their flooded homes, everyone sought out aid from FEMA. Applying for federal disaster assistance was perceived as a necessary first step in the process of recovery, and no one expressed concern about being stigmatized for this form of help-seeking. But local, interpersonal aid is in many ways more fluid than government aid, growing and contracting in different ways and at different paces than state-provided programs. In practice, the perception of local support has a dynamic effect on how individuals make decisions about whether to seek or accept help beyond formal channels.

In Friendswood immediately after the flood the local ecology of aid was robust with offers of help, and flooded residents easily accepted assistance without fear that such aid would be stigmatizing. As time passed, however, the community seemed to move on, and offers of help faded long before most residents had fully recovered. In this new environment defined by fewer offers of assistance, flooded residents started to feel uncomfortable asking their friends, families, and neighbors for help. In trying to understand what makes someone more or less likely to seek and accept aid during a time of crisis or extreme distress, examining the local context matters a great deal. When the local ecology of aid changes, so too do residents' help-seeking attitudes and behaviors.

APPLYING FOR GOVERNMENT AID

The federal government declared Hurricane Harvey a disaster on August 25, 2017, making flooded households in Friendswood eligible for assistance from FEMA.[14] After evacuating their homes, one of the first things residents did was apply for government assistance. Some even applied for FEMA aid within hours of escaping the floodwater, using their cell phones to submit the application as soon as they arrived at local shelters. Both insured and uninsured residents applied for FEMA assistance, and few expressed any concern that contacting FEMA would be considered shameful or asking for a handout. Instead, flooded residents described applying for federal assistance as what they had been "told to do" by other evacuees, friends, and neighbors.

Like most of their neighbors, Carrie and her husband, parents in their thirties, had never had their home flood before. They took cues about what to do from the people around them. Within a day of the flood, Carrie contacted FEMA and her insurance company: "We registered with them immediately, like you're told to do. Not knowing what to do, you just kind of hear what everyone else is doing, and so we all just kind of figured out what we're all doing. . . . You just start making all those phone calls. Yep, so FEMA, registered with them and Allstate and just [got] on everybody's list." Shelters were buzzing with advice for those whose houses flooded, primarily with directions to contact FEMA as quickly as possible.

Grace was encouraged by others at the shelter to apply for FEMA aid even though she arrived before the floodwaters were high enough to enter her home: "Everybody was telling me that my house was going to flood and that I needed to apply for FEMA." Her boyfriend stayed behind to monitor the house, and he agreed that she should "go ahead and apply. He said, if the water doesn't come in the house, then I could always tell them that I didn't end up getting flooded. And I said, 'Okay.'" By the next day her home had flooded, and her boyfriend told her, "'It's a good thing you applied with FEMA.' He said I had six inches of water in the house and, as it turned out, it kept rising and we got about eighteen [inches]."

Only uninsured homeowners are eligible for direct cash payments to repair damage through FEMA's Individuals and Households Program, but all disaster-affected households, both homeowners and renters, can apply for various forms of housing support from FEMA if they are displaced. In other words, disaster aid does not operate like most means-tested welfare programs, which are viewed as highly stigmatizing and are often turned to only as a last resort.[15] Instead, FEMA is more like a universal program, which is typically less stigmatizing because it does not single out any one group as needy.[16] In the aftermath of the storm, everyone was told to apply for assistance, including residents with flood insurance, whose agents often directed them to FEMA for aid. Thomas, a married father in his forties, told us:

> Once we got to the church [shelter], and I felt like my family was safe, then I knew, I said, "What do we got to do to start recovering, to get back in the house?" . . . It was just start ticking off the boxes. The car insurance, the flood insurance, and then calling FEMA, and just going through the process there. Our flood insurance agency was great. They were like, "Here's what we can do. Here's the direct number to FEMA right now. The sooner you call, the better, because they go first in, first out, on a lot of things."

None of our respondents expressed reluctance about registering for FEMA assistance. Instead, they recalled the general sense of urgency among flooded residents about applying as quickly as possible. In other words, there was certainly no stigma attached to this kind of help-seeking, and some residents even described money from the government as something they were due.

Typically, all affected households received around $2,000 in rental assistance, and they were also eligible for vouchers to cover the cost of hotel rooms. Just after the floodwaters receded, however, it was difficult to find a hotel with available rooms that accepted FEMA vouchers near Friendswood. John, a widower in his late fifties, was told that he "could live in a hotel, but none of those hotels that they had lists of had openings." Only seven households in our sample used a FEMA hotel voucher. Instead, as we saw in chapter 2, most of our respondents chose to stay with friends or family when they left local shelters, using their rental assistance to pay for food and transportation and to contribute to costs for those who took them in.

In addition to rental assistance, FEMA provided direct aid to households without flood insurance for home repairs after Hurricane Harvey, capped at $33,300. This assistance "is intended to make the damaged home safe, sanitary and functional," but FEMA will not pay to return a home to its pre-disaster condition.[17] Since it will not cover the full cost of repairs, FEMA directs homeowners to apply to the Small Business Administration for low-interest disaster loans. The amount of money loaned by the SBA to disaster victims dwarfs direct aid from FEMA, and it makes up the majority of federal government assistance for individual recovery.

To determine the exact amount of aid each household is eligible to receive, FEMA inspectors assess and verify structural damage. On average, FEMA inspected the homes of our respondents about one month after the storm. Many people attributed what they viewed as the slow pace of inspections to the occurrence of other disasters in the weeks after Hurricane Harvey. Erin, a married mother in her forties, told us:

> I honestly think the hurricane [Irma] hitting Florida right after we were hit, I think it just messed up the whole system. It was just too much. And then the wildfires going on in California, and then Puerto Rico got hit [by Hurricane Maria], and it's like, boom, boom, boom. FEMA's not that big. There's not that many resources. And so they got stretched.

Erin told us that the FEMA application was "relatively straightforward, [and] easy to use," but that the more difficult part was waiting for inspection. "I think the hardest thing with FEMA was it was a 'hurry up and wait' situation." In general, Friendswood residents found it quite easy to apply, but they expressed some anxiety about the time between application and inspection.

Forcing people seeking aid to wait is a common way in which bureaucracies exercise power. Those in need of aid face what the sociologist Javier Auyero describes as "the pervasive uncertainty and arbitrariness of the lived experience of waiting."[18] The anxiety that households felt while waiting for FEMA inspections was amplified by uncertainty about how much money they would actually receive. Poor individuals and households are more frequently made to wait, but this experience was new for many of the middle-class households in Friendswood, who expressed impatience, confusion, and exasperation at the time it took for FEMA to inspect their homes.

After waiting for weeks, residents were often surprised by the brevity of the FEMA inspections. Kyle, a full-time university student in his twenties who lived with his parents in Friendswood and played an active role in helping his family navigate recovery, told us, "The inspection was about twenty minutes. In and out and that was it." Inspectors measured rooms, checked the water line inside the house, asked about damaged appliances and belongings, and then entered all this information into a form, usually on an iPad. Inspectors were there simply to gather information on structural damage and were unable to tell the homeowners the amount of assistance they would receive. After the inspection, homeowners had to wait again—this time to receive a payment from FEMA, most often as a direct deposit into their bank accounts around two weeks later.

The uninsured households in our sample received a wide range of direct assistance from FEMA, from just under $4,000 to nearly the maximum amount approved for FEMA relief at $33,300. On average, our uninsured respondents received just over $17,000. By and large, the residents of Friendswood found interactions with FEMA to be straightforward, even if the amounts of money they ended up getting were too small to support full recovery.[19]

Residents generally knew that FEMA would not provide enough assistance to fully cover the costs of repairing their homes. Elvis, a single man in his sixties, said, "They're going to give you a hand up, but they ain't going to put you back whole, you know." The fact that FEMA aid would not cover the full costs of repair was readily apparent to Erin and Paul, who received $11,000 in assistance. This did not come close to their expected repair costs. Paul told us that, by his early calculations, it was "going to be about $50,000 to $60,000 to get everything back to working." Erin and Paul chose to apply for a loan from the Small Business Administration to try to close the gap between their FEMA aid and their anticipated repair costs.[20]

Although uninsured households were eligible to apply to SBA, they were not guaranteed a loan. Out of the twenty-eight households we spoke to that did not have flood insurance when Hurricane Harvey hit, nine (32 percent) were turned down for an SBA loan. Overall, in the first three months after Harvey, more applications for SBA loans were denied than approved.[21] Common reasons the SBA gives for why loans are denied include "unsatisfactory credit history" and "lack of repayment ability." This often means the lowest-income households are the most likely to be denied and demonstrates that recovery policies can amplify inequality within communities, as some neighbors have access to greater recovery resources than others.

When Erin and Paul applied to the SBA, they were quickly approved for a loan of $111,000, which Erin told us was "way more than I expected." Unlike FEMA aid, which households receive in full as a direct deposit, SBA loans are disbursed like insurance payouts: funds are paid in small amounts as homeowners provide proof of completed repairs. Describing this process, Erin said, "They give it to you in increments. So now, to get the next installment, you have to submit receipts . . . get like a progress report basically." Paul confirmed that the process was a way of "just essentially showing that we're rebuilding the house." The loan from SBA was critical to Erin and Paul's capacity to rebuild their home, but as Erin told us, they were acutely aware that, "at the end of the day, it's still a loan and you have to pay it back. Even though it's a good interest rate, and you have thirty years to pay it back, it's still a lien on your house. It's not free money."[22] These loan terms kept Erin and Paul focused on finding ways to keep their repair costs low, and to do so they needed help.

It was not only uninsured households that found themselves in need of ongoing help from family, friends, and the local community during recovery. Insured residents also needed aid as they managed the slow insurance payouts and the broader challenges of being displaced from their homes. Elizabeth and Richard, a retired couple in their seventies, received a total of $90,000 in flood insurance payouts to cover repairs and lost belongings. It took months to get the funds, however, and there were plenty of hoops to jump through. Elizabeth was disappointed by all the red tape: "You pay out all this money for your insurance, and you pay and you pay and you pay, and when they do give you the money back, they expect you to show every dollar—that the $90,000 they gave you was spent accordingly." Richard told us that "what rocked my boat" was that "people who didn't have insurance got $30,000 free from the government. And they got money before we did, and that's what put us behind getting started. Waiting on money." The couple got an advance to cover some initial costs but did not get their insurance payout in full until "about the twentieth of December or something like that." Because they had to use their savings to cover construction costs while they waited, work on the house proceeded slowly. (We detail the bureaucratic hassles and complications of receiving insurance money in chapter 5.)

Elizabeth and Richard also relied on help from friends and family to continue moving forward with their repairs while they waited for their insurance payout. For example, Elizabeth told us that it was only "the generosity of our friends" that enabled them to purchase new appliances, "because, you know, at that time we had [limited funds] to operate on. Just, it's just overwhelming." They both felt extremely fortunate, however, that they had been "able to rely on each other and our friends and our family." Even for insured households, local informal sources of assistance were a key part of the recovery process in the months after the storm.

In the aftermath of Hurricane Harvey, all households applied for federal aid without compunction. Applying for assistance was simply one step in the process of shifting from immediate survival to focusing on recovery. FEMA quickly provided nearly all affected residents with rental assistance funds or a hotel voucher to use to secure a safe place to stay. As FEMA began inspecting damaged properties in the weeks after the storm, uninsured residents received additional aid for repairing their homes. Although there was variation in the amount of aid that uninsured households received, none of them received enough to fully recover. Some households tried to fill the gap by using SBA loans, but not everyone was approved. Lacking sufficient funds and facing indeterminate timelines, flooded households also had to rely on other informal sources of support. How they did so depended on the features of the local ecology of aid.

A ROBUST LOCAL ECOLOGY OF AID
IN THE IMMEDIATE AFTERMATH

As flooded residents recognized their need for interpersonal sources of help, they faced a choice: Should they seek out and accept help from local organizations, friends, family, and neighbors? This decision was far more fraught than the decision to apply for FEMA aid. But accepting local help was made easier by the robustness of the offers of assistance in the weeks right after the storm.

For many flooded residents of Friendswood, being in the position of having to ask for help was uncomfortable. They perceived themselves as people who gave help, not people who received it. As Tanya, a married mother in her forties, told us, "We're used to being the ones who go out and help. We're not used to being the people who get help." These self-understandings led some people to feel dispirited by the position of being in need. Lena also described receiving help in the aftermath of Hurricane Harvey: "It was very hard. I think that was the most difficult part of this whole hurricane. Not the physical damage that is seen, but accepting help from others. That was very hard." These statements echo research findings that middle-class households affected by disaster are wary of, and unaccustomed to, accepting charity.[23] Yet their need for help in the aftermath of Hurricane Harvey led these middle-class households not only to apply for federal aid without hesitation but also to accept informal help from local organizations and from their social networks, even when they noted that doing so contrasted with their identities as givers. Molly, a married mother in her fifties, told us that "receiving [help] was a difficult thing for me because I'm a giver." She ultimately accepted help after encouragement from her friends, who told her, "You're blessed by giving, so let somebody else be blessed by giving back to you."

Through September and even into October, the narrow suburban streets of Friendswood were clogged with cars, trucks, and volunteers helping flooded residents. The community was dense with unprompted offers of aid, and there was a strong sense of solidarity within the town at the start of the recovery process.[24] In this context, Molly and all of her flooded neighbors accepted the help that was available.

This outpouring of support also occurred at a critical juncture in the recovery timeline. In the first few days after the water receded, residents needed to muck out their homes—removing wet belongings, carpet, drywall, and insulation to prevent mold and allow their homes to dry out. Most residents in Friendswood had multiple volunteers help with this effort. Kevin, a married man in his fifties, told us that when he was able to return to his home, "in my mind I'm thinking we got to get it out, everything out for the rebuild. We got to stop the mold." He was grateful when members of his church showed up en masse. So many people came to volunteer that he described them as "an army." The volunteers helped remove nearly everything from his house: "That day they were moving furniture out. Everything out. They're taking sheetrock. . . . All we could do was just make the pile big. . . . All the furniture, clothes, everything was gone. Everything in that house was gone." The clarity of the need and the scale of the task spurred Friendswood into action to help flooded households.

Marissa, a married woman in her thirties, said, "the community was wonderful. Everybody was helping everyone. When we would be outside, there would just be random people out there, like, 'Hey, do you guys need help?' . . . Just all that entire month of September was like that." There were so many people out, she said, that "if you needed it, they were there. All you had to do was go outside and flag somebody down. . . . There was no shortage of help. If you needed somebody to come knock your drywall down for you because you couldn't or you're disabled or whatever, there was a group to come do it for you." As Marissa's description makes clear, the community responded with assistance that extended beyond the individual social networks of flooded households.

In fact, quite a few respondents described strangers helping them in those early days after the flood. For Marissa and others, this robust community response made it easy and appropriate to accept help because it was so available. Sarah, a married mother in her forties, told us that there was a big volunteer turnout in the neighborhood the first weekend after the storm. "Saturday we had more, more people in the neighborhood [asking], 'How can we help?' and strangers walking into your house and helping you muck it out."

Because of the overwhelmingly generous volunteer efforts, Valencia, a single woman in her midfifties who lived with an elderly parent, never had to ask for help; instead, she received frequent and even forceful offers of assistance. Even when she initially declined their help, volunteers would continue to press:

> They would come walking up and down the street, or driving up and down the street, and would just stop and ask, "Do you need some help?" And half the time you could say, "No, I don't think so." And they go, "Yes, you do." And just come on and take over. Which was a good thing, because they could see that you didn't know where to go or what, what to do next.

Nick, a retired widower in his sixties, similarly described the importance of church and civic groups and strangers on the street offering help throughout the neighborhood. He told us, "The people from the church group were very helpful. . . . People would just walk up from off the street and say, 'Can I help you?' 'Well, sure.' I mean, a couple of different people did that, and they would just move on down to the next house and see if they could help there." Later he said, "I believe that the whole community really banded together." Between the sheer scale of the community response and the extent of the damage to people's homes, it seemed as though nearly everyone was either helping or being helped.

Importantly, the ubiquity of the help being given and received made it easier for households to seek out and take the help that was offered. Cora and her husband Michael, parents in their forties, explained that "we're not the people that would ever reach out," but in the aftermath of the storm "we never had to ask for help." Instead, the offers of assistance were so plentiful that it felt like "sometimes they would force themselves on you, and you didn't think that you wanted or needed it." Yet this context of repeated offers of help pushed Cora and Michael toward accepting it. Finally, they told us, "we took it."

Similarly, Mia, a married mother in her thirties, said, "Yeah, I mean, it was definitely a weird feeling to be the recipient of help, but at the same time . . . when people were saying, 'I'm bringing you dinner,' I didn't object. It was like, 'Thank you.'" The shared sense among residents of Friendswood that the community as a whole was engaged in asking for, offering, and receiving help enabled flooded households to accept aid without fear of stigmatization or compromise to their identities as independent or as generous givers.[25]

Later that fall, however, as the holidays approached and the weather turned chillier, the robust local aid that had flowed so easily in the first few weeks and months after the storm started to wane. There were far fewer people on the street. Volunteers organized by churches, civic groups, and schools were no longer going door to door to see if people needed help. There was a sense that the community had moved on. In other words, the local ecology of aid changed. Yet most of the households that flooded were still quite far from completing their repairs.

OFFERS OF ASSISTANCE FADE AND STIGMA EMERGES

Over time the local ecology of aid became one in which fewer offers of help were extended. In this new setting, flooded residents had to make decisions about whether or not to actively seek out further help; many expressed a growing sense of discomfort about doing so. In other words, as the availability of aid changed, so too did residents' perceptions of their own and others' need and deservingness. Even when the needs of flooded households were still great—for example, they had outstanding major repairs or had depleted their sources of cash—they began to worry that they would be stigmatized if they asked for help.

Kara, a married mother in her forties, described how offers of assistance faded, even though she and others were still in need:

> Once the holidays hit . . . starting Thanksgiving going forward, it's, it's been, not the same. . . . People have moved on even though we can't move on. . . . In the immediate aftermath people just wanna do whatever it is to help. You know, you would have people show up at your house and just start cleaning out stuff for you. I had a friend who went to go help at a house and didn't realize until like five hours in that she was at the wrong house. . . . So the community was, has been, great in that way. But it fades. And it fades before you need it to fade.

Samantha, a married mother in her thirties, also found the immediate surge of aid extremely helpful but noticed that the offers of help dissipated quite quickly. "It all kind of wears off. All of it kind of wears off. But for the first, like, month and a half . . . we had meals brought to us. I mean, I was blown away . . . people signed up to bring me a dinner. That was so, so helpful." For Georgia and Leo, a married couple in their fifties, their friends and neighbors whose homes did not flood no longer recognized the ongoing need months later. Georgia said:

> It's been how many months now, four months? And so I think people are more back into their routines. That's not nice. And so it's just not fore-front in people's thoughts anymore, you know. It's not an emergency any-more. . . . When something happens, people immediately, with the empathy, want to go out and do something to help. And then eventually, life sort of catches up with people, and they get distracted again.

Other respondents also perceived a marked change in how they were treated. The robust ecology of aid and the community-level sense of cohesion transitioned, becoming more fragmented.

Alicia, a married woman in her sixties, told us that, immediately after the storm, "we had people volunteer from churches, and all these kinds of people were here, and it was awesome. I mean, I could not say enough about the outreach of those people here locally." However, over time there was a growing disconnect between those whose homes had flooded and those whose homes had not; by two years after the flood, she said, "I think the people that were not flooded are way over it." This affected Alicia's relationships with people whose homes had not flooded, even friends who had helped in the early months after the storm. "They're way past that now," she said.

> You know, Harvey is kind of, like, ancient history. . . . I wouldn't talk about Harvey [to] anybody who hadn't flooded because that would be like, "You're so living in the past." You know, "Quit moaning." . . . You don't want to raise something that's pointless and stupid to them, and they will interpret it as "You're just not over it, are you?"

As time passed, even some households that flooded but finished rebuilding relatively quickly started to judge neighbors who were slower to repair their homes. Charles and Barbara, a retired couple in their seventies, had flood insurance and enough savings to begin to pay their contractor to start work even before their insurance payments began. As a result, they were able to complete the majority of the repairs and move back into their home within five months. When we reinterviewed them a year after the storm, they had only a few small tasks and furniture purchases remaining. Meanwhile, a number of their neighbors were further behind in the repair process. Adjacent properties still had piles of debris in their yards from ongoing work as well as trailers in their driveways that their neighbors continued to live in during construction. Although Charles and Barbara recognized that "a lot of people didn't have money, and [when] they don't have money, it's a struggle," they felt frustrated with the slow pace of their neighbors' repairs. Charles told us:

> There comes a point in a subdivision where you're going to say, "Enough is enough." Enough time has gone by, you got to get back to where we were, and there are certain standards that you got to meet, like getting these dang trailers out of here or getting your house fixed up . . . because that affects all of us. . . . There must be ordinances or health and safety standards. At some point you say, "Enough is enough."

Charles's sentiments reflected the general erosion of community support, empathy, and solidarity that had defined the local context immediately after the flood. One year after the storm, Carla, a married woman in her fifties, similarly complained about the lack of progress made on nearby properties. She and her husband moved quickly to hire a contractor after the floodwater receded, and they were ahead in the repair process relative to most of the households we followed. Carla was "very frustrated with the fact that two homes, one on each side of us, hasn't been touched. Very little has been done. Their yards are all grown this high. I mean, our house looks like it did before. So the folks that haven't done anything is frustrating to us."

As variation in households' repair progress grew more visible and offers of help waned, different assessments about those still in need emerged. In this new context, households still in need started to view others' judgments as stigmatizing.[26] Angela, a married mother of three in her forties, provided an example: "I had an uncle . . . I had posted something on Facebook. He just said, 'You're still not done?' like, just really insensitive." Her family was repairing their home without flood insurance, and the process was taking longer than any of them wished. The challenges they faced made such comments even more irksome. She sent her uncle a long email in response, describing her family's experience, and her uncle apologized. However, for Angela and others still in need, these types of responses indicated that collective sentiment had changed, and that they were increasingly likely to face judgment about the pace of their recovery and any expression of ongoing need.

THE STIGMA OF HELP-SEEKING

In this new local ecology of aid defined by fewer offers of assistance and more critical assessments of flooded households' behavior, residents engaged in less help-seeking. Despite continued need, as time progressed people came to see help-seeking as less appropriate. More than a year after the storm, Molly and her husband still had some large repairs to complete on their home, including finishing their master bathroom. Molly acknowledged that help was still available—she could have requested a crew of volunteers from her church, which was still organizing groups to assist households in need on the weekends. She and her husband were no longer comfortable, however, with asking for help. "We could contact them. I mean, they could come and help with the shower. I mean, that's still an option for us to do." Her husband replied, "I'd feel guilty about using them for that." Although they had accepted aid in the immediate aftermath of the storm, Molly and her husband now expressed discomfort with continuing to engage in help-seeking.

One year after Hurricane Harvey, Claire and her husband were living on the second story of their home with their children while repair work continued on their damaged first floor. Even with insurance coverage, repairing their home proved to be a very slow process. They still were unable to use the kitchen, so they were cooking in a microwave upstairs. Despite their continued need, Claire expressed discomfort with accepting food, even though she had accepted this type of help in the immediate aftermath of the storm. She was reluctant to accept help, in part, because people in her social network assumed that her family had completed their repairs:

> They didn't realize, "Wait, you're living upstairs with no kitchen?" I was like, "Oh, we're just eating out a lot, and sandwiches, and peanut butter and jelly. Our microwave can heat up some things, macaroni and cheese, and stuff." But yeah, people offer meals, but I haven't taken a lot of those. I feel awkward having people cook for us. Like, when [Harvey] happened, people were giving us meals, like, there was no time to do anything, so it was kind of more needed then, because I didn't have time to run to the store, run to even grab food from the McDonald's or whatever.

Just as Claire was reluctant to seek out assistance, she also did not feel comfortable accepting offered aid. Right after Harvey, Claire's children were automatically enrolled in the free or reduced lunch program at their school because they were displaced. Although Claire praised this aid program, she was uncertain one year later whether or not it was acceptable to enroll her children in it for another year. Since their repairs were not complete and her family was living without a kitchen, Claire was told that her children were still eligible, but she felt that they were too close to completing repairs to accept this aid for another year. She told us that, while her family wasn't "homeless," they were "technically still displaced." Referring to the paperwork needed to enroll her children in the program, she said, "I don't want to fill that out, knowing that we're gonna be, hopefully, living downstairs, [in the] next couple of months, at least." Claire believed that her family was still recovering: "I'm still, still rebuilding, I'm still paying for everything"; yet she no longer sought help: "I don't want to consider myself needing, or I don't want to take someone else's stuff." As time passed and the local ecology of aid changed, even accepting aid from formal sources began to conflict with Friendswood residents' sense of themselves.[27]

Other respondents were likewise hesitant to accept formal aid. One year after the storm, Karen, a married mother in her forties, told us that she had recently been contacted by an aid association offering assistance.

Although she had received FEMA aid in the aftermath of the storm because her family did not have flood insurance, she refused this offer of further aid. She said, "I was contacted last week. . . . [An association representative] wanted to come to my home, to see if there was anything that they could do for us in any way. I told her, 'I think we're okay.' Besides, you know, I feel like we've gotten a lot of help." Karen asked if she could meet the representative and direct her to others in need, saying, "I know people in tents, and things like that . . . and I get the privilege of going to all the campers and just say, 'Help them, help them, help them.'" Even if households in our sample were still living with some level of need, they often identified their need as less than that of others.[28] As a result, they frequently refused offers of help.

As time passed, not only did households seek and accept help far less than they had in the immediate aftermath of Harvey, but they also described their prior help-seeking behavior as an aberration. When we spoke with Samantha two years after the storm, she explained that her willingness to ask for and accept help was now notably different than before, when her family was mucking out their home and trying to salvage their belongings.

SAMANTHA: Facebook memories pop up and I'm like, "People are asking how they can help, here's a way. Now we need this." And I look at that and I'm like, I can't believe I would even put that on Facebook. Like that's, we're just, I'm just a very private person in that way. And I would never reach out to the mass public. More power to those people who don't feel weird about asking for help like that, but that's just never been me. So I look at these memories, I'm like, "Oh my God, I did that?"

INTERVIEWER: So what is an example of something that you put online that now you have [a] reaction to?

SAMANTHA: Well, it's not even that big of a deal, but I can't believe I was asking for bins. I was like, okay, you know, now we have to take everything out of our cabinets and we need a place to store it, anything we can salvage, we need a place to store it. . . . I didn't ask people to go buy bins, but I was like, "We need bins. If you have any, can you please?" And people brought tons and tons of bins.

Samantha explained her willingness to take people up on offers of help with meal preparation after the flood in similar terms. "When we got back into our house and still didn't have a kitchen, I posted again . . . 'People have offered to cook for us, we finally need it.' . . . And so I asked. I set up my own meal train, which is just crazy. I would never ever, ever do that." Samantha's description of these help-seeking actions as something she "would never ever, ever do" demonstrates that help-seeking can be contingent on need as well as on local ecological factors.

When there was an outpouring of seemingly universal support from flooded households' social networks and the community overall, they more readily sought and accepted help. When help was universal, it was easier to receive. But as offers of help declined and households had to individually seek out assistance, flooded residents increasingly worried about judgment from friends and neighbors who seemed less interested in providing help. As the local ecology of aid changed, flooded households became uncomfortable with help-seeking, and some even reframed their previous help-seeking behavior as an anomalous deviation from their identity as givers. Others chose to forgo offered help, even in the face of persistent need, as a strategy for mitigating potential stigma in the new ecology of aid.

In Friendswood immediately after Hurricane Harvey, flooded residents knew they would have to marshal resources in an effort to recover. Their decisions about whether to seek out or accept help were influenced by the conditions of the local ecology of aid. A great deal of past research after disasters has focused on social networks as an important source—if not the main source—of support necessary for recovery.[29] Denser networks with more social capital provide more aid, which helps affected households recover more quickly. The residents of Friendswood certainly tended to have rich and deep networks, while the town itself also has a robust social infrastructure with many churches and civic organizations.[30] But as we have shown, whether and how those affected by disaster engaged these networks or local groups was complex and changed over time.[31] Put another way, while the availability of resources certainly matters for understanding help-seeking during recovery, so too do the collective sentiments about those resources.

In line with past research that has described a general cultural aversion to being in need in the United States, flooded households in Friendswood viewed themselves as givers and not receivers of aid.[32] However, in the immediate aftermath of Hurricane Harvey, when there was a robust outpouring of support, flooded residents readily sought out and accepted various kinds of help without fear of stigmatization. As time passed and community support within Friendswood faded, more variation emerged in flooded households' progress with repairs, and the stigma of being in need increasingly became a critical concern. When robust, unconditional support was no longer part of the local ecology of aid, households began to question the deservingness of their neighbors, pursued sources of aid less willingly, and refused help when it was offered even if their repairs were still incomplete.

By following households in Friendswood over two years, we were able to directly observe the fluidity of local aid in the wake of a disaster. These changes over time had a dynamic effect on how residents decided whether to seek or accept help. That is, households' opinions and decisions about help-seeking shifted as the availability and robustness of aid changed over time. When unsolicited offers of help waned and residents perceived less interest from their social networks and local civic and religious organizations in providing help, they came to see help-seeking as less acceptable. Indeed, residents became less certain about whether or not they were deserving of further assistance, as well as more disapproving of others' help-seeking, and they framed their own past help-seeking as exceptional and distinct from their normal behavior. As we have shown, understanding why someone may ask for or accept help that will speed recovery at one point but not at another requires attention to the local ecology of aid.

Chapter 5 | Growing Inequality during Recovery

DRIVING AROUND FRIENDSWOOD two years after Hurricane Harvey, the visible signs of the flood were almost entirely gone. It would have been easy to assume from the well-maintained lawns and clean home exteriors that most households had fully recovered, but the storm's impact continued to reverberate. For households with a tenuous hold on their middle-class status before Harvey, the long and costly recovery made their financial position more precarious. Even some residents who described themselves as financially stable before the flood found themselves under extreme financial stress in its aftermath. Those who did not have flood insurance to help cover the costs of repair drained their savings and were saddled with new debt. At the same time, some of their neighbors with flood insurance had completed repairs and even added to their savings. Altogether, inequality grew in Friendswood after Harvey as some households fully recovered and others remained barely able to make ends meet.

In the previous chapter, we described the divergence in households' recovery timelines not long after the storm: some households completed repairs quickly, while others still needed help years later. In this chapter, we examine the long-term recovery process in detail as well as the impact of preexisting differences between Friendswood residents on the pace of recovery and post-flood household finances.

Inequality can be measured in different ways; here we focus on the completeness of home repairs, the material consequences of paying for those repairs, and households' subjective anxieties about their finances.[1] Those with the most pre-flood advantages—higher incomes, wider and more resourced social networks, flood insurance coverage, and more experience with home construction—generally recovered more quickly, while Friendswood residents with fewer resources before Hurricane Harvey fell further behind and faced more financial hardships as time went on. In short, we find that there is indeed a disaster recovery "Matthew effect": households that had less before the storm were less likely to recover than their more advantaged neighbors.[2]

Past research has shown that poorer and non-White households affected by disasters experience greater residential instability, are displaced for longer periods of time, and face larger and longer negative effects on their income compared to more privileged households.[3] The physical damages from disasters are also not distributed equally; again, poorer places tend to be more vulnerable. These inequalities are then exacerbated rather than reduced by differences in the distribution of recovery resources.[4] More advantaged neighborhoods benefit from various federal disaster recovery programs as well as from private development.[5] In many ways, then, Friendswood offers us an example of recovery under some of the best possible circumstances.[6] Past research would suggest that, because it is a small, tight-knit, well-resourced suburb that is middle-class, majority-White, and primarily a community of homeowners, households in Friendswood should have recovered quickly. Instead, the reality of recovery proved to be more complicated, particularly for residents who did not have flood insurance.

After Harvey, insured households could receive payouts of up to $350,000 ($250,000 for structural damages and up to $100,000 for contents), while uninsured households were eligible to receive only up to $33,300 from FEMA's Individuals and Households Program.[7] As a result of this major disparity, some households were able to repair their homes and even improve them—remodeling in desired ways—while others did not have enough funds to complete necessary repairs. As home values continue to recover unevenly, depending on the quality of the repairs from the flood damage and whether they are complete, this inequality will only grow over time.[8]

As we saw in chapter 3, households decided to undertake the long and expensive process of repairing their homes in large part because they planned to remain in Friendswood for the foreseeable future. Few wanted to give up the community's amenities, well-regarded public schools, or "small-town" feel that had led them to move to Friendswood in the first place. But such residential plans can be a double-edged sword in the aftermath of a disaster. On the one hand, returning households maintain all the advantages of residing in a middle-class community, but on the other hand, they are also choosing to remain in a place that is increasingly vulnerable as a result of climate change.

Throughout *Soaking the Middle Class*, we have argued that climate change is making a wider set of places vulnerable to disasters, and this, in turn, will reveal not only the different capacities of communities to recover, but also how and why variation in recovery emerges between households in the same community. When some residents have unfinished repairs and continue to face significant financial insecurity years later, this not only increases their vulnerability to future shocks but also leaves the community as a whole less prepared to recover from another disaster. Put simply, inequality is exacerbated within communities after disasters, and community resilience is diminished.

THE LONG PROCESS OF REBUILDING

In previous chapters, we saw that the first step in repairing a flooded home is "mucking out," or removing wet belongings, ruined appliances, waterlogged sheetrock and insulation, and any flooring or carpet. Most Friendswood households removed walls up to four feet, while many of those living closest to the creek had to strip their homes down to the studs from floor to ceiling. After mucking out, residents had to allow their houses to completely dry out in order to prevent mold. This often took days, sometimes weeks, before moisture levels fell, and residents ran fans, dehumidifiers, air purifiers, and air conditioning systems (if they were still working) to speed the process.

Once a home was dry, the next step was to fix any electrical work, plumbing, and framing before a city inspector authorized closing the walls. Then drywall (also often called sheetrock) could be fully installed, a process that included the difficult task of "taping and floating," or sealing the seams between sheets of drywall, before painting could begin and cabinetry and tiling could be installed. Rebuilding an entire house at one time (or at least the entire first floor) required that homeowners make hundreds of decisions, such as choosing tile and fixtures, wall color, flooring, cabinetry and hardware, and countertop materials, to name just a few. All of these had to be purchased in quick succession, leading to huge expenses for materials as well as labor if homeowners were not completing the work themselves.

By the second anniversary of Hurricane Harvey, residents in our sample fell into one of three categories with respect to their home repairs. One group was fully recovered with all repairs completed, although even some of these households were still navigating the long-term financial ramifications of the repair costs. Among the households that remained in Friendswood to repair their homes, around 47 percent had completed the repairs two years after the storm. A second group was mostly recovered, with some repairs remaining, but the lion's share of the work was behind them. For these residents, the work that remained was largely cosmetic—for example, they had yet to install baseboards or paint walls—and did not affect the general livability of their homes. Two years after the storm, around 24 percent of flooded Friendswood households still had some repairs remaining. Many of them were paying for these final repairs piecemeal, which extended how long they took to complete.

The final group of households still had major repairs remaining two years after Hurricane Harvey and were unable to fully use their homes. Bathrooms remained unfinished, flooring had not been laid, or drywall had yet to be installed. Around 18 percent of the flooded households still needed major repairs to their homes two years later.[9] Residents in this category were still living with the physical aftereffects of Harvey every single day, and owing to financial constraints, many were uncertain when, or if, they would ever finish their repairs.

In the rest of this chapter, we present two cases for each of the three categories of home repair status. They illustrate the factors and resources that determined the speed of recovery, and highlight how recovery exacerbated inequality, even within a well-resourced suburban community. Driving through Friendswood two years after the storm, it was often difficult to tell the houses that were finished from those that still needed major work. Exteriors looked largely the same, and lawns were generally well maintained. Growing inequality was only obvious inside homes and across household budgets.

Fully Recovered

Gina and Derek, a couple in their midseventies, were both retired and felt financially stable when Hurricane Harvey hit. On top of their savings, Derek had a pension and they both inherited money from their parents, which, Gina told us, "made us feel secure." They were longtime residents of Friendswood, having moved into their home in the late 1980s. When they bought it, they knew the house had stayed dry during Tropical Storm Claudette in 1979, and like plenty of other Friendswood residents, Gina thought that "anything that didn't flood in '79 was considered to be safe forever." However, she said, "as Harvey proved . . . now we got a new benchmark."

Gina and Derek had eight inches of standing water in their home at the peak of the flooding. Although this might not seem like much, the water remained in their home for several days and soaked up higher into their walls and destroyed their furniture. They had to remove more than a foot of drywall and insulation in addition to repairing damage to their floors and appliances. Their flood insurance coverage was a crucial component of their recovery. They also received a great deal of assistance from friends, family, and the community. Derek, since he was retired, had the time to do some repairs himself and to supervise the work being done by a contractor. Altogether, their various resources—money from insurance, support from their social network, time, and home construction know-how—facilitated a relatively fast recovery that made little discernible difference to their long-term financial well-being.

In the days after the flood, friends, relatives, and lots of local volunteers showed up to help them muck out. Derek told us, "My son got out here . . . [and] I called some friends and they came over. 'Cause I said, 'This is not a two-person job.'" Gina told us that "the school district had organized kids . . . then the church sent up volunteers." Derek estimated that a total of forty people helped them. With all of that assistance, he said, mucking out was quickly completed: "We had everything out of here the first day." Then they waited for their home to dry.

Gina and Derek hired a contractor to help them complete the repairs, using the money from their flood insurance to cover this expense. After an insurance adjuster came to inspect the property and determine the total amount of their insurance payout, they received a $50,000 partial payment that allowed them to begin repairs. Before Harvey, Gina and Derek had already paid off their mortgage, which facilitated their access to the insurance settlement. When homeowners still have a mortgage, flood insurance payouts are issued to both the insured homeowner and the lender. Households must then request the money from their mortgage company. Lenders usually will not distribute insurance payouts to homeowners without proof that the money is being used for repairs, typically in the form of receipts for labor and supplies. Households with both insurance and a mortgage often complained about the arduous negotiations with their lender to get their insurance money and about what they viewed as a backward process: households had to show they were paying for repairs before lenders would give them money to pay for repairs. Since Gina and Derek no longer had a mortgage, they did not have to show receipts to receive their insurance settlement, which came to them directly.

Derek understood the importance of having immediate access to their insurance money. In telling us about some family members whose house flooded and who had to get their funds from a mortgage company, he said that mortgage companies "act like it's their money. . . . They say, 'You can pay for it and have it repaired and then we'll reimburse you.' Well, they [his relatives] are not in the situation to be able to do that. . . . And here, we had our money, we could go start doing it." By the one-year anniversary of the flood, Gina and Derek had received $180,000 in insurance payouts. This money was more than enough to cover the cost of the necessary repairs and replace their ruined belongings.

Although Gina and Derek had the financial resources to begin rebuilding right away, they still felt impatient about how long it took their contractor to start work on their home. They told us that the contractor began in earnest in October, more than a month after the storm. Despite their annoyance at the repair timeline, the work went faster than it did for many other respondents in our sample whose contractors did not begin work for several months.

Once the repairs on Gina and Derek's house did begin, it was not a smooth process. There were often long delays because their contractor was spread thin across multiple jobs. As a result, Gina said, she and Derek did a lot of waiting: "You might have a person come for three hours a day and then not come for three days." Gina and Derek also saw quickly that they needed to remain attentive to every step of the repair process, supervising the work to make sure it was done correctly. Derek told us that the first thing the contractor did was hang sheetrock, and "it wasn't exactly a quality job." As the repairs stretched on, Derek realized the importance of being present to observe the repair work, and he was thankful that, being retired, he could do so. He told us, "I feel sorry for people who were going back to work and had children. 'Cause we were here and could manage."

Unsatisfied with the pace of the work, Derek also began to do more and more on his own. This had the added benefit of saving money. He told us, "Since I've done so much of it myself . . . we've been fully covered." With his "sweat equity," the total cost of repairs came to less than the amount they received from the insurance company, so in the end, he said, "we made money on the deal." In addition to being able to save some of their insurance settlement, Gina and Derek were also able to claim a large tax break because of the losses they experienced during the storm. Before Derek filed their taxes, his longtime accountant asked, "'Well, have you filed a casualty loss along with this?' And I said, 'No, I didn't bother to.' And he says, 'You need to bother to.' And so, bottom line is . . . we don't owe any taxes for this year."

After the flood, Gina and Derek not only ended up in a better financial position but were extremely pleased with their home after the repairs were complete. "Right now," Derek said, "it's in better shape than the day we bought it." In addition, their home value rebounded to nearly its pre-flood level within two years, if not higher. According to Derek, "the market right now is about 125 dollars a square foot. . . . Before the storm it was lower, probably about 120." The interviewer expressed some surprise and asked for clarification: "So prices have actually gotten a little bit higher?" Gina responded, "People like this town." Derek agreed, telling us that the time to get a deal on a property in Friendswood "was right after Harvey." In

2019, they expected to be able to sell their house for more than it was worth before Harvey without having gone into any debt to complete their repairs. And until they sell, they plan to always maintain flood insurance cover-age. When we spoke to them not long after the second anniversary of the flood, they had recently renewed their policy, paying $485 annually for coverage—an increase of just $30 from their premium in 2018. For Gina and Derek, it was worth every penny.

Gina and Derek represent one end of a continuum in Friendswood. Most of the flooded residents we interviewed were not quite as well off financially within two years. Multiple aspects of Gina and Derek's finan-cial circumstances allowed them to repair their home relatively quickly while also adding to their savings. Having flood insurance was certainly key, but so too was the fact that they owned their home outright—that is, they had no mortgage—and that Derek had construction experience and the time to complete some of the repairs himself. Additionally, advice from their accountant added more savings via a large tax deduction. All of these factors contributed to Gina and Derek's full recovery and improved finances two years after the flood.

Helen, a single woman in her seventies, lived on a relatively tight budget in retirement. Her Social Security checks, which were her only income, totaled around $22,000 a year. When Harvey hit, twelve inches of water flooded Helen's home, and she did not have flood insurance coverage. Still, Helen was one of the first people on her block to move back into her repaired home after Hurricane Harvey. While she had some savings, it was certainly not enough to make up the difference between the expense of necessary home repairs and the approximately $17,000 she received from FEMA. Nor did she possess the knowledge or ability to do home repair work herself. Despite her financial constraints, Helen was able to move back into a finished home a few months after Harvey because of her brother Todd.

As soon as Helen had safely evacuated her home, she called Todd. He lived in a nearby suburb and navigated his truck through high waters and back roads to pick her up. Describing her brother, Helen said, "He's just a doer. He does. I mean, if it needs doing, he's there, and I called him and I told him where I was, and I said, 'I don't know if you can get here.' . . . And the next thing I knew he was there." Once Helen was safely at Todd's home, she told us that there was a period of impatient waiting, since the floodwaters did not recede for days. While her home remained inacces-sible, she fretted about what she would see when she could finally return. "I don't remember a lot about that first day. I was . . . so worried about the house because I didn't know how high the water was gonna get, so I didn't do much. My sister-in-law made me a hot meal, and for the next couple days we didn't do anything."

Upon her return, Helen told us, she was "in a state of shock" at the sight of her home and the feeling of the still sloshy carpet she had installed only a year earlier. Everything Helen owned "had been standing in the water for a couple of days," and she did not know what to do. Todd, however, took charge. He hired several day laborers to help with the mucking-out process. "He got a crew and came back," Helen said, "and they started moving my furniture out. . . . They piled everything I owned into the garage. . . . It was just stacked to the ceiling. . . . Then they rolled up the carpet and put it out by the curb, and then they started on the sheetrock." Helen was immensely grateful for her brother's help.

While Gina and Derek had more than forty people show up to help them muck out their home, Helen was not involved in any local churches or community groups that might have provided volunteer assistance. Instead, help came primarily from Todd. She said, "Had it not been for my brother, I don't know what I would have done." Todd was Helen's main source of financial support during recovery, and he insisted that Helen not apply for an SBA loan or take on any new forms of debt. She also received some financial assistance from a few other family members; her nephew, for instance, "bought me a dishwasher and a washer and dryer and he came over here the first few days that we were in the house and helped out . . . and then a couple of my cousins sent checks, but not big ones." While not every member of Helen's family was in a position to offer a large amount of financial help, her nephew's purchase of major appliances illustrates how a few key well-resourced members of a social network can reduce the cost of recovery. For households in Friendswood, it was common to have ties to people who could make sizable contributions.

After mucking out the house and then running fans for nearly a week, Todd began the repair work. He operated his own hardware supply business and had a clear idea of what needed to be done. Helen told us, "We started cutting sheetrock, and Todd would cut while the guys [the day laborers] would nail it to the walls." If tasks that Todd had little experience with arose, like taping and floating drywall seams, he taught himself how to do them from online tutorials. Helen told us that Todd "had never taped and floated, so he watched something on TV, you know, to find out how to do it." All of the work that Todd did to repair her walls helped Helen save a great deal of money, though she still had to spend some of her savings and her $17,000 FEMA payout to cover the cost of supplies, hire a painting crew, and pay for new carpet. Once the carpet was finally installed—after a few significant delays because of the overwhelming local demand—Todd helped her check the furniture that had been stored in the garage for mold and mildew, and they were able to move many of the pieces back into the house.

Taking us on a tour of her home, Helen pointed out the furniture that she had been able to save and showed us where a faint waterline from the flood could be seen on each piece. "I tried to put stuff on it to see if it would come back to life," she noted, "but it hasn't." Although this visible reminder of the flood was somewhat bothersome, Helen was grateful that she had been able to keep some beloved pieces of furniture. She told us that the waterline was "kind of my badge of honor, so to speak. . . . I just don't care. I just—I mean, I do but I don't. I'm in my house and that's what I really wanted."

When we asked if she always knew she wanted to rebuild and return, Helen admitted to a "split second" of doubt when she first saw the damage caused by the flood:

> You know, in the beginning I didn't know what I was gonna do. I just remember walking in the door and looking at it and like "Oh my God." . . . I knew I wouldn't be able to refinish it myself, so I thought, "Well, I guess I could sell it to one of these WE BUY WET HOUSES or whatever," but then [my brother] said, "No, no, no, we're gonna see what we can do to fix it." So—but had it not been for him, that's probably what I would have done, because I didn't know what else to do. I couldn't do this by myself.

She later said of her brother, "I owe him and he doesn't want anything, but I owe him everything."

Todd was able to start repairs on Helen's home quickly not only because he possessed the skills to manage the work but also because he was in a financial position to pay for supplies before Helen's FEMA check arrived. As Helen put it, "My brother fronted the cost for me until FEMA came through." Even when her repairs were completely finished and Helen had moved back into her home, she told us, she was uncertain about the true cost of the repairs because she did not know exactly how much her brother paid for. She estimated that the repairs cost about $25,000 to $30,000, but, she told us, "my brother did so much of that himself at no cost, except his out-of-pocket expenses. And I guess I just really didn't have any idea what it would cost." But she thought that if she "had to get a contractor to come take care of this house, it would have cost me five times as much." Her brother's assistance also enabled Helen to return to her home faster than nearly all of her neighbors. She told us that the neighbors "on either side of me had flood insurance. They're still not in their houses . . . they're still waiting. They don't even know how much money they're gonna get from their insurance company."

Although Helen received key forms of support from her brother that allowed her to return to her home relatively quickly, the flood still negatively affected her finances. When we interviewed Helen around the one year anniversary of the storm, she told us that she had spent most of her savings to get back into her home: "FEMA gave me some, but not enough, and I still had a little money in the bank, and it took a whole lot of that to finish up." For a retiree living on Social Security, Helen said, the cost of repairs "was a lot of money. . . . It took a big chunk out of my savings, and now every time I write a check on that particular account I really have to think about [it]." In fact, she still hasn't purchased a flood insurance policy because it would add another expense to her already tight budget. "I have something here from the city telling me I should get it," she said, "but I know I just can't afford it right now." On her budget, "the money only goes so far. . . . I pay the necessary bills. There's not that much left over."

Helen was also anticipating some big-ticket expenses in the future. "It won't be that long [before] I'll need a new car," she said. She was still driving her car that flooded during Harvey. "I had it in the shop four times before they finally got it running right, but it was still cheaper than buying a new one." When we spoke again two years after Harvey, Helen's finances remained unchanged. She acknowledged that she needed flood insurance, but she still did not have a policy. "I'm still in the same place. I need to get it, I know I need to get it, I just haven't done it."

Helen now had no financial safety net, could not afford to replace her car, and was generally more anxious about paying her bills in the future. She had little room in her budget to pay for future expenses and still had no flood insurance coverage to protect against the risk of another storm. Although, like Gina and Derek, Helen was back living in her fully repaired home, she was certainly financially worse off as a result of the flood, and she was far more vulnerable to another financial shock. As a single retiree living solely on Social Security, Helen would have been completely ruined by Hurricane Harvey if not for the aid provided by her brother.

Mostly Recovered

Erin and Paul, parents in their forties, live in a newer Friendswood subdivision filled with large, two-story homes. At the time of the flood, Erin worked part-time, while Paul worked full-time in the oil and gas industry. Their annual household income was around $140,000. Erin and Paul's house took on eighteen inches of water during Hurricane Harvey; the entire first floor flooded. Although they were able to save some belongings by moving them upstairs before evacuating their home, Erin and Paul still lost much of their furniture and both of their cars.

Without flood insurance coverage, Erin and Paul applied for assistance from FEMA. They received $2,000 to help with the cost of temporary rental housing and another $11,000 to help with repairing their flooded property. As we saw in chapter 4, they knew repairs would cost considerably more, so they also applied for an SBA loan. They were approved for $111,000, which was dispersed in several installments. To get the funds, Erin and Paul had to document their expenditures and submit receipts.

While they waited for the money, they began to work on the house. When we asked what their home looked like when they were first able to get back inside, Paul told us, "There was a definite waterline across the walls and the doors, [and] just stuff floating everywhere. The living room was not where we'd left it." They were grateful that a large number of volunteers came to help them muck out. "We have a lot of great friends. As soon as the hardware store opened, they were getting crowbars and hammers and saws and fans and just everything you can think of, and we just started hauling stuff out and tearing sheetrock off the walls." He added, "We had easily twenty-five people here." Once their home was mucked out, Paul and the group of volunteers helped others: "We just kept going. We went to the neighbor's house to help them." This expansive volunteer effort was typical in the first few weeks after the flood, and the assistance Erin and Paul received did not end with mucking out. Erin made a list of all the people who came to help so that she could write them thank-you notes. Her list "starts with donations, and it goes all the way through people that brought food, that took care of our kids, that helped in the houses, helped clean out." In the end she had more than one hundred people to thank.[10]

Erin and Paul were deeply connected to the local community, as evidenced by the number of volunteers who came to their aid. Erin said, "We had a lot of people come from church, neighbors . . . the kids' school. [We] had a lot of meals from friends from school. Church was a lot of help. The preschool that my youngest son goes to, they sent a lot of help with labor." When her son's teacher asked if there was anything else they needed help with, Erin told us, "I mentioned our next big project was going to be ripping the hardwoods out." The teacher contacted her church—where Erin and Paul were not congregants—to organize a crew to help them remove the floors. "The next morning I got a phone call from the pastor," Erin recalled. "And he said, 'We're sending a crew your way to help you rip out your floors today.' We weren't expecting it. It was just things like that. People were very proactive in just showing up and helping." The church Erin and Paul did attend also offered assistance with the mucking-out process and provided them with nearly $2,400 in gift cards and cash donations.

Erin told us that they received additional aid from their wider social network. "I mean, people were, goodness, mailing us money left and right, Amazon gift cards. Even with the Christmas cards that we got, this was almost three months, four months after the hurricane, we received Christmas cards from people with checks in them. You know, it was just overwhelming. Even with somebody sending us $10, $20, you're like, it's Christmastime, budgets are tight, and people are still thinking of us." The nearly $10,000 in cash and gift cards that they received reflected the financial capacity of many middle-class households' social networks.

Friends also gave big-ticket appliances as gifts. After living with extended family for weeks, Erin told us, "our friends gave us a fridge." Paul added, "That was enough to be able to move back home." The family lived upstairs for months as the downstairs was being repaired. During this time, the loan of a car from another friend helped Erin and Paul save money in the short term, since they only had to replace one car right away.

Erin and Paul were extremely gratified by the quick offers of assistance from members of the community whose homes had not flooded:

> The community has been amazing. You know, in Friendswood, we had 30 percent of the houses flood. That's a pretty high percentage for a small little town. But I feel like people that didn't flood were quick to bring food. I don't think we cooked for two months. . . . At one point, we had to stop accepting food, because we had nowhere to put it.

Although Erin and Paul received an immense amount of help, it was not enough to cover the costs of recovery. Even with $11,000 from FEMA, more than $10,000 from their social network, help from dozens of volunteers, and donated appliances, Erin and Paul decided that it was necessary to take out an SBA loan. Furthermore, they knew that they would have to remain as frugal as possible as they repaired their home.

They initially considered hiring a contractor and trying to do some larger-scale remodeling work, but ultimately they decided against it. Erin told us, "We had toyed with the idea of doing some more remodel-type stuff in the kitchen. And we actually did get a quote from an actual contractor for all of that. . . . It was going to be like $50,000. . . . Once we saw the price, it was like, 'That's easy to say no to.'" Erin observed that "not having flood insurance really made us look at things a little differently price-wise."

As the repair process began, Paul attempted to do a lot of the work himself. Erin explained that they wanted to minimize how much they would owe on top of their existing mortgage after they had recovered. "We were approved for $111,000 through SBA . . . but I don't want an $111,000 loan that I have to pay back. So we've tried to look at things from a cost perspective. He's pretty handy to begin with. He's been learning all kinds of new skills that he has never used before." Volunteers from their church who had specific construction skills also helped with more challenging tasks, like taping and floating the drywall. Erin and Paul had been quoted $14,000 for that job alone by a contractor, so they were elated when the church volunteers stepped in to do the work. Erin and Paul also saved a lot of money by purchasing their new flooring from an acquaintance. Erin said, "He ended up giving us the flooring at his cost. . . . So we got a huge discount."

After receiving an SBA loan and lots of help, Erin and Paul considered themselves mostly finished with repairs two years after the storm. Their home was back to a livable state, and the remaining repairs were ones they deemed cosmetic. Although they were generally back to their pre-Harvey routines, the flood took a heavy and long-lasting toll on their finances. Not only did they have to cover the costs of expensive repairs to their home, but Paul's work was also affected after Harvey. Their household income still had not fully recovered. As a result, they were budgeting carefully, and many of the cosmetic repairs they still needed to finish were not a priority. Erin said, "If you look, you'll see a lot of detail things that are not done; trim is not painted, doors aren't painted, couple of things still aren't fixed, because we basically ran out of the money. . . . For the moment, everything has just been on hold . . . everything is functional. Everything is, you know, workable. It's just not the finished touch."

In addition to some unfinished repairs, Erin and Paul now had monthly payments on more than $100,000 of debt from their SBA loan. Erin told us, "Well, that's a $400 payment every month that we have to make. So, I mean, it's just tight, I'm not going to lie. It's tight, which is why the other stuff hasn't gotten done." They were also spending around $500 a year on flood insurance coverage. Erin said, "That was part of—I mean, granted I wanted it, but that was part of SBA requirements, is that we had to get it." Erin expressed some ambivalence about the cost but was ultimately grateful that flood insurance was not even more expensive after she learned that the policy for a neighbor who lived just one block closer to the creek recently "went up to almost $1,500 a year."

For Erin and Paul, the fact that they received so much help certainly facilitated their recovery in the face of limited financial resources and no flood insurance. This support included some key forms of skilled labor that reduced costs for specific jobs, like taping and floating drywall, and getting expensive materials, like flooring, at a discount. Yet Erin and Paul continued to feel the financial ramifications of this storm every month as they paid down their SBA loan. Although many of their insured neighbors also had some small cosmetic repairs to complete, none faced the same level of new debt as Erin and Paul. If, as past research has shown, disasters increase inequality, new forms of debt are clearly one cause.[11] More generally, insurance, or the lack of it, is key in determining financial stability post-disaster.

Claire and her husband, parents in their thirties, moved to Friendswood a few years before Hurricane Harvey. When the storm hit, Claire was a stay-at-home mother, and her husband worked in finance. Their household income was around $220,000. Harvey flooded their home with ten inches of water, but they had flood insurance that they hoped would cover the cost of repairs.

When the floodwaters receded and they were able to return and start the process of mucking out, Claire felt completely overwhelmed. She knew that they needed to record the damage to their home and belongings to file an insurance claim. However, this task was complicated by all the volunteers who showed up to help muck out. Describing the chaotic environment, Claire told us that her priority was "documentation. I don't want to lose anything. . . . I was like, oh my gosh, all these droves of people coming in, trying to help, and I'm like, I'm still trying to document." She struggled to focus on this task as volunteers and friends repeatedly asked, "'What do you need? What do you want? And we're bringing you food,' and suddenly all this food's showing up. And I'm like, there's so much food. I don't want it to go to waste." For Claire, the outpouring of support in the early days after the storm was a source of both relief and anxiety: "People just [kept] showing up randomly, and it was very helpful and very nice. . . . It was kind of stressful too."

Claire expected their insurance to cover the cost of repairs, so when the mucking out was complete, she started calling contractors. She was stunned by the long repair timelines they quoted, amazed that some contractors would not even be able to start for months. She told us:

> You start calling people, like contractors. . . . I remember at first when I called, they're like, "We can't start till December." I'm like, "Uh that's not gonna work." . . . I had friends that were like, "Yeah, my husband was calling while it was still raining, and when we saw our house was flooded, he was calling the contractor." . . . Here it is like a week later, and I'm starting to call people, and I'm finding everyone's got people lined up already.

Claire told us that remodeling the downstairs of their home had been part of her family's "five- to ten-year plan," though she admitted that "we've never done any kind of construction, any kind of renovating." Their lack of experience made the contractor bids to do the repair work difficult to evaluate. Claire said, "I ended up having three people come out and give us bids, and we're just kind of all over the place. I'm like, 'I don't even know how much this is supposed to cost.'" The bids came in between $70,000 and $100,000. Claire said:

> When we finally picked our person . . . he said, starting [the work] would probably be like mid-November. I'm like, "Okay, well, I really want to surprise the kids and have the house ready by Christmas," and he goes, "Okay, well, I might, you know, could be livable but not done by Christmas." I'm like, "Great!" You know, I can live with that.

Claire's contractor did not start work until the end of January. Like Claire, multiple respondents had been hopeful that they could return to their homes by the end of 2017—four months after Harvey—but very few were back by then.

Claire's insurance company initially offered $110,000 for repairs after an adjuster came to inspect the damage. Encouraged by some neighbors whose homes also flooded, Claire went through the claim line by line. She told us, "A lot of our neighbors just keep fighting it, you know, do the squeaky wheel kind of thing." In the two years after the flood, Claire and her husband submitted three appeals and did receive some additional funds.[12] Claire told us that, in some instances, "the unit prices that they were giving us wasn't what we paid . . . so we're trying to prove to them that this is what we did. Like, we're not trying to get more money because we're trying to get extra, we need to cover . . . what we paid for with the contractor." Even with a higher total from insurance, however, Claire and her husband still faced issues with the timing of the disbursements from their mortgage company. The bank would not release more money until Claire submitted receipts for completed work, but they could not pay for the work without the money.

In the end, they were forced to spend funds earmarked to replace damaged belongings on structural repairs.[13] Around the one-year anniversary of the storm Claire told us, "We've been using a lot of our content money too, that's another thing, we haven't replaced our couch, a kitchen table and chairs, and dining room, so we've been using some of that money to help pay for things." In addition to the difficulties accessing their insurance funds, Claire and her husband also faced ongoing issues with their contractor.

In 2018, as the work progressed, Claire told us that it was not meeting her expectations. "The work was not, like, quality work . . . so I called him out on it a couple of times, and finally, he said that, you know, we were being nitpicky and expecting perfection, and they said they are not gonna fix certain things." So she and her husband decided to cut ties with their original contractor. "Now we're trying to piecemeal everything back together, to fix what he's done," Claire said, "and then, what he wasn't gonna fix, and then, finishing everything to make it livable downstairs basically."

To fix the shoddy work and finish repairs, Claire and her husband hired a handyman. This left Claire to manage all of the supply orders, which was immensely stressful and at times slowed the repair process. She described taking on these responsibilities as "just very draining. I tell my grandma, 'I'm Harvey tired.' Like, I spend my days in tile shops lately looking at counters. I feel like I live on Pinterest, and my kids are like, 'Why are you always on your phone?' I'm like, 'I'm trying to figure out how to fix things.'" Her husband tried to encourage Claire by telling her that they could always change the house again later, but she wanted to be deliberate because "it's just so final. . . . I don't want to go through this again. I don't ever want to have to deal with flooding again, or like [with] contractors building a house."

After firing their contractor, Claire and her husband also needed funds to repair the mistakes but did not have enough cash on hand. Meanwhile, nearly $20,000 remained on their insurance claim, but they were unable to directly access it without proof of further work:

> CLAIRE: We don't have the money right now to have things redone, so, but then, we can't get money from the bank until we have, like, countertops put on, so it's like, we're trying to, like, find the money to get the countertops put on, to get access to the money that we need. So that's kind of, a bit of a loophole right now, we're dealing with.
>
> INTERVIEWER: And why countertops? Is that—
>
> CLAIRE: They said it's part of structure, they said that once we get countertops, they'll release 95 percent of the remainder.

Navigating this financial quagmire was especially difficult because Claire's husband did not want to dip into their emergency fund to cover the repairs. She told us, "We're a one-income family, I see him stressing, sometimes, about stuff, not wanting to touch some money, just in case kind of thing, . . . I know we have a little bit aside, but he doesn't want to—I know he said we had, like, $10,000 beforehand, before Harvey. He doesn't want to dip into that." Indeed, the devastating effects of Harvey revealed the importance of being prepared for unexpected financial shocks.

The financial stress of recovery also prompted Claire to consider returning to work. Before Harvey, she wanted to wait until her youngest was through the first few years of elementary school to start working again, but as the full financial cost of the storm became apparent she and her husband talked about a shorter timeline. Claire told us that, around the one-year anniversary of Hurricane Harvey, "we were actually just having this discussion the other day. . . . What he said was that he was wanting me to go back next year. . . . He's saying it would be even more beneficial after all the financial issues—not issues, but like, spending. . . . He said it would be helpful, it wouldn't be as stressful for him." By the second anniversary of the storm, Claire was back at work. Although eventually returning to work had always been her plan, the financial ramifications of the storm accelerated the timing and made her paycheck increasingly important for her family.

When we spoke to Claire two years after the storm, she and her husband had finally received the last of their insurance money, which she said had been critical. "We needed that, most of that money, to finish some of the bigger jobs without us having to pay it first and then paying ourselves back." While her husband primarily handled the family finances, Claire said, "I don't think we've taken out any loans." "I know we've used our savings account money." Their plan was to "replace it once we get [the] insurance check."

With the extra cost of fixing the mistakes made by their initial contractor, Claire and her husband spent more than their total insurance payout to repair their home. To avoid taking on new debt, they were completing the remaining repairs one at a time. Claire said,

> We'll go, "Okay, well, the next time we get paid, we're gonna do this area." We're gonna, you know, we don't wanna put anything on credit, or put our-selves in debt because of it. 'Cause everything's functional, so that's like, there's a toilet in the bathroom, you just have to walk to the kitchen to wash your hands kind of thing.

Two years after Harvey, seeing these unfinished repairs was disheartening for Claire. She told us, "When you walk past it, it's like a reminder."

As Claire reflected on the experience of dealing with contractors, insurance, and the bank, she was simultaneously grateful for her insurance coverage and frustrated with the red tape that complicated their access to the payout when they needed it. She told us that flood insurance "helped a lot of us, [we] didn't have to be in as much financial struggle." However, the distribution of insurance funds introduced a different set of challenges; "With flood insurance, like, you're tied, you had to have a contractor . . . you have to turn it into the bank, 'cause they're holding the money, like you have to have . . . paperwork filled out just to—it was a long process to get the money from the bank." Ultimately, however, Claire recognized the impor-tance of flood insurance for covering most of their repair costs:

> I'm sure we'll spend a little of our own money, but not, I mean, if we had
> to replace everything on our own, I mean, then that's an extra $150,000,
> that's basically buying another home. So if we had to spend an extra, you
> know, ten, twenty [thousand], that's, in the grand scheme of things, that's
> not a lot—I mean, it is a lot, but for what we've had to put back together,
> it's not.

Given the importance of their flood insurance, Claire and her husband made sure to keep their policy active. Two years after Harvey, she told us, "We just re-upped . . . still the same price . . . somewhere between four and five hundred." In fact, when her husband realized three weeks after mailing it in that their insurance check had not been cashed, he called the company, and "they said they hadn't received it. . . . [So he] gave them payment over the phone, because at that point we were like, 'Okay, we can't lapse anything.'" (As we saw in chapter 2, it is the homeowner's responsibility to keep a policy up to date.)

Two years after the flood, Claire was grateful to have moved back into the downstairs of their home, even though there was still work left to do. Unlike Erin and Paul, Claire had insurance and her family was certainly in a better financial position as a result. But unlike Gina and Derek, she and her husband had very little experience with home building or dealing with contractors. Moreover, since they still had a mortgage, Claire and her family faced challenges accessing their insurance money. The repairs—and figuring out how to pay for them—certainly caused a great deal of stress. Not only did Claire and her husband ultimately spend more than they received from insurance, but the strain of budgeting also led her to return to work earlier than she had originally planned.

Although Claire and her husband were lucky not to have to take on new debt, their case shows the toll of events like Harvey on even relatively well-resourced households, as well as the stress and complexity of navigat-ing recovery. Still, despite spending some of their savings and finishing repairs slowly in order to avoid new debt, Claire's family was back in a livable home two years after the storm. That was not the case for everyone who flooded in Friendswood.

Major Repairs Remain

Phyllis and Vera, two sisters in their seventies, were both retired and living in a one-story Friendswood home when Hurricane Harvey flooded it with three feet of water. Phyllis and her husband had purchased the house in the 1970s, shortly after it was built. They financed it with a loan from the VA and a one-dollar down payment on a purchase price of $29,000. Both Phyllis and her sister Vera, who moved in after she retired, had been widowed. The sisters were living on fixed incomes from Social Security and had limited savings. Neither of them expected Hurricane Harvey to flood the house. As the water was still rising, they were rescued by boat and taken to the shelter at the local elementary school. When the roads cleared, they went to stay with Phyllis's daughter, who lived about fifty miles from Friendswood.

Phyllis's son-in-law organized the muck out of the house. Phyllis described what she saw after they returned:

> I've been here forty-four years, forty-four years of my belongings were right there in that dead spot in the yard. . . . I wanted to cry, but I looked, and my neighbors were in the same situation, so you know, it's not like it was just me. And I thought, "Well, you know, I got the most valuable things out: myself, my sister, and my dog." And you know, it could have been a whole lot worse.

The sisters knew that they faced a difficult recovery process, since they did not have flood insurance. The home had flooded once before, with six inches of water during Tropical Storm Claudette in 1979. Afterward Phyllis's husband decided that they did not need flood insurance. She recalled their conversation at the time: "We were on a one-hundred-year floodplain, and my husband says, 'Well, we won't be here in a hundred years, so it's not going to flood.'" This thinking reflects how difficult it can be for households to use the flood maps to assess their flood risk (a topic we address further in chapter 6).

After Harvey, Phyllis received $16,000 in aid from FEMA. A contractor she found quoted her a price of $33,000 to do the basic repairs of putting up walls and installing kitchen and bathroom cabinets and flooring. Phyllis noted that, at that price, "we are having to pay more to repair the house than we did when we bought it." The sisters did not have enough cash to pay for the repairs, and they were also turned down for an SBA loan, as Phyllis explained:

PHYLLIS: I did not have flood insurance . . . so we went down and registered with FEMA, and we tried to get this small business loan, which we were turned down because we didn't qualify.

INTERVIEWER: What did they tell you the reason was you don't qualify?

PHYLLIS: Well, they said that I had bad credit, but they wouldn't let me on my own sign up for it because they said I didn't make enough money because I'm only on Social Security, but they said that if we went together we would qualify. Well, we went together and they turned us both down.

Phyllis believed that they were turned down for a loan because she and her sister were older and living on fixed incomes and also because she was still paying outstanding medical bills from her husband's care before he died, which affected her credit. Without this loan, she told us, "I don't think $16,000 is going to be enough to make it. I do have an IRA that I'm going to have to withdraw to finish — to get the house in livable shape."

As they navigated the bureaucracy of FEMA and SBA, Phyllis and Vera continued to stay with Phyllis's daughter and to make the drive back to Friendswood each day. However, after a few weeks of staying with her daughter, Phyllis began to worry that she and Vera were imposing. Additionally, the long drive back and forth was taxing. Phyllis and Vera did not have enough money between them to rent another home while their house was being repaired, and it was difficult to find FEMA-subsidized hotels that were nearby and would allow dogs. Phyllis told us that when they went to look at one hotel, "the lady said she didn't know who I talked to, but they didn't have any room for FEMA. And to be honest with you, I'm glad, because it was not a safe-looking neighborhood." Eventually she and Vera decided to move back to Friendswood and live in the driveway of their home in a camper borrowed from a neighbor.

The house still offered the basic necessities — "both bathrooms work, my kitchen stove works, the refrigerator and freezer work" — so between the camper and the house they were able to stay on the property. The camper had pop-up canvas walls and plastic windows that zipped down. As the weather cooled in the fall the camper remained suitable, but it was not insulated enough for them to stay warm when the temperatures dropped.

It rarely snows in Houston, but 2017 was full of extreme weather for the region. After a rare snowstorm in December, the sisters decided that they needed to move back into their unrepaired home. "We were really cold out there," Phyllis said. The house still had no interior walls or insulation, but it was warmer than the camper. At first, Phyllis said, "we had a lawn chair, and we spread that out and we slept on that a couple of nights." After a few days, they bought a mattress and box spring to put on a metal bed frame Phyllis had saved after the flood. The conditions were not good, but the sisters wanted to remain in their home while they waited for their contractor to begin repairs.

Phyllis never wavered from her plan to repair and return to her home. When we asked, "Was it ever a consideration that you would not come back here?" she quickly responded:

> No . . . this is my home. I've been here for forty-four years. After my husband passed away, my daughters told me I needed to move closer to them. The house just has too many memories for me to just up and leave, and besides, it's paid for. I thought, you know . . . before this ever happened, even if I sell it, I'm going to have to buy something else. It just didn't seem like it was worth it. I was happy here, so this is where I'll stay.

Even as Phyllis remained clear about her plan to return to her home, neither she nor Vera knew how long the repair process would take. Phyllis was slower than many of her neighbors to get quotes from contractors, having not started the process until around a month after the flood. She did eventually find a contractor through a neighbor, but it took more than a year for the contractor to start work.

When we reinterviewed Phyllis and Vera a few days before the one-year anniversary of Harvey, Phyllis told us that "the hardest part was just waiting." Given their limited finances, the sisters' friends and family tried to help as much as possible, offering to take on some of the repair work to reduce the costs. "My friends told me, don't even think about painting. They said we have—family and friends will come over and help with the painting." Friends also provided places for them to stay once the repair work started. These offers of shelter were essential, since they could no longer use the camper. "We got a letter from the homeowners' association," Phyllis said, "saying we had to move the camper . . . we can't stay in that if we have to move it." They stayed at one friend's home to look after her dog while she was out of town. When her friend thanked her for watching her dog, Phyllis responded, "Thank you for the walls, the doors, the privacy." They also received some donated furniture from a friend to replace what they had lost, including an entertainment center, a bedroom suite, and a sofa. Although the sofa wasn't her style, Phyllis said, "the price is right."

Even with some assistance from friends and family, Phyllis totally wiped out her IRA to cover repair costs. When we asked her how much money she had to spend after the contractor started the job, she told us, "Well, let's see, I had, I think, $29,000 in my IRA, and I drew out every penny of it. Gave it to him." The work progressed slowly, with days going by that "they didn't show up . . . didn't call or anything." Phyllis said, "Eventually I ran out of money, and he quit. And he didn't do some of the stuff that we had paid him for." She and Vera felt cheated but were still grateful to be inside their home with a functional kitchen. Yet several large repairs remained unfinished; most notably, the home had no flooring over the concrete slab. Friends helped them paint the concrete and cover parts of it with area rugs so that Phyllis and Vera could move their furniture out of storage and back into the house. When we interviewed them around the second anniversary of the storm, Phyllis told us, "We would like to get flooring. I mean, we're not hurting without it, we can live without it. But that is one thing on our future problem list."

Addressing these "future problems" was going to be very challenging. When we interviewed the sisters in the summer of 2019, Phyllis was carrying a balance of nearly $5,000 in credit card debt, and living in the unrepaired house had caused further problems. A few months earlier, Vera had fallen on the concrete slab. She was not seriously injured, and Phyllis joked that they should get carpet installed for no other reason than that it would be softer to land on. When we asked about their anticipated timeline for getting carpet, Phyllis told us, "Well, we are both on Social Security. That's our only income, so it—we really don't have a timeline." It was unclear if they would ever be able to afford a new floor. Phyllis did, however, prioritize paying for flood insurance coverage, spending $482 a year to make sure that they would have the financial resources to repair the house and replace their belongings in the event of another flood. For now, however, they did not expect to receive any further help with their remaining repairs. Still, Phyllis said, "I'm not planning on leaving. . . . They'll probably take me out of here in a box."

Despite being a community of mostly homeowners, there is great variation in the financial circumstances of Friendswood's residents. Phyllis and her husband were able to live a fairly middle-class life, but after his death her financial position became far more precarious. She and Vera did not have the money, skills, or, like Helen, a helpful and handy relative to weather Harvey unscathed. Instead, the storm left them far worse off: they had spent down what little savings they had and were living in an unfinished, hazardous house. There was no way the sisters could handle another flood, and any future shock would almost certainly be ruinous.

The one-story home of Josie and Parker, a married couple in their fifties, flooded with more than four feet of water during Hurricane Harvey. Before the storm, they were living on Parker's income of around $54,000 from his work as a shift supervisor for a construction company. Josie had worked in food service, but quit a job earlier that year. They did not have flood insurance, and after the storm she focused her energy on home repairs instead of trying to go back to work. Recovery became her full-time job.

The couple inherited their home in Friendswood from Josie's family, who "bought this home with a dollar down with a VA [loan]." Since then, the house had flooded twice, once during Tropical Storm Claudette and again during Tropical Storm Allison. During Allison, Josie said, they saved their "dining room table 'cause we put it up on soup cans, so it was up out of the water." Such measures did little good against Harvey. Josie told us that while they waited to be rescued, "we just kept going around putting up stuff higher 'cause it was coming in higher and higher, and eventually we just ran out of places to put stuff . . . the furniture was floating."

It also took several days for the water to retreat, and Josie knew from experience that the recovery would therefore be more difficult than after previous storms. She said, "In '79 [during Claudette], in Allison [in 2001], the water receded within twenty-four hours." But during Harvey, "the second night . . . it rose another foot from the highest level." When they got back inside the house, they found that they had lost almost everything they owned. "A lot of my parents' stuff . . . everything, all gone. Just wiped out."

Because the floodwater had risen so high inside their house, Josie and Parker stripped it down to the studs from floor to ceiling. Without flood insurance coverage, Josie told us, "We tried for the SBA [loan], but for some reason they turned us down, so we can't get a loan." When we asked why they were denied, Josie told us, "It's for any homeowner, but I guess they go by, you know, credit." Parker interjected to explain, "We don't have credit. We don't have bad credit, we just don't have credit." Josie told us this was because "we've always just bought [using] cash, usually spent cash." Credit, of course, is not distributed equally, and so predicating disaster recovery loans on existing credit clearly puts already struggling home-owners like Josie and Parker—or Phyllis and Vera—at a disadvantage.

Before the flood, Josie and Parker were living on a relatively tight budget as they worked to pay off the remainder of a home equity loan. This forced them to make some tough financial trade-offs. "[We're] just like the elderly people now," Josie said. "Do they buy their medicine or do they eat? . . . It's the same deal." Flood insurance was one expense they thought was too costly, especially since the premium went up after Allison. Parker felt like the tough financial choices they faced put them in a precarious situation: "I don't wanna say you're gamed in one way to lose, but that's how I feel." He added, "And then your luck runs out."

Although Josie and Parker had lived in Friendswood for many years, they were not congregants at a local church and did not have school-age children, so they did not have as broad a social network as some of their neighbors. From the first days of recovery, Josie and Parker primarily relied on family. Seven of their close family members showed up to help muck out the house. They also received some donated cleaning supplies and gift cards from local community groups. "Whenever something happens here in Friendswood," Josie noted with appreciation, "we're like all the Whos in Whoville—we all come out together and help each other."

In total, Josie and Parker received around $1,500 in gift cards and cash from aid organizations like the Red Cross, local churches, and civic groups. They were also one of the only households in our sample that applied for Disaster SNAP benefits; however, Parker told us, "I have not used it yet, 'cause I'm still gonna have too much pride in me." Josie told us that she doesn't have too much pride to use them (they were worth $1,200), but the first time she tried to at a grocery store, Parker had not set up the PIN number for their card and so she ended up having to pay cash.

While they waited to hear from FEMA about how much they would receive for rebuilding, they anticipated having to do at least some of the work on their own. In the meantime, they also needed to purchase new cars so Parker could get to work. He tapped into his retirement savings to cover this expense: "I have to cash in my 401(k) . . . [to] get some vehicles." He took out everything he had saved for retirement but spent only a portion of it on the cars; he held back "a little piece still left over to do other things, like, you know if it comes to it, start sheetrocking and insulation stuff." He anticipated that the FEMA assistance would not be enough to cover the full costs of rebuilding.

Although they were preparing to rebuild their home, it was clear that Josie and Parker would have preferred to leave. Unlike most other residents in our sample who had carefully chosen to move to Friendswood, Josie and Parker had moved back to care for her aging parents and inherited a home they knew had flooded multiple times. They would have preferred to sell the house, particularly since they expected it to flood again in the future. Josie told us, "I know it's gonna happen again." They felt financially trapped, however, since they were still paying off a home equity loan on the property.

Josie told us that selling the house was not likely to solve their financial problems: "The reality is, this house has flooded three times. Selling it is a joke without taking a major loss . . . so, you know, we're kind of stuck with it. . . . They probably wouldn't even offer us enough to pay off what we owe on it to get out." In this way, Josie implied that staying in the house was a matter of finances; however, when we asked where she and Parker would go if they did receive a good offer on their house, she responded, "I don't know. I don't know, but if they gave us enough to start somewhere else, you know to buy, 'cause then you're starting totally new again from the ground up. At least we know what we got here, you know?" The tension in her response exemplified the challenges that households face after disaster. The hypothetical offer that would allow them to purchase elsewhere led to questions about where to go, what it would be like to start over, and whether a new house would be better than what they currently had.

For now, Josie told us, they were going to rebuild and take some time to pay off their home equity loan and form a clearer plan for what to do next. She said, "We've got about five years left to pay what we owe off. After that, maybe we could get an offer, and maybe we could take it and we could go." She was certain that she did not want to be in Friendswood through another flood; "Look, we—I can't do it again. This ain't my first rodeo. This ain't my second rodeo. It's my third rodeo. It's my last rodeo. . . . We're looking at long-term basically, five years at least, pay what we owe, and then we may—if nothing happens by then, maybe, you know, we might be able to sell it and make a little bit of a profit to where we can move."

Josie and Parker ultimately received $32,000 from FEMA—almost the maximum allowed in direct aid to homeowners after Harvey. They decided to forgo using a contractor in favor of doing the repairs themselves to keep costs low. They started with the master bedroom and bathroom so that they could move back in as quickly as possible. After the flood, they stayed with their son and daughter-in-law, contributing $200 a week to household expenses, but Josie told us, "I hate imposing on people." To help them move back into their home, some friends and family members gave Josie and Parker a few key pieces of furniture, including a headboard and some side tables. They were relieved to be able to return to their own house around Thanksgiving.

After moving back in, however, the repair process proceeded slowly. Parker was back at his job and could work on the house only in the evenings or on weekends. The labor, he said, was exhausting. Josie, rather than return to work, put her energy into rebuilding the house. Both felt capable of doing most of the repairs themselves, like installing walls and fixtures. Josie watched home construction videos on YouTube to learn how to tape and float sheetrock. She told us, "We've always been raised to do stuff, which we're lucky . . . we've learned to, you know, do stuff. So, I mean, it's just gonna be time-consuming. Like, he works all week, weekends, and you know just constantly. You know, when do you rest?"

Josie and Parker spent the money from FEMA quickly. Within months they were paying for repairs out of pocket, budgeting portions of Parker's paycheck to purchase necessary materials. They paid cash and tried to avoid taking on debt. Josie said, "We're just trying to budget." Parker told us, "It's getting tight." Around the one-year anniversary of the storm, they were having to redirect funds intended for their property tax bill. Nevertheless, they had made progress: they passed the initial inspection and got approval to close up the walls. But as repairs dragged on, Josie said, they were emotionally in "a little bit of a rut. Kinda got maybe a little depressed."

Parker was intensely worried about their lack of progress and their financial position. Since, by that point, they had used all of his retirement funds, they had no safety net. He told us, "If something happens to me or something, it won't take long before the power is off, the water's off. Cops are beating on the door. You can't pay taxes. You can't do this. No money to fall back on in case." Although they had started repairs more quickly than some neighbors who were depending on contractors, when the FEMA money ran out their progress slowed significantly. By the one-year mark, Josie and Parker's home still needed considerably more repairs than most of their neighbors' homes. They still had to purchase and install kitchen cabinets, countertops, and flooring, as well as redo the roof. Before Harvey, they had planned to use some of Parker's retirement savings for a new roof, but after having spent most of that on repairing flood damage, they did not know if or when they would be able to afford it. They worried that the freshly repaired walls could be ruined by a leak if they did not fix their roof.

It was clear that more assistance would have been incredibly valuable for Josie and Parker, but it was not something they were actively seeking. Parker spoke about the struggle of swallowing his pride to ask for help and about his preference for doing things on their own. When we asked them if they had considered setting up a GoFundMe, as some of their neighbors had done, Parker said, "For one, I'm not technologically smart enough to do it. And two, I got too much pride. I'm already having to swallow my pride by living in other people's places. I've already swallowed my pride by asking the government for, those taxpayers for, the money that they did give to us and all these other folks." He and Josie were focused on completing repairs on their own, even if that meant they proceeded little by little.

At the one-year anniversary, we asked Josie and Parker when they thought they might be done with repairs. "Calling it done?" Josie responded. "I don't know. 'Cause, I mean . . . I physically can't do it. Moneywise, you know, it depends. . . . I would love to have this all completed by, by next year. But I don't know, we'll, we'll just have to see, you know, how things go."

When we spoke again around the second anniversary of Harvey, they still had many of the same large repairs left to complete, including flooring, kitchen cabinets, and countertops. Josie had made progress on the walls, which were nearly all sheetrocked, textured, and painted. She was hoping that they would be able to install floors soon because "this concrete is killing my ankles." We asked how she was feeling about their repair progress. "Just burned out," she said. "I'm just exhausted, and I have to recoup, and then I get back into it again." Josie knew that their neighbors were done with their repairs. "I pretty much think everybody else is all back together. You know, 'cause they had—they had insurance, so they had companies that came in and did the work for them." Knowing that their neighbors were back to normal made their ongoing list of repairs more frustrating, but she was trying to remain positive:

> It just seems a lot more kind of depressing, because you feel like you should be further along. 'Cause you're still, in your mind, you still think, "Oh man, I could get so much more done than I'm getting accomplished." But, you know, like I also tell myself, "Don't worry. As long as you're getting some-thing [done], you're moving forward."

One bright spot was the roof, which was being repaired during our second-anniversary interview. In fact, Parker spent only a few minutes with us because he was supervising the roofers. Josie and Parker were able to pay for the new roof after receiving funds through an aid organization that was providing assistance to households affected by Hurricane Harvey. Their neighbor had encouraged them to apply, and Parker had swallowed his pride and done it, his worry about the roof outweighing any discomfort he had with seeking help. After providing the nonprofit organization with details on their FEMA payout and repairs so far, they received two addi-tional relief checks, one for $9,000 and another for $8,000. Josie told us that without this assistance, "we would've had to go into debt. We would've had to get it financed. One way or the other, but we would've been in debt, and this way we're not." Although they were still tired and burned out from living in a home that had been under construction for two years, the tone of the second-anniversary interview was notably lighter as workers overhead repaired the roof—a repair that, a year earlier, they knew they needed but could not afford.

After the storm, Josie and Parker also had flood insurance coverage, which was paid for out of their FEMA aid. When they renewed the policy, they paid only to insure the structure of the house, not the contents. Coverage cost about $800 a year. In 2019, Josie told us, renewing their coverage was important because "if we were to get flooded again, FEMA says they're not gonna help you unless you at least had that. . . . If you at least have the national flood insurance, then, you know, they'd be able to help you again, but if you didn't, you don't qualify." But when we checked in with Josie in 2021, four years after Hurricane Harvey, she and Parker no longer had an active flood insurance policy. When we asked why, Josie told us, "Well, just—just money." They did not have much room in their budget, and they needed to prioritize their property tax bill, but, Josie said, "hopefully we can get it done, get our taxes done, and all that, and get [coverage] in the spring . . . before the next storm season." After exhausting their financial safety net and spending years directing every available dollar to cover repairs, Josie and Parker had to make decisions about which bills were the most pressing. Yet even though she and Parker did not have flood insurance, she had recently warned new neighbors who moved onto their street that "when it rains, this creek's going to come up and scare the hell out of you. Make sure you get flood insurance. This house has been flooded three times, and it's going to happen again."

Even after receiving additional assistance and finally being able to repair the roof, two years into recovery Josie and Parker were still far from completing their repairs. While Josie was thankful that she and Parker possessed the skills and knowledge necessary to do the repair work themselves, they had spent down Parker's retirement savings and she was drained from years of working on their home. When we asked her to reflect on their decision to return and rebuild their home, she said, "I'm just kind of at this point of having to do what we have to do. Because we couldn't afford to go anywhere else, and like I said, we're just kind of stuck."

Before the storm, Josie and Parker had a moderate income and were paying off a great deal of debt. Two years afterward, they were in an even more precarious financial position. As Parker noted, they were just one shock away from being completely unable to pay their bills. Compared to Gina and Derek, who had a completely repaired home and had more money than before the storm, homeowners like Josie and Parker, or Phyllis and Vera, were far less prepared for another flood. Hurricane Harvey created more inequality in Friendswood: some households were pushed further into debt and struggled to pay for repairs, while others were back in fully renovated houses with rising home values and insurance money left over. The flood altered household finances and individual financial decision-making, sometimes dramatically. Yet the added financial strain was not borne equally. Households with lower incomes, worse credit, higher debt burdens, and less savings tended to struggle the most during recovery. This pattern is not distinct to Friendswood: recent analyses show that, as time goes on, disaster-affected residents with lower pre-disaster credit scores are more likely to experience declining scores and foreclosure than neighbors with better credit scores.[14] Although this finding may not be surprising, it does confirm that disasters and the responses to them often *widen* existing inequalities.

Such growing disparities also make Friendswood as a community more vulnerable and less able to weather future disasters. Recovery depleted resources that may never come back. For example, Helen, because of her age and employment status, was not likely to ever be able to save the same amount of money she had before Harvey. Phyllis no longer had money in her retirement account. Erin and Paul had more than $100,000 of new debt. Altogether, such losses reduce the capacity of a community to recover from another disaster, since going forward, many individual households have fewer resources to help them bounce back.

The amplified inequality in Friendswood was fostered by differences across households in the types of help they received during recovery. Flood insurance costs money, so advantaged households were better able to afford it. Josie and Parker knew that their home was at risk—it had flooded before—but they simply could not afford the yearly payment; as a result, they got one-tenth the amount of money from FEMA that they might have received from insurance. They were also denied an SBA loan because of their credit status. The quality of credit histories generally correlates with other material advantages like more wealth and higher incomes, and since SBA loans are contingent on credit scores, households like Erin and Paul's are more likely to qualify than those like Phyllis and Vera's.[15] Households also need time and know-how to navigate the bureaucratic aspects of getting aid—two resources that are not evenly distributed.[16] Lastly, having a wide set of well-resourced social connections clearly helps, but better-off households tend to be more connected to better-off friends and relatives who can provide material support.[17] To put it simply, recovery from disaster tends to benefit already advantaged households relative to disadvantaged ones in the same community.

In the next chapter, we explore how households that experienced flooding from Harvey thought about their risk and the potential for another flood and why this mattered for their future residential plans and the overall resilience of the town.

Chapter 6 | Risk, Uncertainty, and Future Residential Plans

GIVEN THE SEVERITY of Hurricane Harvey and the long repair process that proved highly disruptive and costly for many flooded households in Friendswood, how did residents assess their risk moving forward? How safe did they think their repaired properties were from future flooding, and what steps did they take to mitigate that risk?[1]

Two years after the storm, we found that Friendswood residents felt extremely uncertain about how to assess their flood risk. Although risk could not be entirely ignored or denied in a place that was recently hit with a massive climate-related disaster, whether or not the community would ever experience another storm like Hurricane Harvey was less clear. In response to this uncertainty, the vast majority of households we spoke to (90 percent) insured their properties against future flood damage, up from just 52 percent before Harvey. But residents also began to hedge their future plans. Although uncertainty about future flood risk was not enough to prompt them to move immediately, in the event of another flood, many households planned to sell and move.

The timing of our interviews around the second anniversary of Hurricane Harvey was fortuitous for understanding households' risk assessments. Just as we began to contact our respondents, another storm hit the area. On September 17, 2019, Tropical Storm Imelda caused historic rainfall. It was the fourth-wettest storm ever in Texas—some places got over forty inches of rain—and in Friendswood ten inches of rain fell in less than sixty hours. Although none of our respondents' homes flooded during Imelda (one had some flooding in the garage), many of them referenced it when we asked about risk. Their perceptions of risk and their desire to keep living in a place with repeated threats of flooding had just been put to the test. Yet we found that even another tropical storm just two years after Harvey did not seem to change most residents' ideas about living in Friendswood.[2] Why?

Residents had just gone through (or were still in the midst of) a massive rebuilding effort that was emotionally and financially draining. In a sense, it is not surprising that, after they recommitted to living in Friendswood following Hurricane Harvey, they were not eager to think about risk. But we also found that residents had a difficult time assessing risk. Indeed, there was a great deal of uncertainty among residents about how to measure the risk of future flooding and what could be done to mitigate it.[3]

FEMA flood maps provide one of the few tools available to residents for understanding their risk. However, FEMA is required to reassess these maps only every five years, so in the context of our changing climate, they may, at best, represent conservative estimates of vulnerability to future flooding. FEMA flood maps also influence insurance rates and can affect property values. As a result, flood maps have become politically contentious and their accuracy is disputed.[4] Friendswood residents were also unsure how to interpret risk from flood maps, so the maps rarely played a role in their household decision-making and planning.

Instead of flood maps, residents tended to rely on past floods as benchmarks to guide their expectations.[5] They labeled Harvey a "freak" storm, and many were uncertain whether the same conditions—particularly the slow movement of Harvey—would occur again. The fact that Imelda was an intense storm but did not flood their homes seemed to prove to many residents that Harvey was unique. Faced with uncertainty regarding the likelihood of another Harvey-like storm, residents were hesitant to leave Friendswood.

Residents also found it hard to measure or quantify how much their future flood risk was affected by processes like upstream development and new construction. The Houston region has grown tremendously in recent decades, and developing land removes vegetation and soil that can absorb water and replaces it with less permeable materials. Asphalt and concrete surfaces expanded by 114 percent in Houston from 2000 to 2003 alone, substantially increasing the risk of flooding in downstream places like Friendswood.[6] Most of our respondents brought up concerns about development unprompted, yet without a clear sense of the extent to which development increased their risk, it was difficult for them to translate this general awareness into actionable information. Furthermore, nearly everyone felt that they had very little influence over development and regional planning.

Meanwhile, Friendswood residents held varied perspectives on the role of climate change. Not all who believed that human activity affects climate change thought that it was directly tied to their flood risk, and even those who were certain that climate change plays a role in increased risk did not believe that the threat of future flooding was strong enough to prompt them to leave the area.[7] Many households also thought that Friendswood's city government was trying to mitigate flood risk. This further complicated things: while climate change and regional development could lead residents to assess an increased risk level, local mitigation efforts reassured them that risk was reduced. In the confusion of these contradictory perceptions, residents stayed put—but they also purchased flood insurance.

Lastly, and perhaps most importantly, most of the policies and programs available to households in Friendswood to aid their recovery were tied to returning and rebuilding. As we showed in chapter 5, much of the money available to flooded households from FEMA, SBA, and flood insurance pays for repairing damaged property. Despite the material pressures to rebuild, households reported relatively little, if any, communication from the local or federal government about the risk of staying. Many saw no changes in their flood insurance premiums, and those who did generally saw them years after Hurricane Harvey struck. One result of this lagged timeline was that residents received little additional information or guidance for assessing any change in risk while they were still making decisions about whether or not to repair and return to their homes. Taken together, all of these factors left residents with a great deal of uncertainty.[8] Whether or not residents said that they felt their homes would flood again, no one seemed particularly sure about their answer.

UNCERTAINTY AND THE RISK OF FUTURE FLOODING

After Harvey, it was impossible for residents to view their properties as entirely immune to flooding. Harvey proved that there was at least some level of risk associated with living in Friendswood near Clear Creek. Helen told us, "I'm hoping it won't happen again . . . but yeah, it happened before, I mean it happened, so I know it could." Residents' assessments of the potential for another flood ranged widely. While some thought that their homes were likely to take on water again, others thought that another storm like Harvey was very unlikely, especially within their lifetimes. Few felt certain about their assessment.[9]

When discussing flood risk, residents often relied on past storms as benchmarks. In particular, Tropical Storm Claudette in 1979 was generally understood as the last major flood in Friendswood before Harvey. Some residents also referenced Allison, a 2001 tropical storm that caused flooding in some areas of the town but did not require home repairs for nearly as many residents as Claudette and Harvey. Residents were less likely to rely on official sources whose purpose is to communicate risk. For example,

FEMA flood maps, which may make sense to policymakers and engineers who have the expertise to interpret them, are less helpful to residents of flood-prone areas, who are often unsure of what to make of different flood zone designations.[10] In fact, households in Friendswood regularly interpreted these maps incorrectly.

For instance, some residents seemed to think that living in a one-hundred-year flood zone meant that a flood might happen every hundred years. In other words, after Claudette in 1979, these residents seemed not to expect another severe flood until around 2079, Harvey notwithstanding. In chapter 5, for example, Phyllis explained why she and her husband did not buy flood insurance after Claudette: "We were on a hundred-year floodplain, and my husband says 'Well, we won't be here in a hundred years, so it's not going to flood.'" In actuality, this flood map designation indicates a one-in–one hundred, or 1 percent, chance of flooding in *any given year*, but this was rarely how residents discussed the risk that these maps were intended to communicate.[11] Even when residents did correctly understand the flood map's assessed risk to their properties, it was challenging to interpret what a 1 percent chance of flooding meant in a practical sense.[12] The terminology of flood map designations created confusion instead of clarity, so residents continued to primarily rely on past storms as benchmarks. Both Harvey and Claudette were perceived as "extreme" or "freak" storms that stood apart from "regular" hurricanes.

In many cases, residents simply did not mention flood maps at all when talking about risk. For example, Diane and Jack, parents in their forties, hoping that the frequency of severe storms would remain relatively stable, felt that the length of time between Claudette and Harvey was an indicator for how long it would be before another flood. Yet neither of them was particularly confident that this was a good heuristic for estimating risk.

> JACK: [Claudette] was in '79, and then this one was in '17, so, I mean, that was a pretty good spread. Uh, (*laughs*) so, I don't know, I think probably, I think the, both of those storms were just kind of freak storms, it wasn't like a regular hurricane, or anything like that. You know, I'm not overly concerned that we're going to flood again in the time that we're here. . . . I don't think that, uh, it's as big of a fear as it was right afterwards.
>
> INTERVIEWER: So, if you had to rate the likelihood of a storm like Harvey hitting again within the next ten years, what would you say?
>
> JACK: I would say it's fifty-fifty. Either it is or it isn't. (*laughs*)

Diane laughed along with Jack at his uncertain response, then tried to clarify, saying she viewed another Harvey as "somewhat likely."

Such uncertain estimations of risk were common. The length of time between storms that caused intense flooding gave many residents some hope that their homes were unlikely to take on water anytime soon, but everyone acknowledged that they were engaged in guesswork. Given the uncertainty, Diane and Jack planned to stay in Friendswood, but they purchased flood insurance after Harvey, just in case.

Two years after Hurricane Harvey, Andrea, a married mother in her thirties, also struggled with uncertainty about her flood risk. She said that she still felt anxious when it rained, but she framed this anxiety as an "emotional" response not tied to an accurate assessment of the vulnerability of her home. To her, a more "analytical" view of risk was one based on the benchmark of Tropical Storm Claudette, which she described as an "extreme" storm that, like Harvey, was unlikely to occur again soon. However, these two conflicting responses left her more uncertain about risk. She told us, "It's really almost PTSD. You know it's not an issue, you know you're not supposed to be freaking out. . . . But it's still there in the back of your mind, you know? It wasn't supposed to happen. It wasn't gonna happen, and then all of a sudden there's a foot [of water] in your house, you're just like, ugh."

When asked, "Do you think it's very unlikely, somewhat likely, or very likely that it will flood again in this house?" Andrea responded, "I think it's pretty much unlikely. I really don't see it happening again. Honestly, like, my analytical mind is like, this is not going to happen again. I mean, of course, it always could." Later in the interview, Andrea further clarified her assessment of flood risk, turning again to a logic based on past benchmarks and the unique nature of Hurricane Harvey: "Honestly, I think it was a historical flood, so, you know, Friendswood wasn't known for flooding beforehand except for extreme storms like hurricanes coming through. The last time I can recall being told it flooded was late seventies. . . . That was the last time they'd had major flooding, so normally it isn't an issue." Andrea saw this history as a reason to view future flood risk as low, yet she still worried.

After Hurricane Harvey, Andrea and her neighbors now knew exactly how high water levels in Clear Creek had to be for their homes to flood, and they regularly checked the county's flood warning system website and mobile phone application to monitor the gauges in the creek. Neighbors texted each other updates about the creek when it rained. Andrea told us:

There's three different versions of flood stage out here, you know. Twelve foot is it's just kind of hitting the banks, fifteen is where they start going, "Oh, the houses along the creek might get in trouble soon." Twenty is when the houses near the creek have water, twenty-four is when it was in our house. So, I mean, we're still pretty far away from the initial flood stage of twelve foot, and it hit that like twice . . . this spring with some of the bad storms . . . we all watched it. It got all the way up to 12.45, and . . . we're like assuring each other. We're texting, "It's not that bad, it's okay." . . . The neighbors all feel it too, you know? Just, you know, it could happen. You never know which way the creek's gonna go.

Andrea may have viewed her reaction to heavy rainstorms as illogical, but it seemed that everyone in the neighborhood shared her anxiety. The worry she felt and the text messages she received with every heavy rain only added to her sense of uncertainty about the risk of future flooding.

When making their risk assessments, Friendswood residents often relied more heavily on past benchmark storms than on official sources of information like the FEMA flood maps, which they misinterpreted or found too abstracted from day-to-day life to meaningfully affect their risk assessments.[13] Their understandings of risk were also influenced by collective interpretations of on-the-ground local conditions more than by officially reported analyses.[14]

FACTORS THAT AMPLIFY RISK AND UNCERTAINTY

Given that nearly everyone expressed uncertainty about how to evaluate their flood risk after Harvey, we wanted to understand what contributed to this lack of clarity. Although inaccurate assumptions about odds, incorrect interpretations of official maps, and local social networks all played some part in providing conflicting information, we found two additional factors that affected how people thought about flood risk and their residential future: development and climate change.

Residents were aware that the chances of flooding were affected by development and that, as a result, their risk did not necessarily remain static over time. Longtime residents of Friendswood had seen dramatic changes in the metro area over the past several decades. Nearby communities had experienced growth and development, including those upstream along Clear Creek.[15] Thus, there was a shared understanding among residents that development played a role in why their houses flooded during Hurricane Harvey and why they might be at risk for future flooding. However, they found the relationship between development and an increased risk of flooding difficult to measure or to translate into actionable information. As a result, the knowledge that development increased their future flood risk primarily fostered residents' uncertainty about if and when they might flood again.

Josie and Parker viewed development as the biggest factor in their future flood risk. Josie, who had lived in Friendswood for much of her life, told us, "The built environment is what they're changing, you know? And like I said, they keep building more and more subdivisions, and they have them all draining off into the creek . . . when the creek couldn't even handle what it had . . . and plus, they're building everything up higher, making us in a bowl." Growth and constant new construction had made flooding worse over time, and from Josie's perspective, it caused the flood-water to drain more slowly. "In '79, when the water was up just almost as high as it was in Harvey, it was gone the next day. Allison, it was in here for a little bit, it was gone the next day. I've never seen anything sit for three days before it went anywhere."

Residents whose older Friendswood homes were built in the 1960s and 1970s were particularly concerned that new development would lead to more runoff. Valencia, a single woman in her midfifties, said, "They're building more and more. They're steady building, and that's gonna push the water right here to us. I mean, I just went down the street the other day. . . . It's gonna be a strip center right there on that street, which means that's gonna be built up high; we're gonna be low." Residents were also concerned about regional development to the north of the watershed. Friendswood is directly between Houston and Galveston Bay, and upstream suburbs like Pearland are growing. Alicia said that "development upstream from us will affect us, you know. When the upper watershed gets developed, that will affect us too." Gina and Derek told us that the flooding in Friendswood was "compounded by everything upstream coming down this way."

Comments about development came up again and again in our inter-views in the two years after Harvey. But climate change, another possible exacerbating factor in flood risk, was conspicuously absent. Indeed, in the first three waves of interviews, only seven residents brought up climate change. So during our fourth wave of interviews around the second anniver-sary of Hurricane Harvey, we asked Friendswood residents directly about climate change and whether they thought it played any role in increasing their flood risk.

The absence of unprompted discussions of climate change could have been due to the politicized nature of the topic and the politically right-ward tilt of the area.[16] It could also have stemmed from the fact that some Friendswood residents did not believe that climate change increased their risk. Even residents who broadly believed in climate change were uncertain of its effects on flooding. Of the forty-six respondents we interviewed around the two-year anniversary of the storm, nearly 40 percent indicated that they did not believe that human activity caused climate change, around 8 percent were unsure, and about 52 percent said that they thought the climate was changing. Not even all of those who said that the climate was changing agreed, however, that it played a role in the flooding caused by Hurricane Harvey or that it would increase the risk of flooding in the future.

Charles and Barbara acknowledged climate change but were unclear how, if at all, it was connected to flooding in Friendswood. When we asked if they thought the changing climate was affecting the storms they experienced, Charles told us, "From everything I see and read, I don't know if it can be extracted all the way down to flooding here, if that's why, but things probably are different than they used to be." Barbara agreed, and Charles went on: "It just seems like things are accelerated. You know, the things that used to take fifteen, twenty, or a hundred years are happening in five or ten." This view of climate change, however, did not make them rethink their decision to repair their home and remain in Friendswood.

Marissa and Jason were unclear about the role of climate change and largely viewed their flood risk as more directly tied to development. When asked specifically whether Harvey and climate change were related, they said:

> MARISSA: I honestly think it was just a freak thing that happened. No one has ever seen it happen before and probably won't see it in that magnitude again. It was the perfect storm that happened. Like the pressure that kept it and it just sat and spun, it never happened before.
>
> JASON: But I will say, though, the development . . . like paving over all the land, that has contributed to the flooding, right? Absolutely.
>
> MARISSA: So, I feel like it's more, it was more man-made than, for instance —
>
> JASON: Man-made in the — in not so much causing the rainfall but causing what happened with the rain that did fall.
>
> MARISSA: Exactly.

For Marissa and Jason, their flood risk was most directly related to new development and changes to the built environment, not to climate change.

Molly, a married mother in her fifties, similarly rejected climate change as a cause and focused her attention on the role of development. When we asked, "Would you say that climate change has played a role in the risk of flooding in Friendswood?" she replied, "Climate change? I don't think so. . . . I mean, I think that the building, the way that the—they give building permits to just take over, like, different things. I think that the change of the land and the building part, yes. I think that that has affected it."

Georgia and Leo, a married couple in their late fifties, also did not believe that there was a clear and strong relationship between climate change and increased risk. Georgia said, "I think that global warming has been going on, global climate change, has been going on since before we even started monitoring it. I think that there are things that man does to mismanage the environment, and I think that plays an impact. I don't know that I believe it has a serious impact on the nature of the storms we're having." Leo agreed with her. Telling us that climate change has become a political issue, he said that it "depends on what side of the politics you get on. If you listen to a lot of well-known scientists, they'll tell you it's been goin' on for a long time. And it's gone up about a degree, okay? And it is not the fault of man, or man may have some impact on it, but it's not catastrophic. We can hurt the environment in many ways, but as far as our warming from emissions and all, that's really not verifiable. And it's a big political thing." Given the politicization of the issue, Leo did not let climate change affect his sense of vulnerability, telling us, "Does it worry me? Nah. . . . Does that make me fearful of living here? Not in the least."

In contrast, Thomas, a married father in his forties, not only believed that the climate is changing but thought that climate change played a role in the flooding from Harvey and should be taken into account as the government tries to reduce flood risk. He told us:

> It's put some interesting conversations into the government side of it. Um, how do we—how do we mitigate for the next one, because there's going to be another one. I mean, if you pay any attention to climate change, there's going to be another one, right? We're going to—the storms have become more intense, more severe. So it's actually elongated that conversation because, obviously, government doesn't move nearly as quickly as individuals.

When we asked Thomas if he thought that his neighbors shared his view, he said that there was a great deal of disagreement, some of which he attributed to the politics of the town. He said, "We're still pretty strong Republicans in the area. So there's still a lot of fake math, fake science involved in the conversations, but there's some that are 100 percent on board."

In fact, other residents were more concerned about climate change than Thomas assumed, but even when they acknowledged the increasing risk of flooding posed by climate change, this risk did not factor into their decision-making. In other words, there was a disparate and relatively weak relationship between certainty and action.[17] Some households perceived themselves to be more at risk than before and expressed some certainty that their risk had changed, but their actions did not look that different from the actions of their neighbors who believed that they were less at risk.[18]

When we began to ask Mia, "Do you see climate change as part of what's driving—," she interrupted to quickly respond, "One hundred percent. As I sit here and drink from my plastic bottle." She laughed and told us that she had listened to podcasts and read news stories that indicated that the impact could be catastrophic if a "cat 5 hurricane [were] to hit us directly." Knowing this, however, did not seem to have affected her decision-making. "Yeah, I don't know. I mean, when I listen to those things, I'm like, 'Okay, well, you know, we're gonna have to move.' . . . Pretty soon Houston's gonna be underwater." Despite this fatalistic view, she also reflected that the increasing flood risk is not at the forefront of her mind; she thought about it only when flooding seemed possible again, as it did during Tropical Storm Imelda.

> Most days I bury my head in the sand. But, you know, when we have a storm like this last one that just popped up, it was, yeah, kind of brings things back to the surface. Not that I was like, feeling, like, "Oh my gosh, we're gonna flood again." But just thinking . . . they said that it was gonna happen again, and here we are, and it's two years later, and some of the houses that flooded in Harvey are actually flooding again. Like, that is probably my worst nightmare.

Imelda, which hit Friendswood just after the second anniversary of Harvey, raised the specter of flooding. But near-miss events can have the perverse effect of reducing individuals' sense of risk.[19] That is, experiencing another severe storm that did not flood their homes reinforced the idea held by residents like Mia that Harvey was unique. As Mia revealed, even a belief in the reality of climate change does not necessarily spur mobility.

Our respondents in Friendswood were not taking steps to move even if they thought the risk of another flood was significant and climate change was making things worse. Instead, some pointed to other factors to justify remaining in place, such as the mitigation efforts taken by the local municipal government, which they believed might reduce their risk. In other words, residents drew on conflicting signals when describing how they assessed their risk.

LOCAL MITIGATION AND RESIDENTIAL STABILITY

Residents' evaluations of future flood risk were informed in part by perceptions that the City of Friendswood and local flood control districts were taking mitigation steps. The city manager of Friendswood, whom we interviewed multiple times, explained that larger-scale mitigation efforts required federal or state funding, which takes time to acquire. In the two years after Harvey, the city applied for grants from FEMA's Hazard Mitigation Grant Program, the Texas Water Development Board's flood assistance program, and the Texas General Land Office to pay for buyouts of severely at-risk properties. Regionally, municipal leaders in the southeastern suburbs of Texas were also discussing the adoption of new flood maps based on a 2018 survey by the National Weather Service called Atlas 14, which showed that the risk of severe flooding was higher than previously thought. The city manager also reported that there were ongoing, cross-municipal efforts to improve drainage in the Clear Creek watershed. In other words, the storm sparked considerable planning at the regional government level, but there was limited capacity for immediate changes to the built environment.

Few flooded residents knew the specific details of local flood mitigation projects, but many had the sense that efforts were being made to alter the creek and drainage systems. Some residents pointed to the huge dump trucks removing earth from Clear Creek in 2019, two years after Hurricane Harvey. As it turns out, these trucks were not part of any effort directly related to Harvey but instead were connected to a longer-term creek maintenance plan that predated the flood. Nonetheless, the trucks were proof to some residents that Friendswood was proactively working to reduce their risk.[20]

Derek asked us, "Did you see any dump trucks when you were coming up?" After confirming that we had, Derek told us that he felt that these efforts from the city were important for residents who were rebuilding.

> I think in general, if Friendswood wasn't doing anything, then I suspect we would be down there raising hell, because we've done that before. (*laughs*) But at this point, Harvey was the kind of event that, you know you don't ever expect to see again, but we didn't expect to see '79 again either. So, no, I think the city has done what it can do. . . . You can add the retention and the drainage improvements they're doing, that gets the water outta here faster.

Although Gina and Derek both lauded Friendswood's mitigation efforts, they were unsure whether the measures would be enough given the pace of development upstream. Gina said, "And what's happening in Pearland that's coming down through here that we have no control over . . . it's huge, Pearland's huge . . . that is just, so many people and so much cement." Derek said, "Nothing you can do about that," and Gina agreed: "Can't stop progress."

Samantha knew right after Harvey that she would constantly be worried about future flooding. She and her husband Greg had decided to rebuild their home, but they did not always see eye to eye about future flood risk. Greg wanted to remain in their home, but Samantha thought that moving would bring them peace of mind. When we spoke to Samantha shortly after Tropical Storm Imelda, she said that this most recent rain event had finally led Greg to consider moving. She told us:

> Part of me wants to, like, jump on the bandwagon. "Okay, if you're ready to sell, let's move. I've always wanted to." But I do, I love my house . . . and then, when Imelda came, the conversation picked back up. . . . At this point it's like, I don't even wanna live in this area anymore. Like, how can we deal with that feeling for the rest of our lives? . . . Every time a storm comes we're just gonna have a panic attack, or feel like we should move, or why didn't we sell our house. . . . And he's like, "I just don't think I can do this every single time a storm is in the Gulf or whatever." But we still both really love our house, so—I mean, you think about, like, what it would really mean to move.

The tension Samantha felt between staying and moving stemmed from trying to balance potential future flood risk against all the things that she and her husband loved about their home and Friendswood—a tension familiar to other residents. Giving up all that Friendswood had to offer would be a major life change.

Indeed, despite how worried she had been since Harvey, Samantha expressed uncertainty about her assessment of their risk. When we asked in 2019, "What do you think is the likelihood of a Harvey-like event happening again?" she responded:

> The rational side of me says we'll never see this again in our lifetime. And that's what I tell my kids. . . . And then the irrational side is like, "Ugh! It coulda happened last week [during Imelda]. It could happen next summer." You know? But realistically, I know it'll probably never happen again, especially with the changes that they're making and the drainage, if they're doing what they should be doing.

Samantha and her husband were anxious enough about future flooding to discuss the possibility of moving, but she nevertheless described this anxiety as irrational and pointed to local mitigation efforts as reason to believe that the risk of flooding would be low in the future. She told us that if a rain event as intense as Imelda did not flood her home—"You're like, 'Okay, well that was a big rain event and we were fine'"—then perhaps Harvey truly was a once-in-a-lifetime storm. Imelda instigated a new conversation between Samantha and Greg about how risky it was to stay in Friendswood, but when it turned out to be a near-miss event, it reduced rather than increased their sense of risk.

Residents of Friendswood whose homes were flooded during Harvey experienced a range of signals about their vulnerability. Many, like Samantha, described Harvey as a unique event, but they were simultaneously quite anxious that flooding could occur again. Although perceived mitigation efforts on the part of the city provided some solace, uncertainty remained high. Just before the second anniversary of Hurricane Harvey, Carrie and her husband received a notice that new flood maps were being adopted for their area. Their home was now in a flood zone that required flood insurance coverage. At the same time, Carrie was aware of local efforts to widen Clear Creek. Together these two pieces of information made it even more confusing to assess their risk. On the one hand, the flood map suggested that their risk had increased; on the other hand, the city's mitigation efforts indicated that their risk might be reduced. Carrie said:

> Well, the latest is the rezoning of the floodplain I guess. Plan. Flood plan? So yeah . . . we got a letter that said we were now in [the] AE flood zone, which requires flood insurance. We already had it . . . but now we will be required, so now the mortgage company wants a copy of it. . . . It's just frustrating to now be in a flood zone. But then it's like, well, aren't they doing a lot of work in the creek? So maybe we won't be? Or, you know, did the flood zone get rezoned before all the work was done? . . . But now [my husband] thinks they've done all this work and we're still in a flood zone.

The public conversation happening on social media did little to clarify Carrie's sense of risk:

> We looked it up and saw the map and all that, and how it cuts through the neighborhood, and it looks pretty close to what flooded [during Harvey] and who got it worse . . . [but] on Facebook I see Friendswood people talking about it, and so it's frustrating, 'cause one person said they flooded, but their letter said that they're now not in a flood zone. Like, how is that even? So it's just confusing.

Rather than making their risk easier to assess, the new flood maps added to Carrie's bafflement, especially in light of the simultaneous mitigation efforts. The lack of clarity made it difficult to determine an appropriate plan. Carrie said that her husband was more concerned. "He wants to move so bad 'cause he thinks we'll flood again because no one's doing any work. Well, they're doing work, but we don't know what. And we don't know what's next. And so, I hate to move just because of fear." The uncertainty that residents felt about future flooding, combined with all of the various pieces of information that fueled even more uncertainty, left flooded households unclear about the right path forward when it came to their homes.

Carrie's confusion about changes to the local flood maps was understandable. FEMA considers its assessments to be conservative estimates of flooding and encourages municipalities to create their own regulations aimed at alerting more households to potential risks. Before Harvey, Friendswood regulations specified that if flood damage to a house is assessed above 50 percent of the house's value and that house stands within the one-hundred-year floodplain of the local flood map, it must be raised at least two feet above the one-hundred-year flood elevation level. That is, the structure had to be detached from its foundation and raised to a level where it would be less likely to flood. The trouble was that, when Hurricane Harvey hit, Friendswood was operating under two different flood maps.

As we explained in the introduction, Clear Creek not only divides the town but serves as the boundary between Harris County (where Houston is) and Galveston County. In 2007, in the wake of Tropical Storm Allison, Harris County updated its flood maps and Friendswood accepted the new levels, which specified that a larger number of homes were in the one-hundred-year floodplain. Galveston County had not made any changes since 1999. After Harvey, about three hundred homes on the Harris County side would have to be elevated by the standards of the 2007 flood map. Raising a house is incredibly expensive, and so, in December 2017, the city council voted unanimously to revert to the 1999 flood map on the Harris County side, a decision that the city said would prevent residents from having to move.[21] More generally, municipalities are not eager to adopt flood maps that indicate an increased risk of flooding, since doing so can lead to higher insurance premiums for homeowners and threaten the property tax base.[22]

For many residents, the changing flood maps added further uncertainty about risk. Indeed, Friendswood's use of flood maps to determine the provision of building permits in the aftermath of Hurricane Harvey sent mixed signals to Lena and her husband Nicholas at different points in time. Recall from chapter 3 that Lena and Nicholas ended up leaving their home because they could not afford to raise it after the flood damage was assessed at more than 50 percent of the home's value. Before they moved, Lena told us about the whiplash process of determining whether they could rebuild without raising their home.

Not long after Harvey, Lena and Nicholas received a notice that the damage to their home was extensive, and that the city would not issue a building permit unless they raised their home to mitigate future flood risk. They went to city hall to discuss the specifics of their situation. As Lena told us, "A couple days later, they called us: 'Here is your permit.' And we were like, 'You're sure? We're living in this AE zone. We had 80 percent loss, according to insurance. You're giving me a permit?'" Lena thought that the city was trying to allow flooded residents to stay even if their properties were at extreme risk of flooding again. She said, "I think they just didn't want to burden people. They wanted to help people." Confused about what the city's decision meant for their home and their future risk, Lena and Nicholas hesitated to go pick up the permit. While they deliberated about what to do, the city reversed its decision, revoking the permit and reiterating the mandate that Lena and Nicholas would have to raise the house if they wanted to rebuild. Lena told us, "I think it's a more fair decision from the city, because the hurricane and flood is going to happen again, and this house as-is will flood again."

Although the financial burden of raising their home forced them to move, the mandate was at least a clear signal of risk. When Lena and Nicholas moved, they made sure to buy a new home "that has never flooded," though they did not leave Friendswood. Despite the risks, Friendswood still offered the same amenities it had before the storm, and with the quick rebound in local real estate prices, Lena and Nicholas made enough from the sale of their home that they could afford to stay in town without too much financial strain.

In light of the uncertainty and the multiple mixed signals about the risk of future flooding after Harvey, residents maintained their pre-flood plans to stay in Friendswood, but nearly everyone purchased flood insurance. Many residents also developed contingent future plans: they would stay only so long as their homes did not flood again.

INSURING AGAINST FUTURE FLOODS

Those who were insured when Hurricane Harvey struck had more resources for completing repairs and were better off financially two years after the storm than their uninsured neighbors. Among the households we interviewed around the second anniversary of the storm, all of those with flood insurance before the storm had maintained their coverage, unless

they moved out of state. And nearly all of the households that were uninsured when Harvey hit purchased a flood insurance policy in the two years
after the disaster. Only four households that flooded and were still living
in Friendswood or nearby suburbs did not have coverage in 2019. In other
words, there was a marked shift in the uptake of flood insurance among
Friendswood residents after Harvey. Although most people remained
uncertain about whether their homes would flood again, for those who
were uninsured before Harvey, flood insurance coverage became a way to
mitigate against possible future losses.

Kevin and his wife, the couple in their fifties whose harrowing escape
from the floodwaters is described in chapter 2, chose not to return to their
flooded home and instead moved into an apartment in the Friendswood
area. However, their experience with Hurricane Harvey changed their
approach to protecting themselves no matter where they lived. Kevin told
us, "We made sure, even [with] our renter's insurance, that we now have
flood coverage. That was part of the first few sentences we talked about
when we decided to lease an apartment. Let's make sure . . . that we're
covered with flood insurance before we do anything. . . . I'm thinking
everyone around here is saying the same thing."

Susanne reflected on what she had taken away from the long recovery
process and the uncertainty around future flood risk by saying:

> I look at it, it's a force of nature, I don't know how . . . you would prepare
> for something like this in the future. I can't think of anything that you could,
> that we could have done to prevent something like this. . . . I think, for just us
> personally, the thing I would do is, I would just encourage people to really
> look at their flood insurance and make sure they have it. That would kind of
> be my biggest thing that I would say.

As we saw in chapter 2, Susanne and her husband did not have flood insurance before Harvey, but after the storm they made certain they had an
active policy.

For some households, the decision to get flood insurance was prompted
by the requirements of their SBA loans. Two years after the storm, when
we asked Thomas if he and his wife had flood insurance now, he replied,
"Yeah . . . you didn't have a choice. There was a secondary loan we took
out through the SBA to finish up the repairs, and one of the requirements
is you have to carry flood. . . . I think it's like $440 a year." Although it
was a requirement of their SBA loan, he told us, "I probably still would've
gotten it because the peace of mind for four hundred bucks a year—worth
every penny." Based on his back-of-the-envelope calculations after repairing their home, Thomas thought that, even if their home did not flood

for another "fifty more years, that's still, the math works out well, right? $20,000 worth of insurance for $100,000 worth of rebuild." These sentiments contrast with those described in chapter 2, where residents reported neighbors and insurance agents minimizing the risk and viewing flood insurance as an unnecessary expense prior to Hurricane Harvey.

All households understood the value of flood insurance in the aftermath of Hurricane Harvey, but for some the cost of repairing their home made the expense of flood insurance more challenging. John did not buy flood insurance before the hurricane based on neighbors' reports that homes in the area had not flooded during past benchmark storms. A year after the flood, John was carrying $90,000 of credit card debt from repairing his home and the rental properties he owned that also flooded. Although he knew that he should insure his homes, "I couldn't afford it in June," he said. Yet faced with another hurricane season, he purchased coverage in July, using some of his rental income. He told us, "I had to wait thirty days for it to go into effect, but it was the start of hurricane season. I thought I better get my butt in gear and get it."

After he paid for coverage on his house and some of his rental properties, John told us that he planned to maintain it: "You know, now that I know there's a chance, you know, it's always a gamble anyway, insurance. So, but we all do it for car insurance, house insurance, or whatever, but this is a lot less of a gamble, you know. You just never know what'll happen. So it's a risk that I'm not willing to take, not with houses." John was uncertain about the risk of future flooding, but he did reference Tropical Storms Claudette and Allison, as well as his experience with Harvey, in explaining his decision. Raising his hand above his head to indicate a higher level of risk, he said, "I mean, if it's happened now three times in fifty years, you know, forty years, then chances of getting water in here are probably there. Having insurance now will make a big difference." In the wake of a long and challenging recovery process, residents like John were acutely aware of the benefits of insurance, and most figured out how to pay for it.

Yet for some households the cost of flood insurance continued to be a barrier. As we saw in chapter 5, Helen still had not purchased flood insurance coverage two years after the storm. Her finances were quite tight, and she did not think she could afford it. Luis, who could not afford insurance before Harvey (see chapter 2), also said that he was waiting to purchase flood insurance until he could pay off debt he had incurred during recovery. Reflecting on the long and expensive process of repairing his home, Luis said, "I should have bought flood insurance." Yet two years after Hurricane Harvey he still had not done so. When we asked why, he answered succinctly, "Money." For now, he told us, "I don't want to spend the money." But he suggested that he would purchase flood insurance in the future: "Once I've paid, paid up all these bills. Yeah."

For those who could afford it, purchasing insurance was a primary way to hedge against future risk. The vast majority of residents who did not have insurance before the flood bought it within two years, and those with existing policies maintained their coverage. In addition to altering most uninsured households' ideas about the value and necessity of flood insurance coverage, Hurricane Harvey and the arduous recovery process also changed how most households in Friendswood thought about their future residential plans.

CONTINGENT FUTURE RESIDENTIAL PLANS

After Hurricane Harvey, most residents whose homes flooded stuck to their pre-flood residential plans. In the face of uncertainty about their future flood risk, many determined that the amenities that Friendswood offered and their strong ties to the community were still incentive enough to remain in place.[23] Additionally, various sources of aid encouraged returning and rebuilding, and available flood insurance policies allowed for most residents to hedge against future risk. Rather than move, residents who repaired their homes and returned to Friendswood instead developed contingent future plans: they would stay unless their homes flooded again.[24]

Mia and her husband Aaron did not want to move away from Friendswood, but their residential plans became less durable after a taxing recovery process. They had initially purchased their home in Friendswood with plans to remain for a long time. A friend recommended the town, describing it as "this magical neighborhood where your kids would have this magical childhood." After moving in, Mia told us, she found that her friend was right. She described Friendswood as having a "small-town feel — everybody-knows-your-name type thing." Mia and Aaron's initial positive assessment was only strengthened immediately after Hurricane Harvey as the community came together to support those affected by the flood.

However, nearly two years of recovery had changed Mia and Aaron's thoughts about the future. Mia was clear that if their home flooded again, she and her family would leave. She said, "I don't know that I could actually go through that again. And I think that my husband and I are both of the mindset that, we don't have to live here, like, we want to live here, and if we want to move, then we can, and if we flood again, like, we're definitely moving." When asked why they would move, she said that recovery was incredibly stressful and she did not want to repeat it. After Hurricane Harvey, it was a year and a half before "things started to feel normal."

Mia and Aaron had the financial resources to make a fairly unconstrained residential choice, and so, for now, they were staying in Friendswood. Their relatively privileged socioeconomic position allowed them to take this risk. Indeed, like many other households in Friendswood, another flood would probably not be ruinous for Mia and Aaron, so for now they could stay and enjoy their community.[25] In other words, only the prospect of another long recovery would push them out.

When we spoke to Nick around the one-year anniversary of Hurricane Harvey about the risk of another flood, he was uncertain as to whether another flood was coming, but he knew that, since it happened once, it could happen again. He made it clear that he would not return if his home flooded a second time.

INTERVIEWER: Do you worry at all about something like Harvey happening again?

NICK: Absolutely. Yeah. It could happen . . . the people who are in the know say that that was a once-in-a-lifetime deal. So, but it could, it could happen, you never know.

INTERVIEWER: How do you feel about that? What would you do in that case?

NICK: So, everything. Just get my insurance money and tuck my tail between my legs and go find something else, you know . . . once burned, twice learned. So, you know, I've been burned once, so if it happens again, it's . . . I'll sell it to a house flipper. Take the insurance and go.

Many other Friendswood residents we spoke to expressed the same sentiments. Elvis told us that he planned to move in the event of another flood. "My plan is that if this happens again, I will call [the insurance company] and say, 'My house flooded, I'm filing a claim,' . . . put a FOR SALE sign in the front yard. I'm not going to do it again. I will not do this again. I can't. I choose not to." As we saw in chapter 3, households with pre-flood plans for mobility were the most likely to move in the aftermath of Hurricane Harvey, so those who developed these more contingent future residential plans in the wake of a long recovery process may be more inclined to leave should they flood again.

In stark contrast to her stated plans right after Harvey, Chachi told us that the drawn-out process of rebuilding her home had led her to form a new plan to move if she flooded again. Recall from chapter 3 that she refused to move despite being urged by her children to do so. She was too attached to her home. However, at the one-year anniversary of the storm we asked Chachi, "Looking back on the past year, what would you say was the most challenging part of all this?" Rather than focusing on the flood itself, or the evacuation, she spoke about the recovery process:

> Finishing the house. Just pushing, pushing, pushing to finish the house. The, the anxiety of like, is it ever going to be finished, or is this guy [her contractor] just going to run away with my money, you know, because there was weeks, I mean, two, one, two weeks at a time that you would not see one soul in here, and you would go, like, "Oh, my God." That was the most challenging time.

Although she felt that through the recovery process "I became a stronger, stronger person," she did not plan on going through it again. "I think that if it happens again, I can walk away."

When we interviewed Chachi again two years after Hurricane Harvey and just after Tropical Storm Imelda, it was one of the only times she ever expressed doubt that her plan to return and rebuild her home might have been a mistake. "It makes you think whether I made the right decision about staying here." However, her relationship to her home and her strong friendships in the community still anchored her in Friendswood and made it difficult to leave. To explain why she was not planning to preemptively sell before another flood occurs, she said, "Where, where do I go? This is pretty much what I have known for twenty years now. My roots are here. . . . So it is a really, really difficult decision . . . to sell the house and move. . . . I'm just going to keep on going and take it as it comes."

For Chachi, this decision was not about feeling financially trapped two years after the storm. Even at the one-year anniversary, when she had been back in her home for only a matter of weeks, she told us that "the value of my house is, it probably went up, maybe 200 percent. . . . So if I was to choose to sell my house, I would pretty much . . . make out as a bandit." And yet, she told us, "I don't want to go through the experience that I already had. I don't want to start over again. . . . I really don't want to lose everything, and it just . . . (*sighs*) start from scratch like I did, you know, two years ago."

For many residents of Friendswood whose homes flooded, moving was a difficult choice. Moving would entail creating distance from social ties and trying to find a place that offered similar qualities and amenities. Without strong convictions in their assessments of risk, most residents planned to stay—at least until another flood.

Immediately after Harvey, most residents who had long-term plans to live in Friendswood quickly decided to come back and rebuild their damaged homes. As recovery progressed, questions about vulnerability to future flooding became highly salient. Yet people struggled to clearly make sense of their risk and often received conflicting signals about the likelihood of future flooding. They spoke about Harvey as a storm with exceptional conditions that were unlikely to be reproduced in a generation, if not a lifetime. Harvey's uniqueness seemed to be confirmed by Tropical Storm Imelda, a severe storm but one that did not cause houses in Friendswood to flood. Nevertheless, many people also acknowledged that if an exceptional storm happened once, it could happen again.

Drawing conclusions about risk from various sources of information proved complicated for residents. They were unclear about how to identify the magnitude of increased risk from factors like nearby development or the potential reduction in risk from local mitigation efforts. There was also broad disagreement about the role of climate change in the area's vulnerability to flooding, and even those who said that the climate was changing were unsure about how such changes directly affected the vulnerability of their homes. As a result, most residents of Friendswood felt very uncertain about their future flood risk.

In the absence of clear signals that it was risky to reside in Friendswood, flooded households stayed in place. After all, Friendswood had not lost much of its social infrastructure, and it still offered many of the amenities that had attracted residents in the first place. Flooded residents like Lena and Nicholas, who moved because the financial costs of staying would have been too great, were the exception. And even they managed to move without leaving the community by purchasing another home in Friendswood.

Additionally, federal recovery programs and local government actions reinforced an orientation toward residential stability, even while offering relatively little information to homeowners about how to understand their flood risk. Indeed, aid policies encouraged rebuilding and reinvestment in houses, and that being the case, many in Friendswood saw the decision to return, rebuild, and stay as a practical one.[26] However, differential access to resources during the costly process of rebuilding made Friendswood more unequal. Better-off residents with insurance faced few long-term financial consequences, but other residents experienced significantly increased financial precarity two years after the storm. Yet they all remained in Friendswood together, equally uncertain about the risk of another flood and collectively hoping that their homes would remain dry.

Since Hurricane Harvey, FEMA has made important changes in the way it assesses and communicates risk to residents. Specifically, FEMA is moving away from the use of flood maps to determine flood insurance premiums, acknowledging that the one-hundred- and five-hundred-year floodplain designations are too easily misinterpreted.[27] In the coming years, residents will face a new risk landscape with more individualized assessments of risk and flood insurance cost, and many will see an increase in their premiums. Time will tell whether such changes offer residents greater clarity around their flood risk or prompt them to move away from vulnerable areas. In this chapter, sentiments expressed by Samantha and Carrie certainly suggest that clearer information about an increase in their flood risk might spur further discussions about selling their houses, while information that suggests a low risk of future flooding would probably give them greater confidence in their decisions to stay.

After Hurricane Harvey, in the absence of clear information about risk, most Friendswood residents purchased flood insurance and developed a contingent future plan—should their homes flood again, they would not rebuild. No one wanted to repeat the extremely taxing experience of recovering from a flood. Over time offers of help faded, neighbors became less sympathetic, and the costs of repairs piled up. With strained finances and interminable arguments with mortgage banks and contractors, residents came to view recovery so negatively that their plans for continued residence in Friendswood became contingent on never having to go through it again. As one respondent put it, he would only stay "God willing and the creek don't rise."

Conclusion | The Future of Disasters and Inequality

WHEN WE FIRST spoke to Lynne in the weeks after Hurricane Harvey, she described the flood as a "slow-motion disaster"—a reference to the seemingly endless rain that eventually flooded thousands of homes in Friendswood. Two years after the storm, Lynne's description was still apt, but in a different way. The impact of the flood reverberated long after the rain stopped, and the financial consequences of the recovery process would continue to affect many households for years to come. Indeed, Harvey was a slow-motion disaster in more ways than one. The storm caused more than $125 billion in direct damage, yet there were also more complicated social costs that emerged through the long process of recovery.

In fact, climate-related disasters are an increasingly central component of stratification in the United States; recovery processes accrue more resources to already advantaged households, which amplifies inequality.[1] There is, indeed, a disaster Matthew effect. And, as we have shown, middle-class, majority-White suburban communities are not immune to these stratifying effects.

Throughout *Soaking the Middle Class* we have focused on the residents of Friendswood, Texas, elucidating and analyzing their stories of experiencing Hurricane Harvey and then struggling to recover from it. The flooding was devastating, but not uniformly so.[2] Two years later, some residents were in an extremely precarious position as they dealt with unfinished repairs, exhausted savings, and growing debts. Meanwhile, some of their neighbors were living in fully renovated homes and reaping the financial benefits of the quick rebound in the local housing market.

Climate change acts as both a financial and social wedge, separating advantaged communities from disadvantaged ones, but also separating advantaged residents from their disadvantaged neighbors within the same community. As middle-class places are increasingly affected by climate-related disasters, the precarious hold many households have on their middle-class status will be threatened. Thus, disasters will play a growing role in further dividing the rich and the poor and also in hollowing out the middle class, propelling some households toward greater wealth and others toward downward mobility.

RECOVERY POLICIES AS DRIVERS OF INEQUALITY

In the aftermath of a disaster like Hurricane Harvey, it is not simply damage to housing or loss of belongings that drives increased inequality. Inequality is also fostered by recovery policy.[3] For residents of Friendswood, flood insurance played a key role in setting neighbors on disparate paths: only 52 percent of the flooded households we interviewed had coverage before Harvey hit, and these households tended to be financially better off than their neighbors. More broadly, a majority of households that flooded during Harvey were not insured, and this distribution of coverage is similar to that of other recent hurricanes, such as Irma, Florence, and Sandy.[4] And generally, higher-income households with better credit scores and higher home values are more likely to have insurance.[5]

At first blush, this low rate of insurance uptake in a middle-class community like Friendswood is surprising given the area's geography and flooding history, and the ability of most households to afford insurance. But as we saw in chapters 2 and 6, the absence of an insurance mandate leaves homeowners with relatively little information about their vulnerability, and what information they do have is often difficult to translate into a definitive conception of risk. It was not always clear to residents that they needed flood insurance. Yet having coverage made all the difference in helping them avoid the most dire financial consequences.

Gina and Derek, for example, were not financially soaked by Hurricane Harvey; instead, flood insurance served to float them. They were able to combine their insurance payout—which they received directly, not through a lender, because they did not have a mortgage—with their existing savings, time available due to retirement, construction know-how, and social capital to fully repair their home and ultimately increase their wealth. Homeowners like Gina and Derek are not unique: more and more research shows that the rich get richer post-disaster, especially in Whiter communities.[6]

Conversely, Friendswood residents without flood insurance faced significant financial consequences in the aftermath of Harvey. FEMA provided some aid, but not enough to fully repair flood-damaged homes.

The difference between the resources available to the insured versus the uninsured can be hundreds of thousands of dollars. Although SBA loans can help some uninsured homeowners bridge the gap, not everyone qualifies for a loan.[7] Because credit histories and current debt play a role in determining loan eligibility, more advantaged households are more likely to be approved, while those with the most severe need are denied. This was indeed the case in Friendswood, where the range of financial circumstances across households led to variation in approval: some households got loans from SBA, while their neighbors did not.

Households in precarious financial positions when disaster strikes are generally not well served by current recovery policies. Two years after Hurricane Harvey, such households in Friendswood were far worse off. Before the storm hit, Phyllis was already saddled with a great deal of medical debt but was making ends meet on a fixed income from monthly Social Security checks. She did not have flood insurance, and she was denied an SBA loan. Two years after Harvey, she had totally depleted her savings, but her home repairs were still incomplete. Trying to recover from Hurricane Harvey increased Phyllis's financial precarity, and given the cost of the remaining repairs, she did not know if she would ever live in a fully intact home again.

Recovery policies thus can leave residents of the same community in vastly different financial positions. The broad hope and expectation of these policies is that local communities will help to meet the remaining needs of households that cannot fully recover on their own. Indeed, we expected that a middle-class, suburban community like Friendswood would be well positioned to do so. In other words, this community offered a best-case scenario for disaster recovery. Yet we continued to find large disparities in households' circumstances two years after the storm, and preexisting patterns of inequality were only further entrenched. Although there was a strong collective response from the community in the immediate aftermath of the flood, as time went on, and as the FEMA funds of many uninsured households ran out, offers of assistance began to fade well before most flooded residents had finished repairing their homes. That flood-affected residents became more concerned about being stigmatized for seeking help demonstrates how aversion to being seen as "in need" can serve as a powerful barrier to help-seeking and thus to collective recovery and community resilience.

Despite being a middle-class community of mostly homeowners, and despite having a strong social infrastructure, Friendswood was made more unequal during the long recovery from Hurricane Harvey. Indeed, recovery policies amplified financial differences instead of mitigating them, and local assistance did not fully close the gaps between the haves and the have-nots. In *Soaking the Middle Class* we have shown that, two years after the storm, insured residents, like Gina and Derek, were able to increase their wealth; others who received SBA loans, like Erin and Paul, were more than $100,000 in new debt; and repairs on the homes of those who only received money from FEMA, like Phyllis, were still incomplete. Altogether, these findings call into question the efficacy of existing disaster recovery policies and reveal the numerous contradictions inherent in how recovery works. Moreover, the current organization of aid not only increases inequality but also encourages people to stay in risky places.

Residential Stability in Risky Places

Even after experiencing a flood, residents of middle-class communities like Friendswood are not quick to move away. In fact, we found just the opposite to be true: most people return to their homes despite the risk. Households' plans for stability combine with policies that encourage homeowners to reinvest in flooded properties to make return more likely.

When families move into middle-class communities, they frequently do so with relatively long-term plans to stay. They seek out homes that will meet their needs and select neighborhoods that offer the institutions, schools, activities, and amenities that they value. These long-term plans for stability, however, can foreclose their thinking about alternative residential options, even after a devastating disaster.

This predisposition toward residential stability is only strengthened by current policies that draw households back to risky places. When flooded homeowners file insurance claims, for example, the payouts are intended to cover the cost of repairing their damaged homes. But homeowners with a mortgage do not receive their insurance payouts directly. Instead, payments are dispersed to their mortgage lenders, which typically require evidence—in the form of receipts, work orders, and invoices—that the homeowners are undertaking repairs before they will release additional funds. In a way, insurance payouts belong to the houses, not the homeowners: mortgage lenders have a vested interest in the repair of the property to protect its value. Even for the uninsured, current policies meant to ameliorate financial loss orient households toward rebuilding and returning to their flooded properties. SBA loans also require homeowners to provide receipts to show progress on repairs before the full loan amount is distributed.

While residential plans for stability and many disaster recovery policies continue to orient households toward return, scholars and policymakers are increasingly advocating for managed retreat as a key part of an adaptive response to climate change.[8] That is, there is a growing interest in fostering mobility away from cities, towns, and neighborhoods that are likely to experience more climate-related disasters in the future. But as we learned in our two years of following households in Friendswood, many residents of middle-class places instead opt for stability.[9] Public policies and personal plans act together to engender households' return to vulnerable places.

The relatively low cost of flood insurance coverage also reduces many homeowners' perceptions of risk. The average cost of an NFIP-backed policy is less than $800 per year. Among our sample of households in Friendswood, the average was just around $400 per year. For households in vulnerable places, such low costs can minimize perceptions of risk.[10] As flooding has become more common across the United States, it is clear that these low rates miscommunicate risk and also that current insurance policies are unsustainable. In fact, the NFIP has been operating at a loss since 2005; in 2020 it was more than $20 billion in the red, despite having had $16 billion of debt canceled by Congress in 2017 after Hurricane Harvey. Critics claim that the program is based on outdated risk assessments that facilitate development and residence in risky places. This has certainly been the case in the Houston metro region: development has skyrocketed in recent decades, and the loss of undeveloped land that could absorb water has made flooding more common in areas that might not otherwise be susceptible. Moreover, flood maps have not been adjusted frequently enough to alert residents to the increased risk.[11] Indeed, the majority of houses that flooded during Hurricane Harvey stood outside the one-hundred-year floodplain. At a time when climate change is leading to slower and wetter storms, flood maps are quickly becoming outdated; in coming years, millions of both uninsured and insured households will take on water, necessitating more investment in the NFIP.[12]

In October 2021, four years after Hurricane Harvey, in an effort to bring much-needed updates to flood insurance policies, FEMA began implementing a more individualized formula for calculating NFIP rates. Instead of simply using flood maps (which base rates on elevation and location in a flood zone), the new rates will be calculated for individual properties and will take into account a broader set of factors, including: flood frequency and type, distance to water, elevation, and the estimated cost of rebuilding the structure. This new system, Risk Rating 2.0, is explicit in its goal to better communicate risk to homeowners, and some advocacy groups have welcomed the changes.[13]

Yet most households that participate in the NFIP will not see substantial increases in their premiums: it is estimated that monthly costs will increase by more than $10 for only 11 percent of current policyholders. The changes have also stirred strong opposition from elected officials from both parties.

Politicians are often loath to support reforms that cost their constituents more money, so raising rates or requiring a wider set of households to purchase insurance is rarely suggested. It remains unclear whether the new system will substantially affect household decision-making, development, or the collective sense of risk in flood-prone places. What is clear is that, as flood events become more common, it is imperative that homeowners and communities understand their risk as clearly as possible.

Still, accurate risk assessment is only one part of more effective mitigation. Currently, there are few programs that facilitate mobility for homeowners who are open to moving. FEMA's Hazard Mitigation Grant Program does allow homeowners to voluntarily leave their properties through buyouts; however, the buyout program remains extremely small relative to the amount of money the government spends on rebuilding, and it is bogged down by bureaucratic impediments. Indeed, homeowners cannot apply directly to FEMA for a buyout. Instead, buyouts are generally facilitated by local governments, using grants from FEMA. Even where residents and communities have actively lobbied for buyouts, they are not necessarily easy to get.[14] A 2018 FEMA news release on buyouts explicitly stated: "It is not a simple process and requires agreement by your local government officials, the state and FEMA. It is important to note that many flooded properties don't qualify for a buyout, funding is limited and requests for funding may exceed available resources."[15] Even for middle-class households in Friendswood, waiting for a buyout while continuing to pay a mortgage on a flooded home and covering the cost of a rental property was generally not financially feasible. Lacking the luxury of time, households have to focus on rebuilding and returning instead of making plans to move away from risky places.

The City of Friendswood submitted multiple applications over several years to access funding for home buyouts. Nearly two years after the storm, FEMA announced a $5.6 million grant to Friendswood for the purchase and demolition of twenty-six homes. In 2020, local news reported that five property owners were closing on home buyouts through the grants program.[16] Out of the thousands of Friendswood homes that flooded during Hurricane Harvey, only an extremely small proportion will be bought out. Additionally, many households that might have been open to considering a buyout were deemed ineligible for participation in the program, reflecting the limited scope of policies designed to facilitate and encourage mobility away from risk.

In the absence of effective buyout policies, most Friendswood residents did not leave. And why would they? Friendswood continued to offer a "small-town feel," well-regarded schools, and rising home values. For households that moved into this community with clear plans to stay long-term, encouraging them to move—even in the aftermath of a disaster—would have required identifying attractive alternatives, places where they could find a similar quality of life. Or it might have required reimagining what a desirable middle-class life looks like altogether, since an increasing number of middle-class communities may simply be unsustainable places to live in a climate-changed future.[17]

THE CLIMATE-CHANGED FUTURE

Friendswood is certainly not alone in confronting the effects of climate-related disasters. Every summer seems to bring ever more extreme heat waves. Drought has plagued many communities for years and led to emergency declarations across the American West. Larger and more severe wildfires are destroying homes, farmland, and entire communities while simultaneously polluting the air thousands of miles away. In 2020, for example, wildfires burned more than 10.1 million acres of land in the United States—the second-most acreage burned in a single year since 1960. Devastating flooding continues from extreme rainfall and tropical cyclones that have swollen in number and size. For the fifth consecutive year, 2020 saw above-average storm activity and recorded the most named tropical storms ever in the Atlantic.[18] In 2019, major rain events and record winter precipitation caused such unprecedented flooding across the Midwest that the *New York Times* called it "the Great Flood."[19] Along the Mississippi River that year the water remained above flood stage in some areas for more than two hundred days, resulting in more than $2 billion in damage. Two years later, in 2021, there were twenty weather- and climate-related events that led to damages of more than $1 billion each. Perhaps the most significant statistic is this: since 2000, property damage from a climate-related hazard has been reported in nearly every single county in the United States.[20]

In 2021, the UN's Intergovernmental Panel on Climate Change (IPCC) released a stark report outlining the current state of climate change and its consequences, as well as the foreboding future we face in the absence of a proactive response.[21] One of the IPCC's conclusions is that "human-induced climate change is already affecting many weather and climate extremes in every region across the globe. Evidence of observed changes in extremes such as heatwaves, heavy precipitation, droughts, and tropical cyclones, and, in particular, their attribution to human influence, has strengthened." The report came out only weeks after deadly flooding in China and western Europe prompted further global conversations about the risks of insufficient action in response to climate change. Even if the international community does take significant steps to address climate change, the IPCC report suggests that more intense disasters are already baked into our future.

In our climate-changed world, many storms are looking more like Hurricane Harvey. Slow, wet storms will overwhelm many communities with water, forcing a reevaluation of how to think about disasters and the places that are vulnerable to them. Hurricane Ida, which made its way from the Gulf Coast to the Northeast in August and September of 2021, provided a vivid illustration. After Ida devastated much of central Louisiana and knocked out power in New Orleans, it moved north and caused serious flooding and dozens of deaths in New Jersey and New York. These northeastern states had spent billions of dollars on resilience after Hurricane Sandy less than a decade earlier. But Ida was more akin to Harvey. It did not lead to significant storm surge—which much of the post-Sandy spending was intended to combat—but instead dumped a record amount of rainfall on the region in an astoundingly short amount of time, flooding homes and severely damaging transit systems. As these types of storms become more common, a growing number of communities will find themselves underwater again and again.[22]

Despite the growing severity and scope of these various climate-related disasters, residents find it difficult to imagine leaving their homes. This is true across various types of hazards. In the wake of the Alameda Fire in Oregon in 2020, the *New York Times* asked affected residents why they had remained in their scorched communities. Many of the responses were strikingly similar to what we heard from people in Friendswood. Parents emphasized their plans to stay put until their children graduated from high school, and others said that they never thought about moving—"leaving was never an option."[23] Similarly, reporting on the Marshall Fire that tore through Colorado in 2021 showed that many residents focused on rebuilding instead of leaving. And just as in Friendswood after Hurricane Harvey, households in Louisville, a majority-White, affluent suburb of Boulder, are finding they were underinsured. Many are faced with deciding whether to take on massive new debt in order to rebuild their houses.[24] Differential pre- and post-disaster resources across households within this community will lead to growing inequality as they navigate the long recovery process.

Climate change is what the pioneering disaster scholar Kai Erikson would call "a new species of trouble."[25] Unlike the industrial accidents that preoccupied disaster scholars in the middle of the twentieth century, climate change is not one discrete event but a prolonged and iterative process that is rapidly altering the vulnerability of communities like Friendswood.[26] In the few years since Harvey, the residents of Friendswood and the surrounding region have already experienced multiple events, from tropical storms to an extreme winter freeze. In 2019, Tropical Storm Imelda was yet another slow, wet storm that moved through the area, dropping nearly forty-one inches of rain. In Friendswood it caused significant street flooding, and the water came close to once again flooding homes. Other communities that flooded during Harvey experienced significant damage from Imelda as well.

Then, in February 2021, a brutal winter storm caused more than one hundred deaths in Texas and knocked out the state's privatized and aged power grid, causing blackouts and leaving residents without heat for days in freezing temperatures. In Friendswood, most households lost power for more than a day, and some experienced burst pipes, which created another set of needed repairs to homes that had been gutted only a few years earlier after flooding from Harvey. The winter storm and blackouts resulted in nearly $200 billion in damage, making it the costliest weather event ever in Texas. Despite their extreme effects, neither Imelda nor the winter freeze prompted residents to move out of Friendswood. Instead, long-term plans for stability continued to shape households' decisions to remain in place.

There is clearly no one change that will make all households safer. Our climate-changed future requires multiple efforts to ensure that we have the resources to be resilient when disaster strikes, and we also need to develop policies and practices that will effectively support mobility away from vulnerable places.

The future of America—and indeed, the world—is one in which climate-related disasters are more prevalent, more powerful, and capable of affecting a wider set of communities. Our aim in *Soaking the Middle Class* has been to show what the fallout will be for middle-class places that are increasingly at risk. The prognosis is clear: without a reconceptualization of what recovery looks like, inequality between neighbors will grow, even in well-resourced communities. Without deep and systemic changes to the process of recovery, Friendswood, Texas, and the country as a whole will become more unequal and more vulnerable.

Methodological Appendix |

WE BOTH MOVED to Houston just a month before the city and much of the southeastern Texas coast were devastated by one of the most catastrophic storms in the nation's history. Neither of us knew exactly what to expect from our first Texas hurricane season. As Hurricane Harvey made land-fall in August 2017, we stayed in our homes and off the roads as flash flood warnings repeatedly popped up on our phones and the streets of our neighborhoods filled with water. We watched a slow-motion disaster unfold over the news and on social media as it rained hard for more than three days. When the rain stopped, we started to think about all of the decisions that flooded households would be facing after such a devastating event. We had both previously studied residential decision-making, and as scholars of neighborhoods and stratification, we often thought about residential context or place as we formulated questions and analyzed our data. Immediately after Hurricane Harvey, we kept returning to one question that became our initial motivation for entering the field: How do households in a middle-class suburb, whose primary source of wealth is likely to be in a home that has just flooded, make the choice to rebuild and return or to sell and move?[1]

ABDUCTIVE ANALYSIS

A long line of research has examined the experiences of disaster-affected households, and we engaged this work as we entered the field. Our approach to this project was abductive. That is, we had some ideas about how recovery might unfold, but no specific hypotheses to test. We wanted to observe a process while also observing and examining any interesting patterns that emerged—especially if they did not fit with what past literature might have predicted.

As we began our project, a growing body of research seemed to indicate that recovery from disasters creates more inequality in various ways. But exactly how it does so remained opaque. In addition, most of this research focused on growing inequality *between* communities instead of *within* communities. To examine how recovery processes might amplify inequality, we knew to pay attention to household finances, of course, as well as social networks, but we were also open to tackling any problems or analytic surprises that were not easily explained by existing theorizing on inequality and disasters. As we spent time with Friendswood households, there were puzzles that emerged in several forms. These surprises became the backbone of "a creative inferential process" through which we generated conversation between our interview data and the theoretical propositions in existing scholarship.[2]

For example, given the emphasis in both research and policy on local social networks in facilitating recovery from disaster and the consistent finding that middle-class places tend to have robust and well-resourced networks, we assumed that there would be relatively little variation in recovery across households in Friendswood in terms of the amounts of help they received. Here our longitudinal data collection proved to be key, since, as time went on, large and consequential differences emerged between households. Erin and Paul received massive amounts of help in the form of labor, donated household goods, and building materials from their social network, while Phyllis and Vera, despite living only a few minutes from Erin and Paul, received comparatively little social network support. Neighborhood of residence, which was central in some past scholarship on networks and recovery, was a less potent force than we initially anticipated. To explain these within-neighborhood differences, we thought about how households varied: by age and stage in the life course, by income and employment (socioeconomic status), by engagement with local institutions, and by length of residence in Friendswood.

Although any of these individual factors could help account for why Erin and Paul received so much while Phyllis and Vera received so little, we believed that an abductive approach—which stresses theorizing beyond the literatures that may have initially motivated the research question—might be more illuminating.[3] Thinking about how all of these differences might be tied together, we began to explore research on how the middle class has changed from the time when Phyllis bought her home to more recently when Erin and Paul moved to Friendswood. The result of this engagement with literature on the squeezed middle class is our argument that stratification and disasters will increasingly become intertwined as the climate continues to change. Living in a middle-class place does not, in and of itself, protect people from downward mobility in the wake of climate-related disasters, because the middle class has changed, becoming more bifurcated and unequal. By directing greater resources toward households that were already more advantaged before disaster struck, disaster policies only serve to further cleave the middle class, allowing some households to grow their wealth in the wake of disaster, while others face downward mobility.

An abductive approach also prompts engagement with a community of inquiry not only in terms of literature but also interpersonally with other scholars who have relevant expertise and experience with similar types of questions, data, or sites. Although we certainly engaged with various scholars about our work at different points of the site selection, data gathering, analysis, and writing (many are thanked in our acknowledgments), we were also fortunate to be conducting our research collaboratively, developing our ideas in concert. Not only did we both conduct interviews and fieldwork—occasionally together—but we also sat together for countless hours discussing our experiences collecting data, developing themes, creating codebooks, and coming to conclusions.

Throughout the process we used qualitative analysis software to facilitate the free flow of ideas. For example, after every interview was transcribed, we used MAXQDA to conduct our analyses, code together, and establish inter-coder reliability.[4] This is to say that every stage of the research process was heavily iterative: we could immediately share and discuss with each other ideas we had or particular observations from an interview.

SITE SELECTION

To study how households in a middle-class community make residential decisions during recovery, we first had to identify a middle-class community that flooded substantially during Hurricane Harvey. On its face this proposition appeared simple, but in practice it proved more challenging than we anticipated.

As we outlined in the introduction, there is little consensus about how to define the middle class, so we first had to come up with a set of parameters to narrow our search. We started with income. The median household income in the Houston metropolitan area at the time of the flood was a little more than $65,000, so we focused on identifying a set of census tracts that were near this median. We also considered some of the cultural factors that people associate with middle-class communities, such as high-performing public schools and relatively high rates of homeownership. We narrowed our focus to three suburban communities and drove out to see these areas for ourselves.

Two things quickly became apparent. First, the reported flooding was sometimes incorrect, and second, some census tracts were identified as having moderate median incomes as a result of micro-segregation: affluent homeowners lived in neighborhoods proximate to lower-income households renting apartments. Prior research has clearly highlighted that divisions of this type between residents can stand in the way of social integration, solidarity, and cross-class (and cross-race) interaction more generally.[5] This led us to seek out a community whose residential environment was more homogeneous and came closer to fitting with broadly shared notions of what middle-class suburban spaces look like—in other words, neighborhoods with detached single-family homes.

When we first visited Friendswood, we noted that, of the suburbs we had viewed, it was closest to the stereotypical suburb in its built environment. It had subdivisions filled with cul-de-sacs lined with tract homes recessed from the street with front yards. As noted in chapter 1, this particular kind of spatial layout and built environment is laden with cultural meaning about stability, upward mobility, and middle-classness. Part of our project was interrogating these cultural meanings and analyzing whether and how they influenced recovery. As such, Friendswood turned out to be the most appropriate research site we could find.

SAMPLING STRATEGY

Conducting rapid-response research introduces a unique set of both opportunities and constraints, which became clear as we worked to identify an appropriate sample for our study. In the immediate aftermath of Hurricane Harvey, an accurate list of flooded households in Friendswood was not available. Yet it was possible to drive through the neighborhoods closest to Clear Creek and see the edges of the flooding. We would pass rows of houses with piles of belongings and construction debris still sitting in their front yards, and then suddenly there were no more piles, the first uncluttered yard unofficially demarcating where houses had been spared from the floodwater. These boundaries helped us know where to knock on doors and which homes within our visually assessed area of flood damage to mail letters to. Had we arrived in the community weeks later, observing the boundaries of the flooding would have been much more challenging.

Leveraging this knowledge, we adopted a multipronged approach to generating a heterogeneous sample of respondents. Although our entry into the field during the immediate aftermath of the storm precluded certain sampling strategies, such as stratified random sampling from a preexisting list of flooded households, it also enabled us to observe an increased level of community interaction around recovery. This turned out to be beneficial for gathering respondents through snowball sampling. Put another way, residents, whether they flooded or not, were out on the street helping neighbors with recovery tasks, chatting with each other about recovery strategies, checking on one another, and interacting with volunteers and local community groups. These types of interactions faded as the weeks went on, and so, by arriving in Friendswood not long after Harvey, we had the benefit of meeting potential respondents at the height of these community interactions.

Given the traumatic event that these residents had just survived and the intense work they faced of mucking out their homes in the first weeks after Hurricane Harvey, we decided to delay our formal interviews until six weeks after the storm. We assumed that talking about their experiences with the storm could be challenging for some people who had been affected so recently. As the immediate first step of deciding what to do about their wet homes and belongings came to an end, many households began waiting for the next step (for their homes to dry, for insurance money to come through, for FEMA inspectors to show up), and it seemed an appropriate point at which to begin recruitment. Indeed, people were ready to talk, and they had time to do so. We noted this in our application to Rice's institutional review board (IRB) for research on human subjects; we wanted our recruitment approach to carefully consider that residents had just experienced a traumatic event. Because we delayed recruitment and formal interviews until affected households had completed the physically and emotionally taxing work of mucking out, we generally made first contact while residents were in this waiting period.

To recruit potential respondents, we began by talking to people who were outside on the streets closest to Clear Creek. In Friendswood, it certainly seemed to be the norm for neighbors to greet each other and chat regularly. It was not strange for us to approach people sitting in their front yards and ask how things were going—particularly in the first few months after Harvey, when many volunteer groups were going door to door offering help. Everyone we approached said hello, and even those very few who said they were not willing to be interviewed would still chat with us for anywhere between five and thirty minutes about their experiences during Harvey and the weeks after. This is all to say that our recruitment began by approaching people and then snowballed by asking those people who agreed to be interviewed to connect us with neighbors and friends in town whose homes had also flooded.

As we began conducting the initial interviews, it was clear that, though some respondents were willing to provide contact information for their friends—or to reach out to them to make a connection—relying solely on a snowball strategy would make recruiting a robust sample difficult, particularly if we wanted to interview households embedded in distinct social networks. In other words, by relying just on snowball sampling, we worried that our respondents would be similar across important demographic characteristics, and that the sources from which they received aid would be similar as well. Identifying households within a varied set of networks as well as those who might have few if any network connections became a pressing recruitment task. We began to knock on the doors of homes that we could identify as flooded, and using our own knowledge, we mailed recruitment letters to a list of addresses for homes we suspected of having flooded in several of the worst-hit subdivisions in the census tracts adjacent to Clear Creek. This strategy of directly reaching out to a broad set of flooded households was ultimately successful in identifying households with relatively few social ties to the community. Finally, several participants agreed to post our recruitment materials to a Facebook group for flooded residents and also to send those materials to a church support group for flooded residents. Each of these approaches yielded new interviews, and with each new interview we continued snowball sampling.

One strength of a multipronged sampling strategy is the capacity to adapt. Although we ultimately interviewed residents on both sides of Clear Creek, we began data collection on the Harris County side. (As mentioned in the introduction, Clear Creek divides Harris County from Galveston County, so the town of Friendswood sits across two counties.) In some of our early interviews with residents on the Harris County side, respondents reported that since the majority of the town, as well as city hall, the police station, and the central fire station, are on the Galveston County side, households on that side seemed to have been picked up by rescue boats earlier than flooded residents on the Harris County side. That is, those who lived farther from where most municipal services were located assumed that those who lived closer had a shorter wait before they were evacuated from their homes. This perception of internal variation within the community led us to expand our sampling to households in neighborhoods in two census tracts on the Galveston County side of Clear Creek.

Certainly, some residents on both sides of the creek perceived differences across households on the two sides, though residents on the Harris County side were more likely to mention such perceived differences unprompted. And there are indeed differences: the census tracts adjacent to Clear Creek on the Galveston County side have higher median incomes and housing prices. As we conducted more and more interviews, however, we came to see that other factors mattered more during recovery. Put another way, the factors playing a role in recovery were largely the same for all households, regardless of which side of the creek they lived on. Living on one side of the creek or the other, which some residents of Friendswood perceived as a social boundary line, was not determinant of how households recovered from Hurricane Harvey.

The extension of our sampling to include households along the Galveston County side of Clear Creek also increased our confidence that we had reached a point of saturation in our interviews. When the main factors affecting recovery began to repeatedly come up in discussions we were having with respondents on both sides of the creek, we knew that our sample size was sufficient.[6] Our confidence in this sample was reinforced by the variation in the households it represented, from young families to single older retirees and many in between. We also accomplished our goal of recruiting households with varying levels of connection to the community and varied social networks.

The majority of our data were gathered through interviews with flooded households; our data collection also included observations. Over the span of two years we collectively visited Friendswood hundreds of times, spending many hours in town. We watched residents rebuild their homes, saw repairs updated, witnessed interactions with contractors, and joined in shared conversations on the curb among neighbors as we arrived or left. Watching families navigate their homes in the midst of repairs, we saw parents feeding their children in makeshift kitchens and giving instructions about where it was safe to play. We also watched the neighborhood change as homes were either rebuilt or seemingly abandoned.

We observed as many town events related to the flood as we could. These events ranged from city council meetings to city-organized meetings about grant applications for elevating homes and eligibility for buyouts, to neighborhood-organized block party celebrations of making it through the first year of recovery. These observations provided key contextualizing information for our interviews. By attending community events, we could more clearly understand the information available to residents and ask them specifically about the steps the city was taking to aid them in recovery and to mitigate future flood risk. In subsequent interviews, respondents would sometimes mention seeing us at the city's informational events, opening the door to conversations about what they took away from these sessions. The questions raised at these informational meetings and the discussions among residents before and after helped us assess the extent to which our interviewees' takeaways reflected those of Friendswood residents more generally. Attending these events also provided us with other sources of information on what actions the city was taking to support recovery. We could then compare these official reports with what our respondents were saying to identify what residents misunderstood or what was being poorly communicated by the city.

After observing these community events, meetings, and civic gatherings, we would record field notes, which helped frame and contextualize our interview data and also shaped our thinking about what questions to ask in future rounds of interviews.

POSITIONALITY AND ACCESS

Neither of us grew up in a community that looked like Friendswood, but our Whiteness and our association with Rice University aided in opening doors and recruiting interviewees. Rice is broadly respected within the Houston metropolitan area as an elite university with strong academics. The people we spoke to in Friendswood knew about Rice, and their regard for the institution gave our research endeavor credibility. During one interview, the respondent took a phone call, but quickly told the caller to call back later because he was "being interviewed by Rice." The institution represented something positive and prestigious enough that a phone call could wait.

As we walked the streets of Friendswood, knocking on doors and speaking to neighbors, our Whiteness almost certainly allowed us to appear as though we belonged. In the early days of interviewing, Friendswood residents seemed to perceive us as local volunteers. In other words, we did not stand out, and as a result, people were rarely wary when we approached. At the time, residents were used to strangers participating in recovery, offering help, and sometimes offering to buy their homes, and after we had a chance to explain the process, we found that the vast majority of people we spoke to were open to participating in an interview. Our interviews typically lasted around two hours, and we offered $50 cash for their time to those who agreed to be interviewed.

LONGITUDINAL DATA

We knew from the outset of this project that we were going to conduct multiple interviews with the same households over time. Recovery, after all, is a process, and some of the most compelling research after past disasters has been work that tracked individuals, households, or neighborhoods over long periods.[7] However, we did not know when we would (or should) stop conducting interviews. If we had based our plans on our respondents' early and hopeful estimations that they would be back in their homes by Christmas of 2017, we might have conducted only one or two interviews in the first year after Harvey. Most households, however, had to adjust this timeline as it became clear in the months after the storm that the road to recovery was going to be much longer than anticipated. Our goal was to continue following these households until most, if not all, were back in their homes and they generally reported that their recovery from the storm was complete. It took two years, and even then, some households still had major repairs to finish. Conducting longitudinal interviews also allowed our questions to become more sophisticated and nuanced as time went on.[8] Tracking respondents over time allowed us to see how events early after Harvey—like looking for a contractor later than neighbors, or asking for assistance from social network ties and local organizations—could affect recovery in the long term.

We began visiting Friendswood not long after the water receded. Our interviews began the first week of October 2017, when some households had finished mucking out but most had not started with their repairs. These earliest respondents were still waiting to hear back from FEMA, SBA, and their insurance companies about how much money they would be getting. Thus, we were unable to account for how these funds would influence their decision-making and their early steps in recovery. In contrast, households that we interviewed later typically either had payouts from the federal government in hand or knew what resources they could count on in the near future. To address this disparity in our baseline information we added an interim set of interviews with our earliest respondents to gather this financial information and check in about the role these resources were playing in their recovery decision-making. These interim interviews allowed us to establish a financial baseline for each of the households in our sample. Then, moving forward, we conducted interviews with as many of the households in our original sample as possible around the first two anniversaries of Hurricane Harvey.

By conducting our follow-up interviews around the one-year and two-year anniversaries of Hurricane Harvey, we knew that our respondents were already being reminded, to some extent, about the storm. Every year at these times, discussions of Harvey were back in the news as local reporters took stock of recovery efforts across the metropolitan area. The storm was also back in public discussion within Friendswood at the one-year anniversary, when the city organized events to celebrate first responders and others who had volunteered with the rescue and recovery efforts.

In our interviews around the one-year anniversary, we began to see some respondents turning a corner after moving back into their homes with only minor outstanding repairs. But these interviews also highlighted the growing gulf between neighbors as the recovery process perpetuated and indeed amplified disparities. It was clear at the one-year anniversary that we needed to follow households for a second year.

By year two, a substantial number of households were, by their own description, essentially finished with recovery. Harvey and the recovery process were no longer part of their day-to-day lives, and they had largely moved on. Yet some households had major repairs remaining, and this group had often made only minor progress from the previous year. Finances were tight, and it was clear that they had very little sense of when repairs would be finished or how they would cover the costs. For many of these residents, a state of ongoing repair—or more accurately, ongoing disrepair—had become the new normal. Thus, while recovery for these households remained unfinished, we felt that we could follow them for years to come and still see little change. And indeed, we have kept in touch with some of these households; Phyllis and Vera, for instance, described their circumstances in 2020 in much the same way as the last time we formally interviewed them in 2019. Taken together, these factors allowed us to stop systematic data collection after two years and turn our attention to analysis.

INTERVIEW CONTENT

Interviews can take many forms and explore various aspects of social life, and they can be useful for understanding reactions to disasters. Disasters upend "normal" and often taken-for-granted ways of interacting with others, as well as social practices within communities and personal social networks.[9] This disruption is often so acute that disaster-affected people are processing the steps they need to take not only to recover but also to navigate the shaken cultural norms, identities, and boundaries within their neighborhoods and communities that are related to recovery. Our goal was to capture Friendswood residents' attitudes about these different topics.

Proponents and even critics of interviewing as a method agree that interviews are apt for understanding individuals' beliefs.[10] But critics are often skeptical that what people do neatly matches up with what they say they do.[11] That is, individuals can tell an interviewer that they believe a certain thing, but then act in ways that conflict with that belief. As such, interviewers must be careful about the kinds of claims that individuals make about their actions.

There are, however, various strategies for ensuring that the data gathered through interviews are representative of behavior and accurately capture individuals' understanding of that behavior. Our interviews began with broad and open-ended questions like "Tell me how you came to Friendswood," or "Tell me about what you were expecting before Hurricane Harvey hit." These questions allowed our respondents to frame their experiences—that is, to begin by expressing what they thought was important, which is certainly key to analyzing households' responses to Harvey. In opening with such questions, we were following what Stefanie DeLuca, Susan Clampet-Lundquist, and Kathryn Edin call "narrative interviewing," which they describe as "the technique of asking broad, open-ended questions and then probing for the more specific information as respondents tell their stories." Narrative interviewing, they point out, "has the added advantage of inviting such unanticipated themes to bubble up."[12] Our interview protocols were long and followed a general topical logic, that is, questions were generally related to the previous ones. They were also semistructured, however, and that allowed us to follow up on interesting statements or to probe more deeply into a particular aspect of a respondent's answer while still gathering consistent information across cases.

Our interview questions were designed to capture some aspects of respondents' objective reality and also their more subjective assessments of what it was like to live through the flooding from Hurricane Harvey and then recover. We prioritized asking questions about *how* respondents navigated different processes during recovery, rather than asking them *why* they took certain actions. This subtle shift elicits detailed examples and longer narratives of these events and the factors that were incorporated into their decision-making. This approach also included less direct questions about meaning-making, attitudes, or feelings. However, we found that when we probed well enough to generate a rich description of how the experience unfolded, respondents also naturally described their attitudes, their feelings, and how they made meaning of these events.

More specifically, we made certain that we asked for details about the processes that respondents were describing. If we were asking about getting money from FEMA, for example, we asked for the dates of application and inspection, how long the inspector viewed the damaged home, which rooms the inspector viewed, what the inspector told the respondent, when the money was deposited, and so on. Answers to these questions were more than simply minutiae to be sorted out during analysis; they also provided timelines, dollar amounts, and other narrative elements that could then be easily compared to the narratives of other respondents.

We had three other strategies for contextualizing interview data and assessing its accuracy in describing what respondents had done during the recovery process. First, at the end of every interview we asked respondents a series of what might be described as demographic, categorical, or numerical survey questions about the composition of their household, their sources of financial support during recovery, and the money they were spending to rebuild their house and replace their belongings. Although much of this information was obtained during the interview, asking for this information directly and probing for more detailed figures (for example, "Tell me again, what was the dollar amount you received from FEMA?") allowed us not only to compare respondents to each other but also to their own self-reports over the multiple waves of interviews. That is, because we asked for this information in detail at every interview, we could easily enter it into a spreadsheet and see whether the amounts reported by a respondent had changed over the years.

Second, we also asked respondents to show us the objects and spaces they were referring to when they were reporting on the damage from Harvey or on the rebuilding process. For example, if a respondent said that a contractor had performed shoddy work, we asked the respondent to point it out. We asked respondents to take us around their homes, and we continued the interviews during these walkthroughs, which allowed us to match respondents' descriptions to actual items and situations. This methodology—asking respondents about their physical surroundings in their homes and linking these answers with the financial data provided in interviews—has also been used to study household finances outside of the context of disasters. For example, Sarah Halpern-Meekin and her colleagues interviewed 115 poor households in Boston about how they spent tax refunds from the IRS.[13] They tried to conduct interviews in people's homes so that interviewees could point to household goods or other items purchased with the money they received.

Third, we created field notes on a digital recorder after every interview. These recordings lasted between ten and twenty minutes and were made as we drove to the next interview or were on our way out of Friendswood. In these recordings, we described the physical appearance of the respondents, the physical state of the home and surrounding homes, and the neighborhood. Recorded after having just interviewed respondents about their homes, these field notes allowed us to compare respondents' assessments to our own observations and provided key contextual information. We also used our field notes to highlight anything covered in the interviews that we thought was particularly interesting, inconsistent with other data, or otherwise notable. For example, in our second-anniversary interviews, many respondents were reporting that dump trucks were moving earth through the town as part of a post-Harvey flood mitigation effort organized by the city. After noting reports like this in multiple post-interview recordings, we made sure to ask the city manager about it when we interviewed him a second time. He replied that the trucks were part of a municipal project that was initiated well before Hurricane Harvey. This discrepancy highlighted respondents' misunderstandings and led us to think more about some of the topics developed in chapter 6. We also listened to the recordings we made in past rounds of interviews while preparing for subsequent interviews with respondents. Finally, these recordings served as quick refreshers when we were analyzing cases across time. Altogether, these data collection strategies allowed us to link respondents' statements to our observations and provided detailed narratives about the processual aspects of recovery.

Questions across Waves

The initial wave of interviews focused on eliciting a clear narrative from each respondent about how long they had lived in Friendswood and their reasons for moving to the community. We also asked respondents to tell us what they were expecting before Hurricane Harvey hit, and then about their actual experiences with the storm, the flooding, evacuation, and, if pertinent, their shelter stay. We asked about the community response to the storm from local organizations and churches, city officials, and their social networks of neighbors and friends. These first interviews also covered the process of returning to flooded homes and mucking out wet belongings, as well as descriptions of all that was lost and what was salvageable. We heard from residents about how they decided where to stay when they had to leave shelters and find more stable arrangements for the long haul of the recovery process. We asked renters about their interactions with landlords during the early phase of recovery, and how they navigated the process of deciding where to live. We also asked respondents what they were going to do with their flooded homes and whether they were going to rebuild and return or try to sell their property.

These interviews probed what forms of assistance respondents knew were available, and we asked about their decisions to apply for aid from FEMA, the Red Cross, or other groups. We also asked about their flood insurance coverage and their reasons for having coverage or not; if relevant, we asked about their interactions with their insurance companies and the process of filing claims. We asked those who were uninsured whether they applied for an SBA loan. We inquired about home inspections by insurance adjusters and how much each household's insurance settlement ultimately was going to cover. In our interviews in November 2017 and afterward, we were often able to ask about FEMA and insurance inspection processes and the financial aid or payouts received; however, such questions often could not be answered until the spring 2018 wave of interviews, as many households had not yet received the money or had their homes inspected.

We asked parents of school-age children how they were managing their children's engagement with the recovery process and how their children were coping. We asked about how schools were responding to the flood and what support they were offering, or not offering, to students and families. For many parents, the primary reason for living in Friendswood had been the schools, so discussions about schools in the aftermath of the storm often prompted discussions about their reasons for remaining in Friendswood. These types of conversations emerged across many of our interviews as families, both with and without children, used the language of "planning" or having "a plan" to live in Friendswood until some future event, such as retirement or the graduation of their children from high school.

In our first wave of interviews, we did not explicitly ask our respondents about their residential plans, but we heard about plans from nearly everyone as they explained their decision to rebuild and return to their homes or to sell and move away. Those with long-term plans typically chose to rebuild and return, and they emphasized that this decision was aligned with their pre-flood plans. We subsequently integrated this emergent theme—the extent to which recovery altered residential plans—into future interview guides in subsequent waves of data collection. This is one example of the adjustments we made to our semistructured interview guide in each successive wave of interviews, based on what we learned in the previous waves. For each respondent, we reread the prior interview transcript before conducting a follow-up, both to ground ourselves in that household's specific circumstances and to be better able to tailor our questions to their stage of recovery as of the last interview.

As we began our subsequent waves of data collection, households had largely settled into their recovery paths: those who were repairing their homes were in the thick of the repairs, while those who chose to sell and move had done so by the first-year anniversary. At this point, then, our interviews focused much more on the work of recovery and the timeline of repairs. We asked how households were navigating the financial cost of repairs and how far they expected their resources to stretch. We also again asked people about their social networks and the support they were receiving from friends, family, and neighbors. We talked about managing contractors and other workers employed in making repairs and asked respondents about what, if any, work they were completing themselves. We asked respondents what they were thinking about their risk and vulnerability to another flood. We wanted to understand how assessments of risk informed their decision-making at multiple points in the process, and to discover whether they were taking any specific mitigation steps. We asked again about the role of the city government and its efforts during cleanup and recovery to support residents. We also asked about the steps the city was taking to mitigate against future flood risk and inquired whether any of our respondents were engaged in public conversations around the steps that should be taken in the future.

In the second, third, and fourth waves of our interviews, we often heard about growing tension between neighbors over time. The emergence of these types of revelations through repeated interviews, besides showing the power of longitudinal data collection, illustrates that respondents did not feel the need to portray their relationships with friends, family, and neighbors in only a positive light. Often the interview became an opportunity to air concerns that would have been difficult to share with friends or family. We, as empathetic listeners who were disconnected from their immediate social networks, could serve as sounding boards. People spoke about their financial struggles, relationship challenges, and frustrations with their neighbors and the community.

One couple told us that they had been anxious before the one-year anniversary interview that we might be judgmental about their lack of progress on rebuilding. At the end of the interview, they said that they had been relieved when we had noted all the progress they had made. Few people knew how slowly it was going, they said, and over the course of several hours we talked through all of the struggles they were facing. At the end of one interview, the respondent noted that it had almost been like a therapy session. We often forget how rare it is to have someone pay careful attention to you for hours, asking questions that focus on your individual experiences, decisions, and feelings. Other respondents made similar comparisons, presumably because therapy is a primary cultural reference for these kinds of focused conversations. These responses demonstrate the power of longitudinal, semistructured, in-depth interviews. They make it possible to have detailed, nuanced discussions that follow change over time and provide space for a type of attention that is quite rare even in our day-to-day interactions with our closest friends and family.[14]

In our final wave of interviews, when most respondents were largely done with their repairs, the topics of conversation began to include the return to normal family routines. We also continued to ask about assessments of risk and the steps that individuals or the city were taking to mitigate risk. Up until this point, very few of our respondents had mentioned climate change in our discussions of risk. In our interviews around the second anniversary, we asked each respondent about their views on climate change and whether they thought climate change was connected to Hurricane Harvey and flooding more generally. We also checked in with households about their financial circumstances and how the repairs had affected their savings, spending, and debt. We asked how, if at all, the recovery process had altered their financial planning. In these interviews, we worked to understand how complete their repairs were, what repairs remained, and how respondents planned on finishing the remaining work. We also asked how their neighbors were faring and inquired about home sales and changes in their assessment of the value of their own home, as well as how much longer they thought they would live in Friendswood. Finally, we asked residents whether they had continued to receive any forms of assistance in the past year, and we asked whether their experience with the flood and receiving aid had changed how they thought about giving or receiving help in the future.

As we mentioned earlier, at each wave we collected a few details at the end of each interview, using a survey-style questionnaire. This helped us gather information about how the respondent identified their race and gender, their household size and composition, their education level, and their employment and income, as well as other information like insurance coverage and total payout, sources of assistance, and the amount and type of assistance received. Over time these questionnaires allowed us to update information about any additional forms and amounts of assistance as well as changes in insurance coverage, household composition, and income after the storm.

The residents of Friendswood who participated in our study invited us into their homes and their lives for years. They shared many personal details about their financial circumstances, relationships, and the challenges of recovery. They shared their stories to help us understand how households in a community like theirs make decisions, as well as the challenges they faced in the aftermath of a disaster. Their graciousness and openness gave us the opportunity to write a book that we hope sheds light on the complicated process of recovery from disaster in middle-class communities. We are extremely grateful to them all.

Notes |

INTRODUCTION

1. NOAA National Centers for Environmental Information 2022a, 2022b.
2. Collier 2018.
3. Intergovernmental Panel on Climate Change 2021, 41.
4. Abatzoglou and Williams 2016; Emanuel 2005; Klinenberg, Araos, and Koslov 2020; Sobel et al. 2016.
5. Bender et al. 2010; Patricola and Wehner 2018.
6. Risser and Wehner 2017.
7. Emanuel 2017.
8. Cutter and Emrich 2006; Cutter and Finch 2008; Kousky 2018. Indeed, many of the neighborhoods that flooded during Harvey had never flooded before, not even during the Memorial Day flood of 2015 and the Tax Day flood of 2016.
9. Tierney 2014.
10. Mileti 1999; see also Freudenburg et al. 2009.
11. Baddour 2016.
12. Klineberg 2020.
13. NOAA National Centers for Environmental Information 2022a.
14. Bullard 2000, 2008; see also Arcaya, Raker, and Waters 2020; Blaikie et al. 2005; Bolin 2007; Cutter, Boruff, and Shirley 2003; Cutter, Mitchell, and Scott 2000; Fothergill and Peek 2004; Tierney 2019.
15. Billings, Gallagher, and Ricketts 2022; Fitzpatrick and Spialek 2020; Kimbro 2021.
16. Cutter and Emrich 2006.
17. Klinenberg, Araos, and Koslov 2020.
18. Pattillo-McCoy 1999, 13.
19. Kochhar 2018.
20. Fontenot, Semega, and Kollar 2018.
21. Even when focusing solely on income, there is no consensus about how to define the middle class. Some definitions use household distance from the

median income or the poverty line, while others focus on position within the income distribution (Reeves, Guyot, and Krause 2018).

22. Lacy 2007; Lamont 1992; Mayer 1975.
23. Reeves 2018.
24. For a review, see Atkinson and Brandolini 2013.
25. Wuthnow 2017.
26. Freund 2007; McCabe 2016; Pattillo 2013; Townsend 2002.
27. Pattillo-McCoy 1999, 13.
28. Pattillo 2007.
29. Lacy 2007, 39; see also Lareau 2003.
30. Bourdieu and Passeron 1977; Calarco 2018.
31. Lacy 2007, 224; see also Landry and Marsh 2011.
32. Ehrenreich 1990; see also Newman 1988.
33. Fothergill 2003, 2004.
34. Pattillo-McCoy 1999, 14.
35. Douds 2021; Warikoo 2020.
36. Pattillo 2005, 2007; Sharkey 2014.
37. Bonam, Yantis, and Taylor 2020; see also Bader and Krysan 2015; Krysan and Bader 2007; Krysan et al. 2009; Murphy 2012.
38. Freund 2007; Kenny 2000.
39. Sherman 2021.
40. Dwyer 2018; Gottschalk and Danziger 2005; Leicht 2012; Mishel and Shierholz 2013a, 2013b; Sierminska, Smeeding, and Allegrezza 2013.
41. Bucks 2012; Duncan 1984; Hodson, Dwyer, and Neilson 2014; Warren and Thorne 2012.
42. Chetty et al. 2017; see also Bernhardt et al. 2001; Kenworthy 2013. On how these changes have created more precarity and financial insecurity, see Danziger and Gottschalk 1995; Hacker 2012; McCloud and Dwyer 2011; Nau and Soener 2019; Neckerman and Torche 2007. On the growing necessity of higher education credentials for economic mobility and middle-class financial stability, see Hertel and Pfeffer 2020; Torche 2011. On changes to the labor market that have made full-time employment and employee benefits less available, see Dwyer 2013; Kalleberg 2011, 2018. On declining pension benefits for middle-class workers, see McCarthy 2017. On how the decline in labor unions' power created more financial insecurity for middle-class workers, see Rosenfeld 2014.
43. Anthony 2012; Conley and Gifford 2006; Dwyer and Lassus 2015. With differences in homeownership rates and home values across racial groups (see Flippen 2001), increased reliance on housing equity has exacerbated the racial wealth gap (Shapiro 2017).
44. Allard 2017.
45. Tierney 2014, 6. Tierney also highlights, however, that resilience has been defined in many different ways, both by scholars studying environmental

hazards and within scientific and policy discourse more broadly (see also Berke and Campanella 2006). The same is true of the term "vulnerability." Social vulnerability refers not just to demographics but also to additional organizational and economic factors that influence a place's rate of recovery after a disaster (Cutter, Boruff, and Shirley 2003; Cutter and Emrich 2006; Finch, Emrich, and Cutter 2010).

46. Bullard and Wright 2012.

47. Cherry and Cherrys 1997; Craemer 2010; Reid 2013a. In contrast, as the poor pursue both formal and informal sources of aid, they become stigmatized and are made to conform to organizations' expectations about appropriate conduct (Kohler-Hausmann 2018; Lipsky 1980; Piven and Cloward 1971; Wacquant 2009). The poor are also made to wait for unspecified amounts of time in order to receive help and entitlements (Schwartz 1975; see also Auyero 2012; Sullivan 2018). Residents of middle-class places rarely encounter such overt forms of control.

48. Klinenberg 2002, 2018. See Small and McDermott (2006) for more on the relationship of local poverty and racial composition to local organizations.

49. Carré and Heintz 2013; Newman 1988. Financial risk more generally has shifted to individual households as state welfare provision has declined (Hacker 2006; Sullivan, Warren, and Westbrook 2000).

50. Dwyer and Lassus 2015; Hacker 2012; McKernan and Ratcliffe 2005; Preston 2013.

51. Federal Emergency Management Agency 2011; see also Comerio 2014; Kick et al. 2011.

52. Aldrich 2012; Hurlbert, Beggs, and Haines 2001.

53. Howell and Elliott 2019, 465; see also Domingue and Emrich 2019; Elliott and Howell 2017; Fussell and Harris 2014; Grube, Fike, and Storr 2018; Kamel and Loukaitou-Sideris 2004.

54. Billings, Gallagher, and Ricketts 2022; Bullard and Wright 2012; Ortega and Taspinar 2018; Ratcliffe et al. 2020; Zhang 2016; Zhang and Peacock 2009. After Hurricane Katrina, there was an explosion of research on the various forms of economic and racial exploitation that cause disasters to disproportionately affect disadvantaged households and places; see, for example, Cutter et al. 2014; Dyson 2006; Fussell 2015; Hartman and Squires 2006.

55. Ethan Raker's (2020) finding that after communities are affected by tornadoes they become more White and socioeconomically advantaged demonstrates that disasters drive mobility processes in unequal ways (see also van Holm and Wyczalkowski 2019).

56. Merton 1968; see also Tilly 1998.

57. Some small businesses are also eligible for the NFIP.

58. However, the increasing risk of flooding brought on by climate change has not been taken into account, as insurance rates have largely remained the

same since the NFIP's inception. Billions of dollars in the red for decades, the program has become increasingly controversial (Elliott 2021; Michel-Kerjan 2010). Critics argue that such heavily subsidized premiums do not adequately communicate flood risk, and in 2021 FEMA announced updates to its rating methods (Federal Emergency Management Agency 2021a, 2022). Yet these changes remain constrained by congressional statutory caps on rate increases. It was not until the creation of the Hazard Mitigation Grant Program in 1985 that FEMA had a disaster response tool that allowed home-owners to voluntarily leave their properties through buyouts. After a buyout, the property remains uninhabited, that is, it is removed from the housing stock entirely because of its vulnerability to flooding (Loughran, Elliott, and Kennedy 2019). The program remains small, however, and often cannot overcome bureaucratic impediments even when residents want buyouts (Koslov 2016).

59. The reliance on flood maps to determine the mandatory purchase require-ment for flood insurance will remain in place even as the NFIP adopts a new ratings system (Federal Emergency Management Agency 2021a, 2022).

60. Federal Emergency Management Agency 2021b.

61. Lave and Lave 1991; Savitt 2017.

62. Adriano 2018; Larsen 2017. Hurricane Katrina was exceptional in that nearly 70 percent of flood-affected households had insurance. Flood insurance allowed many New Orleans homeowners to pay off mortgage debt and avoid long-term financial burdens (Gallagher and Hartley 2017).

63. Atreya, Ferreira, and Michel-Kerjan 2015; Brody et al. 2017; Hung 2009; Li and Landry 2018; Michel-Kerjan and Kousky 2010; Savitt 2017.

64. Federal Emergency Management Agency 2018a. The amount of aid to affected homeowners for repairing property is adjusted every year.

65. After Harvey, the interest on SBA loans for households was generally 1.75 percent. An FAQ pamphlet from SBA released just days after Hurricane Harvey said that affected residents could contact SBA to inquire about funds for relocation (though it did not describe application requirements, detail the process, or guarantee that loans would be available for this purpose), but all of our respondents understood SBA loans as intended for home repair (Small Business Administration 2017).

66. There are broad inequalities in access to SBA loans, and less advantaged households are less likely to get loans (Begley et al. 2021; Billings, Gallagher, and Ricketts 2022).

67. Comerio 2014.

68. Wright et al. 1979.

69. Frank Jacob Brown and Thomas Hadley Lewis officially registered the settle-ment at the Galveston County courthouse. Two residents of Friendswood have written histories of the town that describe the early settlement and the growth of the community in the years since its founding (McGinnis 1947; Baker 1994).

70. All aggregate statistics are drawn from the U.S. Census American Community Survey (ACS) estimates.

71. The Texas Parks and Wildlife Department advises people not to consume fish from Clear Creek owing to concerns about the presence of dioxins and polychlorinated biphenyls.

72. In Friendswood overall in 2017, the share of residents working in manufacturing was 12.6 percent, and the share working in professional, education, and health-care services was over 36 percent. These estimates are drawn from decennial census and ACS data. Both census tract boundaries and industry categories have changed over the years, so estimates are drawn from all census tracts in Friendswood that border Clear Creek in any given decade. Industry data for the 1970s are derived from the categories "manufacturing, durable," "manufacturing, nondurable," and "professional and related service," while 2017 data are derived from the "manufacturing," "educational services, and health care and social assistance," and "professional, scientific, and management, and administrative, and waste management services" categories.

73. In Friendswood overall in 2017, over 80 percent of the adult population had some college education and 16.2 percent had advanced degrees.

74. In contrast, the Houston Independent School District received a C rating for student achievement in the 2017–2018 school year.

75. Studies have shown that after a flood a gendered division of labor arises, even in the mucking-out process. Women are more often tasked with dealing with damaged belongings while men focus on demolition and construction (Enarson 2001).

76. On individuals' heightened exposure to airborne microbes, toxins, and particulates while mucking out, see Hoppe et al. 2012.

77. Kai Erikson (1994) has written about the need for researchers to foreground the experiences of those affected by disasters in order to understand their long-term effects.

78. See Edin and Lein 1997; Small 2009a.

79. On the importance of following individual, household, and community recovery over time, see Waters 2016.

80. This is all to say that our respondents were not a random sample of Friendswood residents whose homes were flooded, but they were somewhat consistent demographically with the population of Friendswood. In the census tracts closest to Clear Creek—where the residents we interviewed lived—household incomes and house values were slightly lower than the town's overall. In 2017, according to ACS data, Friendswood was nearly three-quarters non-Hispanic White; over 67 percent of households were married couples; the median household income was $99,000; over 20 percent of the households made over $200,000; over 95 percent of adult residents had at least a high school degree or GED; over 85 percent of the housing units were

single-family houses; slightly under 65 percent of the owner-occupied households had mortgages; and the median monthly housing costs were $2,119 for owners with a mortgage, $825 for owners without a mortgage, and $1,150 for renters.

81. Curtis, Fussell, and DeWaard 2015; Graif 2016; Loughran and Elliott 2019; see also Massey 1996.

CHAPTER 1: THE CHANGING MIDDLE CLASS IN FRIENDSWOOD, TEXAS

1. Jackson 1985, 288. See also Baldassare 1986; Duany, Plater-Zyberk, and Speck 2000; Hayden 1984; Wuthnow 2013. Homeownership, particularly of stand-alone houses in suburbs, is tied to various other pernicious cultural ideals (Gans 1965), including traditional gender roles and masculine economic provision (Luken and Vaughan 2005; Townsend 2002; Wuthnow 2017), good citizenship (Freund 2007; Goetz 2007; McCabe 2016), and Whiteness as a valorized racial identity (Lipsitz 2011). See Zavisca and Gerber (2016) on the distinct cultural meanings of housing in different countries.

2. A vast body of scholarship has revealed how and why White neighborhoods tend to be more advantaged than Black neighborhoods, as well as the various ways in which the real estate industry, housing technologies, local munici-palities, and federal housing policy have worked to maintain residential seg-regation; see Besbris 2020; Besbris and Faber 2017; Besbris et al. 2015; Besbris, Faber, and Sharkey 2019; Besbris et al. 2022; Besbris, Schachter, and Kuk 2021; Boeing et al. 2021; Faber 2020; Korver-Glenn 2021; Krysan and Crowder 2017; Massey and Denton 1993; Rothstein 2017; Taylor 2019.

3. Freund 2007; Glotzer 2020; Taylor 2019. On racial projects, see Omi and Winant 1986.

4. On how federal policies throughout the twentieth century largely benefited White people over non-White people, see Goetz 2013; Katznelson 2005; Taylor 2019.

5. Massey and Tannen 2018, 1603; see also Frey 2014.

6. On diversity across the Houston metropolitan area, see Emerson et al. 2012; Klineberg 2020. On growing diversity in suburbs across the country over the past forty years, see Alba et al. 1999; Fowler, Lee, and Matthews 2016; Frey 2011, 2014; Lacy 2016; Lewis-McCoy 2014; Parisi, Lichter, and Taquino 2015; though see Massey and Tannen 2018. Whiteness, however, is not simply about demographics but about the institutional forces—laws, discrimination, culture—that reify Whiteness as the highest-status racial category (Harris 1993). This hierarchy is reproduced even in diverse neighborhoods (Douds 2021; Mayorga-Gallo 2014).

7. For more on the effects of HOAs, see Clarke and Freedman 2019; Freund 2007; McCabe 2005, 2011.

8. Data are drawn from the 2017 five-year ACS estimates.

9. To be sure, Friendswood remains a largely advantaged place. As poverty is becoming an increasingly suburban problem (Allard 2017; Holliday and Dwyer 2009; Kneebone and Berube 2013; Murphy 2010), Friendswood's poverty rate of about 4 percent is less than one-third of the Houston metro area's rate of close to 13 percent.

10. Anthony 2012; Madden and Marcuse 2016; Wisman 2013.

11. The U.S. Department of Veterans Affairs provides guarantorship on private mortgages for those who have served in the armed forces. Most VA home loans do not require a down payment.

12. When people move, they tend to end up in places that are demographically quite similar to their past neighborhoods (Krysan and Crowder 2017; Sharkey 2012). On how residence in similar places over multiple generations can negatively affect those in disadvantaged neighborhoods, see Sharkey 2013.

13. Besbris 2020; Besbris and Korver-Glenn 2022; Collins and Margo 2003; Faber and Ellen 2016; Flippen 2001, 2004; Howell and Korver-Glenn 2018, 2020; Kim 2003; Krivo and Kaufman 2004; Macpherson and Sirmans 2001; Thomas et al. 2018; though see Hipp and Singh 2014; Moye and Thomas 2018. In fact, even in relatively high-income suburbs with good-quality schools and well-maintained housing stock, race and house price appreciation are related, with Whiter places experiencing faster rising prices (Coate and Schwester 2011). This relationship between housing prices and race has been theorized as part of a larger racial system in which Whiteness not only affords privileges but also appropriates value from and exploits non-White, particularly Black, people and places (Bonilla-Silva 1997; Connolly 2014; Du Bois 1935; Harris 1993; Lipsitz 2011; Robinson 2021). Indeed, Black people pay higher amounts for lower-quality financing and lower-quality housing in disadvantaged neighborhoods that lack investment and development (Ihlanfeldt and Mayock 2009; Myers 2004; Taylor 2019).

14. Not only do Black households have a more difficult time entering the middle class, but there are also racial differences in the connection between household middle-class status and residence in middle-class communities. Black middle-class neighborhoods, unlike White ones similar to Friendswood, tend to be spatially proximate to disadvantaged Black neighborhoods (Pattillo 2005, 2007; Pattillo-McCoy 1999; Sharkey 2014). So if middle-class Black households are to enjoy the full advantages of residing in middle-class neighborhoods, they, more than White households, have to move to places where they are in the racial minority (Lacy 2007; Sharkey 2014).

15. Some of the land north of the road to Friendswood from I-45 is a former superfund site. Between 1956 and 1982, the Brio Refinery Corporation, which no longer exists, operated a chemical reprocessing plant on the land. The pollution caused numerous health problems in a nearby subdivision (not in

Friendswood) that led to a multimillion-dollar settlement (Marshall 2019). The undeveloped look of the land—Brio's buildings were demolished in the early 1990s—obscures its toxic history (see Frickel and Elliott 2018).

16. Harvey et al. 2020.

17. Unlike poorer households, middle-class households are rarely faced with making trade-offs during their home search (Harvey et al. 2020; Lareau 2014; see also Winger 1969). For how poorer households make these trade-offs, see DeLuca and Jang-Trettien 2020; DeLuca, Wood, and Rosenblatt 2019; Rhodes and DeLuca 2014; Rosen 2017; Rosenblatt and DeLuca 2012.

18. Goetz 2008; Goetz, Williams, and Damiano 2020; Harris 2013; Kirp, Dwyer, and Rosenthal 1995; Lipsitz 2011; Tighe 2012. Put another way, the suburban ideal is predicated on cultural notions of racial hierarchy (Korver-Glenn 2021).

19. Perceived school quality is also largely tied to race. Parents associate Whiteness with school quality (Holme 2002; Lareau 2014; Weininger 2014), while non-White schools are assumed to be of poor quality (Hess and Leal 2001; Lewis-McCoy 2014; Saporito 2003; Smith and Meier 1995; Wrinkle, Stewart, and Polinard 1999).

20. In the United States, the far higher rate of increase in the cost of housing relative to increases in wages has made housing more expensive now than in past decades (Glaeser, Gyourko, and Saks 2005; Madden and Marcuse 2016; Wisman 2013).

21. As social spending has decreased, homeownership continues to provide status while equity acts as a form of insurance (Ansell 2014; Conley and Gifford 2006; McCabe 2016).

22. White home-seekers generally have greater access to better mortgages than non-White home-seekers (Faber 2018; Quillian, Lee, and Honoré 2020).

23. Conley 1999; Killewald and Bryan 2016, 2018; Oliver and Shapiro 2006; Spilerman 2000.

24. Ortega and Taşpinar 2018; Zhang 2016; Zhang and Peacock 2009; see also Kuk et al. 2021.

CHAPTER 2: "A SLOW-MOTION DISASTER"

1. Samenow 2017.

2. National Oceanic and Atmospheric Administration 2017.

3. Kennedy 2018.

4. Erikson 1994. On how event intensity matters for changes to social structure more generally, see Collins 1981; Ermakoff 2015; Sewell 1996; Wagner-Pacifici 2017.

5. Besbris 2016, 2020; Logan and Molotch 1987. For more on housing post-disaster, see Merdjanoff 2013; Merdjanoff et al. 2022; Morrice 2013.

6. Hurricane Rita hit the Texas coast in 2005, less than a month after Hurricane Katrina devastated New Orleans and the Louisiana coast. In the wake of Katrina, Rita spurred a mass evacuation, with the governor and local officials encouraging residents to leave (Zhang et al. 2007). During the evacuation, people were trapped in gridlock traffic for nearly a full day trying to get out of the Houston metropolitan area, and dozens of people died of heat stroke on the roads (Levin 2015). Since Rita, there have been various calls to minimize evacuation notices (Baker 2018; Lindsay 2010; Miller 2018).

7. Bubeck, Botzen, and Aerts 2012. More generally, people who have less experience with flooding tend to underestimate the risk of future flooding (Siegrest and Gutscher 2008; Tulloch and Lupton 2003; Wilkinson 2001).

8. Dillon, Tinsley, and Cronin 2011.

9. Wachinger et al. 2013. For summaries of the psychological and neurological processes of drawing on the past to predict the future, see Dougherty et al. 2005; Schachter, Addis, and Buckner 2007.

10. Adriano 2018; Larsen 2017.

11. Brody et al. 2013.

12. Households with higher incomes and higher property values are generally more likely to have flood insurance (Atreya, Ferreira, and Michel-Kerjan 2015; Michel-Kerjan and Kousky 2010; Savitt 2017).

13. Insurance agents can receive a commission on the flood insurance policies that clients purchase, and the insurance companies that manage these policies profit from their participation. In other words, there is no clear financial incentive to discourage flood insurance coverage. Instead, this advice most likely indicates that insurance agents may also underestimate flood risk for houses outside the one-hundred-year floodplain.

14. On who is more or less likely to evacuate an area before an impending disaster, see Bowser and Cutter 2015; Boyd, Wolshon, and van Heerden 2009; Thiede and Brown 2013.

15. Research across disasters shows that residents with pets are less likely to evacuate their homes than those without (for a review, see Thompson, Garfin, and Silver 2017). Initially city rescue boats did not allow pets on board, and some residents waited until citizens with boats arrived in order to leave their homes with their pets.

16. Klinenberg 2018.

17. The local schools include campuses in both Friendswood Independent School District and Clear Creek Independent School District. The storm did damage one school, but it was able to reopen after the storm because the water primarily affected only the gym. Similarly, a few churches suffered some damage, but most were unaffected. Moreover, very few deaths in Friendswood were attributed to the storm (George et al. 2017).

18. Klinenberg 2002, 2018.

19. Erikson 1976; see also Kick et al. 2011.
20. Green, Kouassi, and Mambo 2013; Long 2007; Nigg, Barnshaw, and Torres 2006.
21. Friendswood residents were advantaged enough to have well-resourced social networks, but not necessarily rich enough to be able to afford to rent a second home during recovery. There are parallels in other conceptualizations of the middle class. In her study of how families pay for college, Caitlin Zaloom (2019), for example, defines middle-class households as ones that make too much money to be eligible for financial aid but still have difficulty affording the full cost of sending a child to college.
22. Residents of more resourced and Whiter places tend to have richer social networks that provide more help for longer periods of time after a disaster (Aldrich 2012; Elliott, Haney, and Sams-Abiodun 2010; Meyer 2017).
23. A household affected by a federally declared disaster can ask its bank for a mortgage forbearance, but the lender is not obligated to grant it. Furthermore, the lender gets to determine the terms of the forbearance—how long it will last and by how much the monthly payment will be reduced. Furthermore, interest still accrues for the duration of the forbearance, and the lender can determine how missed payments will eventually be paid, including asking for a lump sum at the end of the forbearance period.
24. Doubling up is common across households after a disaster (Lowe, Rhodes and Scogilo 2012; Smith 1996). The practice tends to create more stress for disadvantaged households, however, since their homes tend to be smaller (Morrow 1997; Reid 2013b; Riad and Norris 1996; Weber and Peek 2012).

CHAPTER 3: WHY DO PEOPLE RETURN TO VULNERABLE PLACES?

1. Elliott 2015; Elliott and Howell 2017; Hunter, Luna, and Norton 2015; Morrow-Jones and Morrow-Jones 1991.
2. Koslov et al. 2021.
3. Understanding residential mobility is also key for understanding trends in residential segregation. Like others doing recent work on segregation (for example, Besbris, Schachter, and Kuk 2021; Bruch and Swait 2019; Krysan and Crowder 2017; Schachter and Besbris 2017), we are interested in the decision-making processes that lead to either mobility or stability outcomes for households.
4. Poorer households tend to have more unstable income and employment, which leads to more mobility (Crowder and South 2005; DeLuca and Jang-Trettien 2020; DeLuca, Wood, and Rosenblatt 2019; Kull, Coley, and Lynch 2016; Phinney 2013), as well as a far higher likelihood of experiencing other residential mobility pushes like eviction or nearby violence (Boggess and

Hipp 2010; Carrillo et al. 2016; Clark and Withers 1999; Desmond and Gershenson 2017; Rosen 2017; Skobba and Goetz 2013).

5. Clark, Deurloo, and Dieleman 2006; Coulter, van Ham, and Findlay 2016.
6. Harvey et al. 2020; Lareau 2014.
7. Ard and Smiley 2021; Bolin and Kurtz 2018; Bullard 2000; Crowder and Downey 2010; Freudenburg et al. 2009; Fussell 2007; Taylor 2014.
8. Social psychologists have long shown that people rely on their past experiences when establishing preferences and taking action (Mead 1932). See Goffman (1974) on how individuals frame situations based on past experience and Weick (1995) on how retrospection provides individuals with the ability to make sense of themselves and their roles in relation to others.
9. Mische 2009; see also Cottle and Klineberg 1974; Hart 2021; Tavory and Eliasoph 2013.
10. Rhodes and Besbris 2021.
11. Plans are defined in part by their temporal reach (how far into the future they extend) and their contingency (how durable they are in the face of obstacles and constraints). For other dimensions of plans, see Mische 2009. For how sociologists examine perceptions of the future more generally, see Beckert and Suckert 2021.
12. People do not always move when they say they believe they are going to, but there does tend to be a stronger correlation between intended and actualized moves when residents are homeowners and have more education—markers of middle-classness (Lu 1999).
13. Clark and Lisowski 2017.
14. Harvey et al. 2020.
15. Recent research on immobility after flooding points to numerous factors, including feelings of connection to local social networks and particular amenities as reasons that residents might stay (see Binder, Baker, and Barile 2015; Chamlee-Wright and Storr 2009; Haney 2019). Here we are more interested in how these connections lead residents to imagine a particular residential future that they then use as a guide for decision-making.
16. Clearly, relocation decisions cannot be explained by simple rational-actor models or cost-benefit analyses that do not take into account the various factors that enable residents to create bonds to places and form plans in relation to those places (cf. Henry 2013).
17. See Clark and Lisowski 2019.

CHAPTER 4: HELP-SEEKING AND THE LOCAL ECOLOGY OF AID

1. Wright et al. 1979.
2. Aldrich 2012; Fothergill 2004; Quarantelli 1999.
3. For a review, see Aldrich and Meyer 2015.

4. Social networks are a key aspect of recovery after disasters (Aldrich 2011, 2019; Hurlbert, Beggs, and Haines 2001). Affected households' friends and family often provide informal forms of support. As previous studies have shown, however, examining networks alone does not explain variation across affected households in the amount of help they receive; community-level factors also matter (Beggs, Haines, and Hurlbert 1996; Klinenberg 2002).

5. Research in other domains has similarly been critical of network-based approaches that are too static and has advocated instead for reconceptualizing various aspects of social life, like brokerage, as ongoing processes instead of discrete events (see Besbris 2020; Small 2009b).

6. Here we draw on an existing theory (see Besbris and Khan 2017): the first Chicago School's human ecology framework (Hawley 1986; Liu and Emirbayer 2016; McKenzie 1924; Park 1936; Park and Burgess 1921/1969). Examining social phenomena entails understanding how interactions among members of a spatially bound group can shift over time; the ecological perspective we use here focuses on the dynamic ways in which social context and individual action are related, with an emphasis on the potential temporal changes in these relations. As relations change, the meaning ascribed to particular forms of interaction changes as well (Abbott 1995; Emirbayer 1997).

7. See Waters 2016.

8. Community-level processes are key for understanding how individuals and households react to new environmental conditions (Bell 1994; Jerolmack 2021). For example, after a devastating toxic flood and forced relocation in 1972, members of the Buffalo Creek community in West Virginia were unable to recover because they lacked spatial proximity to neighbors and friends (Erikson 1976). After Katrina, whether or not households stayed in the places to which they had relocated largely depended on community-level factors like local labor markets and perceived discrimination—factors that changed over time (Asad 2015).

9. Besbris 2015; Goffman 1963; Link and Phelan 2001; Major and O'Brien 2005; Pescosolido and Martin 2015.

10. Dauber 2005, 395. And yet, what aid these disaster-affected households are thought to deserve is historically contingent. Many of the policies that are today associated with direct aid to disaster victims, such as FEMA payments and SBA loans, were not available until the second half of the twentieth century (Platt 1999; Tierney 2007).

11. See Fothergill 2003, 2004.

12. According to the ACS, in 2017 only 3.5 percent of households in Friendswood received SNAP benefits.

13. Newman 1988; Owens 2014; Sherman 2013. This reluctance is due in part to a broader cultural disdain for the poor in the United States (Gilens 1999; Katz 1989; Piven and Cloward 1971; Rogers-Dillon 1995; Schram et al. 2009), and

for the Black poor in particular (Hancock 2004; Quadagno 1994; Reese 2005; Wacquant 2009).

14. Garrett and Sobel 2003.
15. Edin and Lein 1997; Fong, Wright, and Wimer 2016; Sherman 2006; though see Sykes et al. 2015.
16. Clemens and Cook 1999; Rainwater 1982; Rothstein 1998.
17. Federal Emergency Management Agency 2018a.
18. Auyero 2012, 109. See also Piven and Cloward 1971; Schwartz 1975; Sullivan 2018.
19. Uninsured residents' experiences after Harvey contrast with the findings of some research on poorer households navigating the aid process post-disaster. For example, Megan Reid (2013b) shows that disaster aid policies assume that affected households have a normative middle-class family structure (see also Cherry and Cherrys 1997). Consequently, those in extended family households are made to wait longer for formal assistance. After Hurricane Katrina, aid providers' association of Black survivors with highly stigmatized Black welfare recipients created further procedural hassles and stigma for those in need.
20. On direct government aid rarely being enough to recover and how households compensate, see Aldrich 2012; Berke and Campanella 2006; Pierre and Stephenson 2008.
21. Small Business Administration 2018.
22. The interest rate on SBA home loans was generally 1.75 percent after Harvey.
23. Fothergill 2003. This orientation is not surprising given broader attitudes toward being downtrodden in the United States, where middle-class people are less likely than the economically vulnerable to be supported by organized aid efforts (Hasenfeld and Rafferty 1989).
24. On the shared experience of disaster prompting feelings of solidarity, see Oliver-Smith 1999. More generally, disasters tend to prompt novel forms of giving and new behaviors (Dynes and Quarantelli 1980).
25. These sentiments parallel findings on government programs as well. Although there is a great deal of variation in universal social welfare programs, they tend to be more popular than means-tested programs across advanced industrialized democracies (Brooks and Manza 2008). At various levels, then, aid that is readily provided regardless of individual circumstances is more easily accepted and less stigmatizing to those who receive it.
26. Reduced empathy is a key component of stigmatization (Batson et al. 1997; Goffman 1963).
27. On identity conflicts post-disaster, see Poulshock and Cohen 1975.
28. Comparison across groups is an inherent part of stigmatization (Pescosolido and Martin 2015, 90; Quinn, Bowleg, and Dickson-Gomez 2019). In Friendswood we found that even comparisons between flood-affected households played a role in stigmatization (see Rice et al. 2018; Watkins-Hayes 2019).

29. Aldrich 2012; Aldrich and Meyer 2015. On how networks can also create drawbacks post-disaster, see Fernandez, Barbera, and van Dorp 2006; see also Aldrich and Cook 2008; Smiley, Howell, and Elliott 2018.
30. Poorer and non-White households often have limited social network connections relative to residents of more advantaged places (Elliott, Haney, and Sams-Abiodun 2010).
31. Haney 2018.
32. Halpern-Meekin et al. 2015; Lamont 2000; Sherman 2009.

CHAPTER 5: GROWING INEQUALITY DURING RECOVERY

1. To some extent, the question of internal variation, or differences across households in the same community, contrasts with some major threads in disaster scholarship, which focus on the unequal distribution of vulnerability across places and on how different kinds of places recover after disaster. For example, before Hurricane Katrina, development and municipal policies in New Orleans had segregated the city in such a way that neighborhoods with higher shares of poor and Black residents were the most vulnerable to flooding (Freudenburg et al. 2008, 2009; see also Blaikie et al. 2005; Donner and Rodríguez 2008; Fussell 2007; Go 2018; Horowitz 2020). Afterward, wealthier and Whiter neighborhoods repopulated more quickly, owing in part to the fact that local and federal rules prevented residents from returning to poorer neighborhoods for longer periods of time after the storm. As battles raged over the permanent closure of public housing developments, some of the most vulnerable New Orleans residents affected by Katrina were deprived of their homes (Long 2007).
2. Merton 1968. The sociologist Charles Tilly (1998) argues that contemporary society is structured in such a way as to provide already advantaged actors with the means to reproduce their advantages across time. For reviews of disaster recovery and inequality, see Arcaya, Raker, and Waters 2020; Fothergill and Peek 2004; Reid 2013b; Tierney 2019.
3. Elliott and Howell 2017; Elliott and Pais 2006; Fussell and Harris 2014.
4. Raker 2020.
5. Billings, Gallagher, and Ricketts 2022; Elliott, Brown, and Loughran 2020; Elliott and Clement 2017; Gotham and Greenberg 2014; Howell and Elliott 2019; Loughran and Elliott 2019; Pais and Elliott 2008; van Holm and Wyczalkowski 2019.
6. If middle-class households and communities, which are often prioritized and privileged by state policies, are left insufficiently supported during recovery, then more disadvantaged places undoubtedly suffer more and are left more vulnerable (Bullard 2008; Bullard and Wright 2012).

7. The amount of aid to affected homeowners for repairing property is adjusted every year. After Harvey, FEMA aid was capped at $33,300 (Federal Emergency Management Agency 2018a). Similarly, the total amount of insurance available through the National Flood Insurance Program is fixed, and households can receive payments for damages only up to the policy limit. The NFIP encourages the purchase of both structural and contents coverage, but they are purchased separately.

8. Disaster aid policies often privilege White middle- and upper-class communities like Friendswood (Bullard and Wright 2012). They also typically privilege already advantaged households, suggesting that they can amplify patterns of pre-storm inequality even within communities like Friendswood (see Billings, Gallagher, and Ricketts 2022; Ratcliffe et al. 2020). Places with higher inflows of FEMA aid are characterized by more racial wealth inequality and more wealth inequality overall (Howell and Elliott 2019), indicating not only that aid is distributed inequitably but also that programs meant to help after disasters exacerbate existing differences across households (Domingue and Emrich 2019; Grube, Fike, and Storr 2018; Kamel and Loukaitou-Sideris 2004).

9. In addition to those households among our respondents that were still making repairs two years after the storm, eight households sold their flooded homes, and we do not have information on the state of repairs for five households.

10. Past research has found that demonstrating gratitude to those who gave aid helps flooded households save face and avoid loss of status (Fothergill 2003, 2004).

11. From a broader perspective, this finding makes sense: credit and debt—as opposed to direct provision of goods or a more robust welfare state—are the preferred forms of financing household consumption in the United States (Dwyer 2018; Kus 2015; Prasad 2012; Wiedemann 2021).

12. Successful advocacy for additional resources during recovery often requires skill interacting with bureaucracies—skill that may be more common among middle-class and affluent households than among poorer ones (Cherry and Cherrys 1997). These same relatively affluent households are also more likely to have insurance. This was certainly the case among our sample; households with insurance had members with a BA degree or higher, and the majority had annual incomes over $100,000. As such, inequality emerged in Friendswood after Harvey not because of differences in self-advocacy but because of differences in insurance coverage and access to other forms of direct support. Additionally, residents who, like Claire, appealed their insurance payouts to request more resources typically did so because they had already paid more for supplies or labor than was covered by their itemized insurance assessment.

13. On why it is difficult to put earmarked household monies toward different ends, see Zelizer 1994, 2012.

14. Ratcliffe et al. 2020.
15. Billings, Gallagher, and Ricketts 2022.
16. See Cherry and Cherrys 1997. Formal aid programs increasingly treat those affected by disaster as consumers who must seek out products themselves and adjudicate which forms of aid are applicable and appropriate (Adams 2013; Gotham 2012).
17. McPherson, Smith-Lovin, and Cook 2001. Past work has focused on differences in social network support across neighborhoods (see, for example, Elliott, Haney, and Sams-Abiodun 2010). Here we show that within-community differences are key for predicting growing inequality after a disaster.

CHAPTER 6: RISK, UNCERTAINTY, AND FUTURE RESIDENTIAL PLANS

1. Assessments of risk, particularly post-disaster, are often contentious; see Clarke 1989; Lakoff and Klinenberg 2010.
2. Cf. Lawrence, Quade, and Becker 2014.
3. We describe residents who were sure that their homes would flood again as certain, and those who were less sure (for example, they answered "somewhat likely" when asked if their home would take on water) as uncertain. More broadly, we use the word "uncertain" to capture households' general confusion and lack of information about the risk of flooding (see Kellens, Terpstra, and de Maeyer 2013). Some research suggests that residents of the Gulf Coast, including the Houston-Galveston area, overestimate their risk of flooding, though in general the findings on the relationship between perceived risk and past exposure are mixed (for a review, see Allan et al. 2020).
4. Elliott 2017, 2019, 2021; Koslov 2019. On the importance of local culture in interpreting state assessments of risk, see Cornia, Dressel, and Pfeil 2016.
5. Even when residents of flood-prone areas overestimate the risk of flooding events, they tend to underestimate the expected severity of future floods (Mol et al. 2020).
6. Khan 2005.
7. Generally, personal experience of an environmental disaster yields perceptions of higher risk (Wachinger et al. 2013), though the relationship between flood exposure and concern about climate change is less clear. Older research found little difference in concern over climate change across individuals whose homes had flooded and those whose homes had not (Whitmarsh 2008). More recent work posits that experiential factors are key determinants for climate change risk perceptions (van der Linden 2015).
8. Lave and Lave 1991.
9. Perceived risk is not evenly distributed, even among people who have some experience with flooding. Women, younger people, and poorer people tend

to express more perceived risk than men, older people, and people with more money (Ho et al. 2008). Flooding experience does heighten some concern over climate change (Hamilton-Webb et al. 2017; though see Whitmarsh 2008) and increases preferences for government action on flood mitigation (Lawrence, Quade, and Becker 2014).

10. Elliott 2021.

11. This common misperception is one reason why FEMA has adopted the Risk Rating 2.0 strategy, which will offer households a more individualized risk assessment (Federal Emergency Management Agency 2022).

12. Indeed, individuals generally have difficulty assessing risk when probabilities are low (Schade, Kunreuther, and Koellinger 2012).

13. See Tierney 1999; Wilkinson 2001.

14. Past work has shown that when changes in flood maps are more clearly linked to material considerations (such as property values), homeowners become more aware of the potential financial consequences (Elliott 2019, 2021).

15. Haney 2021.

16. In the 2020 election, Trump beat Biden by double digits in Friendswood, and the area is represented by Republicans in the state legislature. Friendswood's U.S. representative, Randy Weber, is a recipient of many donations from the fossil fuel industry and is a known climate science denier. More generally, local political context is predictive of climate change skepticism (Whitmarsh 2011).

17. Certainty is theorized as motivating action (Tormala 2016), while uncertainty is more often thought to be paralyzing and anxiety-provoking (Arkin, Oleson, and Carroll 2010; Burke and Stets 2009; though see Frost 2019).

18. Theorists have noted that both individuals and societies are able to continue routine practices even in the face of increased risk (Beck 1986/1992, 2009; Erikson 1994; though see Kasperson et al. 1988).

19. Dillon, Tinsley, and Cronin 2011.

20. Perceived mitigation efforts can raise awareness of risk and the likelihood that people will prepare for future flooding (Terpstra and Lindell 2012), though many people's difficulty with predicting the emotional toll that disaster will take limits their motivation to press for municipal mitigation efforts (Siegrest and Gutscher 2008).

21. Collette 2018.

22. Pralle 2019.

23. After Katrina, some households also chose to return to New Orleans in spite of the risks. The city's unique cultural amenities offered a sense of place that could not be replicated elsewhere (Chamlee-Wright and Storr 2009).

24. We draw on the idea that privilege allows households to accept more risk in the face of uncertainty. In a study of middle-class parents in Boston, Shelley Kimelberg (2014) found that residents who wanted to continue living

in the city were willing to take a chance on local public elementary schools, assuming that they could augment their children's education at home when necessary. However, these parents also knew that they could move to the suburbs or enroll their children in private school. Thus, their privileged position allowed them to take a "risk" with public school enrollment in the early grades, knowing that they could opt out at any time. Friendswood residents, many of whom had the resources to move to less risky places, wanted to stay for the foreseeable future in order to enjoy all of the amenities, institutions, and community qualities that initially attracted them to Friendswood in the first place. Residents like Josie and Parker, who wanted to leave but did not have the money to do so, were in the minority. Most repaired their homes and returned, knowing that if the town flooded again, they could choose to relocate somewhat easily. That is, simply by virtue of their socioeconomic status, many households in Friendswood could run the risk of experiencing another flood. On the unequal distribution of risk, see Curran 2013.

25. Kimelberg (2014, 210) describes the privilege of risk as the financial, human, and cultural capital that middle-class families can activate if their plans do not come to fruition. Middle-class households can *afford* to take risks. This is true even of their residential mobility decisions.
26. See Kick et al. 2011.
27. Federal Emergency Management Agency 2022.

CONCLUSION

1. Arcaya, Raker, and Waters 2020; Ratcliffe et al. 2020.
2. Our findings show why a more in-depth approach is necessary for understanding post-disaster inequality. Looking simply at community averages masks important heterogeneity (Billings, Gallagher, and Ricketts 2022) and can hide the susceptibility of already vulnerable households to further financial hardships post-disaster, like bankruptcy and increased debt burdens.
3. Bullard 2008; Comerio 2014; Howell and Elliott 2019.
4. Hurricane Katrina is exceptional in that the majority of affected homeowners had flood insurance.
5. Atreya, Ferreira, and Michel-Kerjan 2015; Savitt 2017.
6. Bullard and Wright 2012; Domingue and Emrich 2019; Howell and Elliott 2019; Raker 2020; Ratcliffe et al. 2020; Zhang 2016; Zhang and Peacock 2009.
7. SBA loans may actually serve to increase debt inequality post-disaster (Billings, Gallagher, and Ricketts 2022).
8. Mach and Siders 2021.

9.   Rhodes and Besbris 2021; see also Gardiner 2021.
10. Lave and Lave 1991; Savitt 2017.
11. Khan 2005.
12. Elliott 2021; Michel-Kerjan 2010.
13. FEMA 2022; Flavelle 2021.
14. Koslov 2016.
15. Federal Emergency Management Agency 2018b.
16. Degrood 2020.
17. Climate change analysts have described suburban lifestyles as "one of the most serious threats to the climate" (Badger 2011). A full managed-retreat policy would encourage residents of communities defined by single-family houses and sprawl to move into denser, more sustainable housing and neighborhoods in less vulnerable places.
18. National Oceanic and Atmospheric Administration 2021.
19. Almukhtar et al. 2019.
20. Howell and Elliott 2019.
21. Intergovernmental Panel on Climate Change 2021, SPM-10.
22. Klinenberg, Araos, and Koslov 2020.
23. Gardiner 2021.
24. Eastman and Campbell-Hicks 2022; Reinke 2022. In an unfortunate and somewhat ironic turn of events that highlights the need for more policies that equitably foster mobility away from vulnerable places, some residents are finding that local building regulations that were introduced before the fire and are meant to reduce carbon emissions are raising the cost of rebuilding homes (Brasch 2022).
25. Erikson 1994.
26. Climate change poses a challenge to sociological theorists, who generally view ruptures as key to understanding how individuals mark time and describe events (see Hernández 2021; Wagner-Pacifici 2017). With the steady, ongoing changes wrought by a warming planet, more work on how individuals experience and interpret climate change is sorely needed (Tavory and Wagner-Pacifici 2021).

METHODOLOGICAL APPENDIX

1.   Rhodes and Besbris 2021.
2.   See Tavory and Timmermans 2012, 2014.
3.   Mears 2017.
4.   See Deterding and Waters 2021.
5.   Tach 2014.
6.   See Small 2009a.

7.   Fothergill and Peek 2015; Waters 2016.
8.   See Armstrong and Hamilton 2013.
9.   Bucher 1957.
10. Jerolmack and Khan 2014; Lamont and Swidler 2014.
11. Deutscher 1973.
12. DeLuca, Clampet-Lundquist, and Edin 2016, 216.
13. Halpern-Meekin et al. 2015, 222.
14. Small 2017.

References |

Abatzoglou, John T., and A. Park Williams. 2016. "Impact of Anthropogenic Climate Change on Wildfire across Western U.S. Forests." *Proceedings of the National Academy of Sciences* 113(42): 11770–75.

Abbott, Andrew. 1995. "Things of Boundaries." *Social Research* 62(4): 857–82.

Adams, Vincanne. 2013. *Markets of Sorrow, Labors of Faith: New Orleans in the Wake of Katrina*. Durham, N.C.: Duke University Press.

Adriano, Lyle. 2018. "Majority of Harvey Victims Did Not Have Flood Insurance: Experts." Insurance Business America, January 2. https://www .insurancebusinessmag.com/us/news/catastrophe/majority-of-harvey-victims -did-not-have-flood-insurance-experts-88416.aspx.

Alba, Richard D., John R. Logan, Brian J. Stults, Gilbert Marzan, and Wenquan Zhang. 1999. "Immigrant Groups in the Suburbs: A Reexamination of Suburbanization and Spatial Assimilation." *American Sociological Review* 64(3): 446–60.

Aldrich, Daniel P. 2011. "The Power of People: Social Capital's Role in Recovery from the 1995 Kobe Earthquake." *Natural Hazards* 56(3): 595–611.

———. 2012. *Building Resilience: Social Capital in Post-Disaster Recovery*. Chicago: University of Chicago Press.

———. 2019. *Black Wave: How Networks and Governance Shaped Japan's 3/11 Disasters*. Chicago: University of Chicago Press.

Aldrich, Daniel P., and Kevin Cook. 2008. "Strong Civil Society as a Double-Edged Sword: Siting Trailers in Post-Katrina New Orleans." *Political Research Quarterly* 61(3): 379–89.

Aldrich, Daniel P., and Michelle A. Meyer. 2015. "Social Capital and Community Resilience." *American Behavioral Scientist* 59(2): 254–69.

Allan, Jinan N., Joseph T. Ripberger, Wesley Wehde, Makenzie Krocak, Carol L. Silva, and Hank C. Jenkins-Smith. 2020. "Geographic Distributions of Extreme Weather Risk Perceptions in the United States." *Risk Analysis* 40(12): 2498–2508.

Allard, Scott W. 2017. *Places in Need: The Changing Geography of Poverty*. New York: Russell Sage Foundation.

Almukhtar, Sarah, Blacki Migliozzi, John Schwartz, and Josh Williams. 2019. "The Great Flood of 2019: A Complete Picture of a Slow-Motion Disaster." *New York Times*, September 11. https://www.nytimes.com/interactive/2019/09/11/us/midwest-flooding.html.

Ansell, Ben. 2014. "The Political Economy of Homeownership: Housing Markets and the Welfare State." *American Political Science Review* 108(2): 383–402.

Anthony, Jerry. 2012. "Home Burdens: The High Cost of Homeownership." In *Broke: How Debt Bankrupts the Middle Class*, edited by Katherine Porter. Stanford, Calif.: Stanford University Press.

Arcaya, Mariana, Ethan J. Raker, and Mary C. Waters. 2020. "The Social Consequences of Disasters: Individual and Community Change." *Annual Review of Sociology* 46: 671–91.

Ard, Kerry, and Kevin Smiley. 2021. "Examining the Relationship between Racialized Poverty Segregation and Hazardous Industrial Facilities in the U.S. over Time." *American Behavioral Scientist* (May). DOI: https://doi.org/10.1177/00027642211013417.

Arkin, Robert M., Kathryn C. Oleson, and Patrick J. Carroll, eds. 2010. *Handbook of the Uncertain Self*. New York: Psychology Press.

Armstrong, Elizabeth A., and Laura T. Hamilton. 2013. *Paying for the Party: How College Maintains Inequality*. Cambridge, Mass.: Harvard University Press.

Asad, Asad L. 2015. "Contexts of Reception, Post-Disaster Migration, and Socio-economic Mobility." *Population and Environment* 36(3): 279–310.

Atkinson, Anthony B., and Andrea Brandolini. 2013. "On the Identification of the Middle Class." In *Income Inequality: Economic Disparities and the Middle Class in Affluent Countries*, edited by Janet C. Gornick and Markus Jäntti. Stanford, Calif.: Stanford University Press.

Atreya, Ajita, Susana Ferreira, and Erwann Michel-Kerjan. 2015. "What Drives Households to Buy Flood Insurance? New Evidence from Georgia." *Ecological Economics* 117(September): 153–61. DOI: https://doi.org/10.1016/j.ecolecon.2015.06.024.

Auyero, Javier. 2012. *Patients of the State: The Politics of Waiting in Argentina*. Durham, N.C.: Duke University Press.

Baddour, Dylan. 2016. "The Trouble with Living in a Swamp: Houston Floods Explained." *Houston Chronicle*, May 31. https://www.houstonchronicle.com/local/explainer/article/The-trouble-with-living-in-a-swamp-Houston-7954514.php.

Bader, Michael D. M., and Maria Krysan. 2015. "Community Attraction and Avoidance in Chicago: What's Race Got to Do with It?" *Annals of the American Academy of Political and Social Science* 660(1): 261–81.

Badger, Emily. 2011. "The Missing Link of Climate Change: Single-Family Suburban Homes." *Bloomberg CityLab*, December 7. https://www.bloomberg.com/news/articles/2011-12-07/the-missing-link-of-climate-change-single-family-suburban-homes.

Baker, Joycina Day. 1994. *Friendswood: A Settlement of Friendly Folks*. Austin: Nortex Press.

Baker, Karen. 2018. "Reflection on Lessons Learned: An Analysis of the Adverse Outcomes Observed during the Hurricane Rita Evacuation." *Disaster Medicine and Public Health Preparedness* 12(1): 115–20.

Baldassare, Mark. 1986. *Trouble in Paradise: The Suburban Transformation of America.* New York: Columbia University Press.

Batson, C. Daniel, Marina P. Polycarpou, Eddie Harmon-Jones, Heidi J. Imhoff, Erin C. Mitchener, Lori L. Bednar, Tricia R. Klein, and Lori Highberger. 1997. "Empathy and Attitudes: Can Feeling for a Member of a Stigmatized Group Improve Feelings toward the Group?" *Journal of Personality and Social Psychology* 72(1): 105–18.

Beck, Ulrich. 1992. *Risk Society: Towards a New Modernity.* London: Sage. (Originally published in 1986.)

——. 2009. *World at Risk,* translated by Ciaran Cronin. Cambridge: Polity Press.

Beckert, Jens, and Lisa Suckert. 2021. "The Future as a Social Fact: The Analysis of Perceptions of the Future in Sociology." *Poetics* 84(February): 101499.

Beggs, John J., Valerie A. Haines, and Jeanne S. Hurlbert. 1996. "Situational Contingencies Surrounding the Receipt of Informal Support." *Social Forces* 75(1): 201–22.

Begley, Taylor A., Umit G. Gurun, Amiyatosh Purnanandam, and Daniel Weagley. 2021. "Disaster Lending: 'Fair' Prices, but 'Unfair' Access." Posted March 22, 2018; updated September 22, 2021. DOI: http://dx.doi.org/10.2139/ssrn.3145298.

Bell, Michael Mayerfeld. 1994. *Childerley: Nature and Morality in a Country Village.* Chicago: University of Chicago Press.

Bender, Morris A., Thomas R. Knutson, Robert E. Tuleya, Joseph J. Sirutis, Gabriel A. Vecchi, Stephen T. Garner, and Isaac M. Held. 2010. "Modeled Impact of Anthropogenic Warming on the Frequency of Intense Atlantic Hurricanes." *Science* 327(5964): 454–58.

Berke, Philip R., and Thomas J. Campanella. 2006. "Planning for Postdisaster Resiliency." *Annals of the American Academy of Political and Social Science* 604(1): 192–207.

Bernhardt, Annette, Martina Morris, Mark S. Handcock, and Marc A. Scott. 2001. *Divergent Paths: Economic Mobility in the New American Labor Market.* New York: Russell Sage Foundation.

Besbris, Max. 2015. "Stigma." In *The Sage Encyclopedia of Economics and Society,* edited by Frederick F. Wherry and Juliet B. Schor. Thousand Oaks, Calif.: Sage Publications.

——. 2016. "Romancing the Home: Emotions and the Interactional Creation of Demand in the Housing Market." *Socio-Economic Review* 14(3): 461–82.

——. 2020. *Upsold: Real Estate Agents, Prices, and Neighborhood Inequality.* Chicago: University of Chicago Press.

Besbris, Max, and Jacob William Faber. 2017. "Investigating the Relationship between Real Estate Agents, Segregation, and House Prices: Steering and Upselling in New York State." *Sociological Forum* 32(4): 850–73.

Besbris, Max, Jacob William Faber, Peter Rich, and Patrick Sharkey. 2015. "Effect of Neighborhood Stigma on Economic Transactions." *Proceedings of the National Academy of Sciences* 112(16): 4994–98.

Besbris, Max, Jacob William Faber, and Patrick Sharkey. 2019. "Disentangling the Effects of Race and Place in Economic Transactions: Findings from an Online Field Experiment." *City & Community* 18(2): 529–55.

Besbris, Max, and Shamus Khan. 2017. "Less Theory. More Description." *Sociological Theory* 35(2): 147–53.

Besbris, Max, and Elizabeth Korver-Glenn. 2022. "Value Fluidity and Value Anchoring: Race, Intermediaries, and Valuation in Two Housing Markets." *Socio-Economic Review*. DOI: https://doi.org/10.1093/ser/mwac012.

Besbris, Max, John Kuk, Ann Owens, and Ariela Schachter. 2022. "Predatory Inclusion in the Market for Rental Housing: A Multi-City Empirical Test." *Socius* 8: 1–16.

Besbris, Max, Ariela Schachter, and John Kuk. 2021. "The Unequal Availability of Rental Housing Information across Neighborhoods." *Demography* 58(4): 1197–1221.

Billings, Stephen B., Emily Gallagher, and Lowell Ricketts. 2022. "Let the Rich Be Flooded: The Distribution of Financial Aid and Distress after Hurricane Harvey." *Journal of Financial Economics* (January 5). DOI: https://doi.org/10.1016/j.jfineco.2021.11.006.

Binder, Sherri Brokopp, Charlene K. Baker, and John P. Barile. 2015. "Rebuild or Relocate? Resilience and Postdisaster Decision-Making after Hurricane Sandy." *American Journal of Community Psychology* 56(1/2): 180–96.

Blaikie, Piers, Terry Cannon, Ian Davis, and Ben Wisner. 2005. *At Risk: Natural Hazards, People's Vulnerability, and Disasters*. London: Routledge.

Boeing, Geoff, Max Besbris, Ariela Schachter, and John Kuk. 2021. "Housing Search in the Era of Big Data: Smarter Cities or the Same Old Blind Spots?" *Housing Policy Debate* 31(1): 112–26.

Boggess, Lyndsay N., and John R. Hipp. 2010. "Violent Crime, Residential Instability, and Mobility: Does the Relationship Differ in Minority Neighborhoods?" *Journal of Quantitative Criminology* 26(February 4): 351–70. DOI: https://doi.org/10.1007/s10940-010-9093-7.

Bolin, Bob. 2007. "Race, Class, Ethnicity, and Disaster Vulnerability." In *Handbook of Disaster Research*, edited by Havidán Rodríguez, Enrico L. Quarantelli, and Russell R. Dynes. New York: Springer New York.

Bolin, Bob, and Liza C. Kurtz. 2018. "Race, Class, Ethnicity, and Disaster Vulnerability." In *Handbook of Disaster Research*, edited by Havidán Rodríguez, William Donner, and Joseph E. Trainor. New York: Springer.

Bonam, Courtney, Caitlyn Yantis, and Valerie Jones Taylor. 2020. "Invisible Middle-Class Black Space: Asymmetrical Person and Space Stereotyping at the Race-Class Nexus." *Group Processes & Intergroup Relations* 21(1): 24–47.

Bonilla-Silva, Eduardo. 1997. "Rethinking Racism: Toward a Structural Interpretation." *American Sociological Review* 62(3): 465–80.

Bourdieu, Pierre, and Jean-Claude Passeron. 1977. *Reproduction in Education, Society, and Culture*. Thousand Oaks, Calif.: Sage Publications.

Bowser, Gregg C., and Susan L. Cutter. 2015. "Stay or Go? Examining Decision Making and Behavior in Hurricane Evacuations." *Environment: Science and Policy for Sustainable Development* 57(6): 28–41.

Boyd, Ezra, Brian Wolshon, and Ivor van Heerden. 2009. "Risk Communication and Public Response during Evacuations: The New Orleans Experience of Hurricane Katrina." *Public Performance & Management Review* 32(3): 437–62.

Brasch, Sam. 2022. "As Marshall Fire Victims Rebuild, Louisville's New Green Building Codes Are Increasing Costs and Raising Tensions over Local Climate Rules." *CPR News*, February 9. https://www.cpr.org/2022/02/09/marshall-fire-louisvilles-green-building-codes/.

Brody, Samuel D., Russell Blessing, Antonia Sebastian, and Philip Bedient. 2013. "Delineating the Reality of Flood Risk and Loss in Southeast Texas." *Natural Hazards Review* 14(2): 89–97.

Brody, Samuel D., Wesley E. Highfield, Morgan Wilson, Michael K. Lindell, and Russell Blessing. 2017. "Understanding the Motivations of Coastal Residents to Voluntarily Purchase Federal Flood Insurance." *Journal of Risk Research* 20(6): 760–75.

Brooks, Clem, and Jeff Manza. 2008. *Why Welfare States Persist: The Importance of Public Opinion in Democracies*. Chicago: University of Chicago Press.

Bruch, Elizabeth, and Joffre Swait. 2019. "Choice Set Formation in Residential Mobility and Its Implications for Segregation Dynamics." *Demography* 56(5): 1665–92.

Bubeck, Philip, Wouter Botzen, and Jeroen C.J.H. Aerts. 2012. "A Review of Risk Perceptions and Other Factors That Influence Flood Mitigation Behavior." *Risk Analysis* 32(9): 1481–95.

Bucher, Rue. 1957. "Blame and Hostility in Disaster." *American Journal of Sociology* 62(5): 467–75.

Bucks, Brian K. 2012. "Out of Balance? Financial Distress in U.S. Households." In *Broke: How Debt Bankrupts the Middle Class*, edited by Katherine Porter. Stanford, Calif.: Stanford University Press.

Bullard, Robert D. 2000. *Dumping in Dixie: Race, Class, and Environmental Quality*. Boulder, Colo.: Westview Press.

———. 2008. "Differential Vulnerabilities: Environmental and Economic Inequality and Government Response to Unnatural Disasters." *Social Research* 75(3): 753–84.

Bullard, Robert D., and Beverly Wright. 2012. *The Wrong Complexion for Protection: How the Government Response to Disaster Endangers African American Communities*. New York: New York University Press.

Burke, Peter J., and Jan E. Stets. 2009. *Identity Theory*. New York: Oxford University Press.

Calarco, Jessica McCrory. 2018. *Negotiating Opportunities: How the Middle Class Secures Advantages in School.* New York: Oxford University Press.

Carré, Françoise, and James Heintz. 2013. "Employment Change and Economic Vulnerability in the U.S." In *The Squeezed Middle: The Pressure on Ordinary Workers in America and Britain,* edited by Sophia Parker. Chicago: Policy Press.

Carrillo, Laura, Mary Pattillo, Erin Hardy, and Dolores Acevedo-Garcia. 2016. "Housing Decisions among Low-Income Hispanic Households in Chicago." *Cityscape* 18(2): 109–50.

Chamlee-Wright, Emily, and Virgil Henry Storr. 2009. "'There's No Place Like New Orleans': Sense of Place and Community Recovery in the Ninth Ward after Hurricane Katrina." *Journal of Urban Affairs* 31(5): 615–34.

Cherry, Andrew L., and Mary Elizabeth Cherrys. 1997. "A Middle Class Response to Disaster: FEMA's Policies and Problems." *Journal of Social Service Research* 23(1): 71–87.

Chetty, Raj, David Grusky, Maximilian Hell, Nathaniel Hendren, Robert Maduca, and Jimmy Narang. 2017. "The Fading American Dream: Trends in Absolute Income Mobility since 1940." *Science* 356(6336): 398–406.

Clark, William, Marinus Deurloo, and Frans Dieleman. 2006. "Residential Mobility and Neighbourhood Outcomes." *Housing Studies* 21(3): 323–42.

Clark, William A. V., and William Lisowski. 2017. "Decisions to Move and Decisions to Stay: Life Course Events and Mobility Outcomes." *Housing Studies* 32(5): 547–65.

———. 2019. "Extending the Human Capital Model of Migration: The Role of Risk, Place, and Social Capital in the Migration Decision." *Population, Space and Place* 25(4): e2225.

Clark, William A. V., and Suzanne Davies Withers. 1999. "Changing Jobs and Changing Houses: Mobility Outcomes of Employment Transitions." *Journal of Regional Science* 39(4): 653–73.

Clarke, Lee. 1989. *Acceptable Risk? Making Decisions in a Toxic Environment.* Berkeley: University of California Press.

Clarke, Wyatt, and Matthew Freedman. 2019. "The Rise and Effects of Homeowners Associations." *Journal of Urban Economics* 112(July): 1–15. DOI: https://doi.org/10.1016/j.jue.2019.05.001.

Clemens, Elisabeth S., and James M. Cook. 1999. "Politics and Institutionalism: Explaining Durability and Change." *Annual Review of Sociology* 25: 441–66.

Coate, Douglas, and Richard Schwester. 2011. "Black-White Appreciation of Owner-Occupied Homes in Upper Income Suburban Communities: The Cases of Maplewood and Montclair, New Jersey." *Journal of Housing Research* 20(2): 127–39.

Collette, Mark. 2018. "After Harvey's Floods, Friendswood Will Allow Residents to Rebuild at Ground Level." *Houston Chronicle,* February 3. https://www.houston chronicle.com/news/houston-texas/houston/article/After-Harvey-s-floods -Houston-area-city-will-12540769.php.

Collier, Kiah. 2018. "Federal Report: Hurricane Harvey Was a Climate Change Harbinger." *Texas Tribune*, November 23. https://www.texastribune.org/2018/11/23/hurricane-harvey-climate-change-federal-report/.

Collins, Randall. 1981. "On the Microfoundations of Macrosociology." *American Journal of Sociology* 86(5): 984–1014.

Collins, William J., and Robert A. Margo. 2003. "Race and the Value of Owner-Occupied Housing, 1940–1990." *Regional Science and Urban Economics* 33(3): 255–86.

Comerio, Mary C. 2014. "Disaster Recovery and Community Renewal: Housing Approaches." *Cityscape* 16(2): 51–68.

Conley, Dalton. 1999. *Being Black, Living in the Red: Race, Wealth, and Social Policy in America*. Berkeley: University of California Press.

Conley, Dalton, and Brian Gifford. 2006. "Homeownership, Social Insurance, and the Welfare State." *Sociological Forum* 21(1): 55–82.

Connolly, N.D.B. 2014. *A World More Concrete: Real Estate and the Remaking of Jim Crow South Florida*. Chicago: University of Chicago Press.

Cornia, Alessio, Kerstin Dressel, and Patricia Pfeil. 2016. "Risk Cultures and Dominant Approaches towards Disasters in Seven European Countries." *Journal of Risk Research* 19(3): 288–304.

Cottle, Thomas J., and Stephen L. Klineberg. 1974. *The Present of Things Future: Explorations of Time in Human Experience*. New York: Free Press.

Coulter, Rory, Maarten van Ham, and Allan M. Findlay. 2016. "Re-thinking Residential Mobility: Linking Lives through Time and Space." *Progress in Human Geography* 40(3): 352–74.

Craemer, Thomas. 2010. "Evaluating Racial Disparities in Hurricane Katrina Relief Using Direct Trailer Counts in New Orleans and FEMA Records." *Public Administration Review* 70(3): 367–77.

Crowder, Kyle, and Liam Downey. 2010. "Interneighborhood Migration, Race, and Environmental Hazards: Modeling Microlevel Processes of Environmental Inequality." *American Journal of Sociology* 115(4): 1110–49.

Crowder, Kyle, and Scott J. South. 2005. "Race, Class, and Changing Patterns of Migration between Poor and Nonpoor Neighborhoods." *American Journal of Sociology* 110(6): 1715–63.

Curran, Dean. 2013. "Risk Society and the Distribution of Bads: Theorizing Class in the Risk Society." *British Journal of Sociology* 64(1): 44–62.

Curtis, Katherine J., Elizabeth Fussell, and Jack DeWaard. 2015. "Recovery Migration after Hurricanes Katrina and Rita: Spatial Concentration and Intensification in the Migration System." *Demography* 52(4): 1269–93.

Cutter, Susan L., Bryan J. Boruff, and W. Lynn Shirley. 2003. "Social Vulnerability to Environmental Hazards." *Social Science Quarterly* 84(2): 242–61.

Cutter, Susan L., and Christopher T. Emrich. 2006. "Moral Hazard, Social Catastrophe: The Changing Face of Vulnerability along the Hurricane Coasts." *Annals of the American Academy of Political and Social Science* 604(1): 102–22.

Cutter, Susan L., Christopher T. Emrich, Jerry T. Mitchell, Walther W. Piergorsch, Mark M. Smith, and Lynn Weber. 2014. *Hurricane Katrina and the Forgotten Coast of Mississippi*. New York: Cambridge University Press.

Cutter, Susan L., and Christina Finch. 2008. "Temporal and Spatial Changes in Social Vulnerability to Natural Hazards." *Proceedings of the National Academy of Sciences* 105(7): S.2301–6.

Cutter, Susan L., Jerry T. Mitchell, and Michael S. Scott. 2000. "Revealing the Vulnerability of People and Places: A Case Study of Georgetown County, South Carolina." *Annals of the Association of American Geographers* 90(4): 713–37.

Danziger, Sheldon, and Peter Gottschalk. 1995. *America Unequal*. New York: Russell Sage Foundation.

Dauber, Michele. 2005. "The Sympathetic State." *Law and History Review* 23(2): 387–442.

Degrood, Matt. 2020. "Five Friendswood Homeowners Take Buyouts." *Galveston County Daily News*, July 13. https://www.galvnews.com/news/free/article _bbd54e6e-1c0b-5d21-8f24-e82560f7a427.html.

DeLuca, Stefanie, Susan Clampet-Lundquist, and Kathryn Edin. 2016. *Coming of Age in the Other America*. New York: Russell Sage Foundation.

DeLuca, Stefanie, and Christine Jang-Trettien. 2020. "'Not Just a Lateral Move': Residential Decisions and the Reproduction of Urban Inequality." *City & Community* 19(3): 451–88.

DeLuca, Stefanie, Holly Wood, and Peter Rosenblatt. 2019. "Why Poor Families Move (and Where They Go): Reactive Mobility and Residential Decisions." *City & Community* 18(2): 556–93.

Desmond, Matthew, and Carl Gershenson. 2017. "Who Gets Evicted? Assessing Individual, Neighborhood, and Network Factors." *Social Science Research* 62(February): 362–77. DOI: https://doi.org/10.1016/j.ssresearch.2016.08.017.

Deterding, Nicole M., and Mary Waters. 2021. "Flexible Coding of In-Depth Interviews: A Twenty-First-Century Approach." *Sociological Methods & Research* 50(2): 708–39.

Deutscher, Irwin. 1973. *What We Say/What We Do: Sentiments and Acts*. Glenview, Ill.: Scott, Foresman.

Dillon, Robin L., Catherine H. Tinsley, and Matthew Cronin. 2011. "Why Near-Miss Events Can Decrease an Individual's Protective Response to Hurricanes." *Risk Analysis* 31(3): 440–49.

Domingue, Simone J., and Christopher T. Emrich. 2019. "Social Vulnerability and Procedural Equity: Exploring the Distribution of Disaster Aid across Counties in the United States." *American Review of Public Administration* 49(8): 897–913.

Donner, William, and Havidán Rodríguez. 2008. "Population Composition, Migration, and Inequality: The Influence of Demographic Changes on Disaster Risk and Vulnerability." *Social Forces* 87(2): 1089–1114.

Douds, Kiara Wyndham. 2021. "The Diversity Contract: Constructing Racial Harmony in a Diverse Suburb." *American Journal of Sociology* 126(6): 1347–88.

Dougherty, Michael R., Petra Scheck, Thomas O. Nelson, and Louis Narens. 2005. "Using the Past to Predict the Future." *Memory & Cognition* 33(6): 1096–1115.

Duany, Andres, Elizabeth Plater-Zyberk, and Jeff Speck. 2000. *Suburban Nation: The Rise and Decline of the American Dream*. New York: North Point Press.

Du Bois, William Edward Burghardt. 1935. *Black Reconstruction in America: An Essay toward a History of the Part Which Black Folk Played in the Attempt to Reconstruct Democracy in America, 1860–1880*, vol. 6. Oxford: Oxford University Press.

Duncan, Greg J. 1984. *Years of Poverty, Years of Plenty: The Changing Economic Fortunes of American Workers and Families*. Ann Arbor: Survey Research Center, Institute for Social Research, University of Michigan.

Dwyer, Rachel E. 2013. "The Care Economy? Gender, Economic Restructuring, and Job Polarization in the U.S. Labor Market." *American Sociological Review* 78(3): 390–416.

———. 2018. "Credit, Debt, and Inequality." *Annual Review of Sociology* 44: 237–61.

Dwyer, Rachel E., and Lora A. Phillips Lassus. 2015. "The Great Risk Shift and Precarity in the U.S. Housing Market." *Annals of the American Academy of Political and Social Science* 660(1): 199–216.

Dynes, Russell R., and Enrico L. Quarantelli. 1980. "Helping Behavior in Large-Scale Disasters." In *Participation in Social and Political Activities*, edited by David Horton Smith and J. McAulay. San Francisco: Jossey-Bass.

Dyson, Michael Eric. 2006. *Come Hell or High Water: Hurricane Katrina and the Color of Disaster*. Cambridge, Mass.: Basic Civitas.

Eastman, Katie, and Jennifer Campbell-Hicks. 2022. "Their Dream Home Burned in the Marshall Fire, and Now They Plan to Rebuild." *9News*, February 21. https://www.9news.com/article/news/local/wildfire/marshall-fire/marshall-fire -ferrington-family/73-d96b2b64-3db7-4a2c-a3bb-d34d0ba363df.

Edin, Kathryn, and Laura Lein. 1997. *Making Ends Meet: How Single Mothers Survive Welfare and Low-Wage Work*. New York: Russell Sage Foundation.

Ehrenreich, Barbara. 1990. *Fear of Falling: The Inner Life of the Middle Class*. New York: Harper Perennial.

Elliott, James R. 2015. "Natural Hazards and Residential Mobility: General Patterns and Racially Unequal Outcomes in the United States." *Social Forces* 93(4): 1723–47.

Elliott, James R., Phylicia Lee Brown, and Kevin Loughran. 2020. "Racial Inequities in the Federal Buyout of Flood-Prone Homes: A Nationwide Assessment of Environmental Adaptation." *Socius* 6(February): 1–15. DOI: https://doi.org/10 .1177/2378023120905439.

Elliott, James R., and Matthew Thomas Clement. 2017. "Natural Hazards and Local Development: The Successive Nature of Landscape Transformation in the United States." *Social Forces* 96(2): 851–76.

Elliott, James R., Timothy J. Haney, and Petrice Sams-Abiodun. 2010. "Limits to Social Capital: Comparing Network Assistance in Two New Orleans

Neighborhoods Devastated by Hurricane Katrina." *Sociological Quarterly* 51(4): 624–48.

Elliott, James R., and Junia Howell. 2017. "Beyond Disasters: A Longitudinal Analysis of Natural Hazards' Unequal Impacts on Residential Instability." *Social Forces* 95(3): 1181–1207.

Elliott, James R., and Jeremy Pais. 2006. "Race, Class, and Hurricane Katrina: Social Differences in Human Responses to Disaster." *Social Science Research* 35(2): 295–321.

Elliott, Rebecca. 2017. "Who Pays for the Next Wave? The American Welfare State and Responsibility for Flood Risk." *Politics & Society* 45(3): 415–40.

——. 2019. "'Scarier than Another Storm': Values at Risk in the Mapping and Insuring of U.S. Floodplains." *British Journal of Sociology* 70(3): 1076–90.

——. 2021. *Underwater: Loss, Flood Insurance, and the Moral Economy of Climate Change in the United States.* New York: Columbia University Press.

Emanuel, Kerry. 2005. "Increasing Destructiveness of Tropical Cyclones over the Past 30 Years." *Nature* 436(7051): 686–88.

——. 2017. "Assessing the Present and Future Probability of Hurricane Harvey's Rainfall." *Proceedings of the National Academy of Sciences* 114(48): 12681–84.

Emerson, Michael O., Jenifer Bratter, Junia Howell, P. Wilner Jeanty, and Mike Cline. 2012. "Houston Region Grows More Ethnically Diverse, with Small Declines in Segregation: A Joint Report Analyzing Census Data from 1990, 2000, and 2010." Rice University Kinder Institute for Urban Research. DOI: https://doi.org/10.25611/bjy0-nr0n.

Emirbayer, Mustafa. 1997. "Manifesto for a Relational Sociology." *American Journal of Sociology* 103(2): 281–317.

Enarson, Elaine. 2001. "What Women Do: Gender Labor in the Red River Valley Flood." *Global Environmental Change Part B: Environmental Hazards* 3(1): 1–18.

Erikson, Kai. 1976. *Everything in Its Path: Destruction of Community in the Buffalo Creek Flood.* New York: Simon and Schuster.

——. 1994. *A New Species of Trouble: The Human Experience of Modern Disasters.* New York: W. W. Norton.

Ermakoff, Ivan. 2015. "The Structure of Contingency." *American Journal of Sociology* 121(1): 64–125.

Faber, Jacob William. 2018. "Segregation and the Geography of Creditworthiness: Racial Inequality in a Recovered Mortgage Market." *Housing Policy Debate* 28(2): 215–47.

——. 2020. "We Built This: Consequences of New Deal Era Intervention in America's Racial Geography." *American Sociological Review* 85(5): 739–75.

Faber, Jacob W., and Ingrid Gould Ellen. 2016. "Race and the Housing Cycle: Differences in Home Equity Trends among Long-Term Homeowners." *Housing Policy Debate* 26(3): 456–73.

Federal Emergency Management Agency (FEMA). 2011. "A Whole Community Approach to Emergency Management: Principles, Themes, and Pathways for Action." FDOC 104-008-1. Washington, D.C.: FEMA (December). https://www.fema.gov/sites/default/files/2020-07/whole_community_dec2011__2.pdf.

———. 2018a. "Fact Sheet: FEMA Assistance Is a Supplement to Private Recovery Efforts—Not a Substitute." Washington, D.C.: FEMA (June 14). https://www.fema.gov/press-release/20210318/fact-sheet-fema-assistance-supplement-private-recovery-efforts-not.

———. 2018b. "Fact Sheet: Acquisition of Property after a Flood Event." Washington, D.C.: FEMA (November 13). https://www.fema.gov/news-release/20200220/fey-enfomasyon-akizisyon-pwopriyete-apre-yon-inondasyon.

———. 2020. "FEMA—Harvey Flood Depths Grid." Accessed April 7, 2022. https://www.hydroshare.org/resource/e8768f4cb4d5478a96d2b1cbd00d9e85.

———. 2021a. "FEMA Updates Its Flood Insurance Rating Methodology to Deliver More Equitable Pricing." Washington, D.C.: FEMA (April 1). https://www.fema.gov/press-release/20210401/fema-updates-its-flood-insurance-rating-methodology-deliver-more-equitable.

———. 2021b. "Flood Risks Increase after Fires." Washington, D.C.: FEMA (March 22). https://www.fema.gov/fact-sheet/flood-risks-increase-after-fires.

———. 2022. "Risk Rating 2.0: Equity in Action." Updated February 18, 2022. https://www.fema.gov/flood-insurance/risk-rating.

Fernandez, Lauren S., Joseph A. Barbera, and Johan R. van Dorp. 2006. "Spontaneous Volunteer Response to Disaster: The Benefits and Consequences of Good Intentions." *Journal of Emergency Management* 4(5): 57–68.

Finch, Christina, Christopher T. Emrich, and Susan L. Cutter. 2010. "Disaster Disparities and Differential Recovery in New Orleans." *Population and Environment* 31(4): 179–202.

Fitzpatrick, Kevin M., and Matthew L. Spialek. 2020. *Hurricane Harvey's Aftermath: Place, Race, and Inequality in Disaster Recovery.* New York: New York University Press.

Flavelle, Christopher. 2021. "The Cost of Insuring Expensive Waterfront Homes Is about to Skyrocket." *New York Times*, September 24. https://www.nytimes.com/2021/09/24/climate/federal-flood-insurance-cost.html.

Flippen, Chenoa. 2001. "Racial and Ethnic Inequality in Homeownership and Housing Equity." *Sociological Quarterly* 42(2): 121–49.

———. 2004. "Unequal Returns to Housing Investment? A Study of Real Housing Appreciation among Black, White, and Hispanic Households." *Social Forces* 82(4): 1523–51.

Fong, Kelley, Rachel Wright, and Christopher Wimer. 2016. "The Cost of Free Assistance: Why Low-Income Individuals Do Not Access Food Pantries." *Journal of Sociology & Social Welfare* 43(1): 71–93.

Fontenot, Kayla, Jessica Semega, and Melissa Kollar. 2018. "Income and Poverty in the United States: 2017." *Current Population Reports*, P60-263. Washington, D.C.: U.S. Census Bureau (September).

Fothergill, Alice. 2003. "The Stigma of Charity: Gender, Class, and Disaster Assistance." *Sociological Quarterly* 44(4): 660–80.

———. 2004. *Heads above Water: Gender, Class, and Family in the Grand Forks Flood.* Albany: State University of New York Press.

Fothergill, Alice, and Lori A. Peek. 2004. "Poverty and Disasters in the United States: A Review of Recent Sociological Findings." *Natural Hazards* 32(1): 89–110.

———. 2015. *Children of Katrina.* Austin: University of Texas Press.

Fowler, Christopher S., Barrett A. Lee, and Stephen A. Matthews. 2016. "The Contributions of Places to Metropolitan Ethnoracial Diversity and Segregation: Decomposing Change across Space and Time." *Demography* 53(6): 1955–77.

Freudenburg, William R., Robert Gramling, Shirley Laska, and Kai T. Erikson. 2008. "Organizing Hazards, Engineering Disasters? Improving the Recognition of Political-Economic Factors in the Creation of Disasters." *Social Forces* 87(2): 1015–38.

———. 2009. *Catastrophe in the Making: The Engineering of Katrina and the Disasters of Tomorrow.* Washington, D.C.: Island Press.

Freund, David M. P. 2007. *Colored Property: State Policy and Racial White Politics in Suburban America.* Chicago: University of Chicago Press.

Frey, William H. 2011. *Melting Pot Cities and Suburbs: Racial and Ethnic Change in Metro America in the 2000s.* Washington, D.C.: Brookings Institution.

———. 2014. *Diversity Explosion: How New Racial Demographics Are Remaking America.* Washington, D.C.: Brookings Institution.

Frickel, Scott, and James R. Elliott. 2018. *Sites Unseen: Uncovering Hidden Hazards in American Cities.* New York: Russell Sage Foundation.

Frost, Jacqui. 2019. "Certainty, Uncertainty, or Indifference? Examining Variation in the Identity Narratives of Nonreligious Americans." *American Sociological Review* 84(5): 828–50.

Fussell, Elizabeth. 2007. "Constructing New Orleans, Constructing Race: A Population History of New Orleans." *Journal of American History* 94(3): 846–55.

———. 2015. "The Long-Term Recovery of New Orleans' Population after Hurricane Katrina." *American Behavioral Scientist* 59(10): 1231–45.

Fussell, Elizabeth, and Elizabeth Harris. 2014. "Homeownership and Housing Displacement after Hurricane Katrina among Low-Income African-American Mothers in New Orleans." *Social Science Quarterly* 95(4): 1086–1100.

Gallagher, Justin, and Daniel Hartley. 2017. "Household Finance after a Natural Disaster: The Case of Hurricane Katrina." *American Economic Journal: Economic Policy* 9(3): 199–228.

Gans, Herbert J. 1965. *The Levittowners: Ways of Life and Politics in a New Suburban Community.* New York: Columbia University Press.

Gardiner, Aidan. 2021. "Wildfires Took Their Homes. Here's Why They Stay." *New York Times*, September 8. https://www.nytimes.com/interactive/2021/09/07/us/oregon-wildfires.html.

Garrett, Thomas A., and Russell S. Sobel. 2003. "The Political Economy of FEMA Disaster Payments." *Economic Inquiry* 41(3): 496–509.

George, Cindy, Margaret Kadifa, Lindsay Ellis, and Keri Blakinger. 2017. "Storm Deaths: Harvey Claims More than 75 in Texas." *Houston Chronicle*, August 29. https://www.chron.com/news/houston-weather/hurricaneharvey/article/Harvey-Aftermath-Houston-police-officer-dies-19-12159139.php.

Gilens, Martin. 1999. *Why Americans Hate Welfare: Race, Media, and the Politics of Antipoverty Policy*. Chicago: University of Chicago Press.

Glaeser, Edward L., Joseph Gyourko, and Raven E. Saks. 2005. "Why Have Housing Prices Gone Up?" *American Economic Review* 95(2): 329–33.

Glotzer, Paige. 2020. *How the Suburbs Were Segregated: Developers and the Business of Exclusionary Housing, 1890–1960*. New York: Columbia University Press.

Go, Min Hee. 2018. "The Tale of a Two-Tiered City: Community Civic Structure and Spatial Inequality in Post-Katrina New Orleans." *Journal of Urban Affairs* 40(8): 1093–1114.

Goetz, Edward G. 2007. "Is Housing Tenure the New Neighborhood Dividing Line?" In *Chasing the American Dream: New Perspectives on Affordable Homeownership*, edited by William M. Rohe and Harry L. Watson. Ithaca, N.Y.: Cornell University Press.

——. 2008. "Words Matter: The Importance of Issue Framing and the Case of Affordable Housing." *Journal of the American Planning Association* 74(2): 222–29.

——. 2013. *New Deal Ruins: Race, Economic Justice, and Public Housing Policy*. Ithaca, N.Y.: Cornell University Press.

Goetz, Edward G., Rashad A. Williams, and Anthony Damiano. 2020. "Whiteness and Urban Planning." *Journal of the American Planning Association* 86(2): 142–56.

Goffman, Erving. 1963. *Stigma: Notes on the Management of Spoiled Identity*. Englewood Cliffs, N.J.: Prentice-Hall.

——. 1974. *Frame Analysis*. Cambridge, Mass.: Harvard University Press.

Gotham, Kevin Fox. 2012. "Disaster, Inc.: Privatization and Post-Katrina Rebuilding in New Orleans." *Perspectives on Politics* 10(3): 633–46.

Gotham, Kevin F., and Miriam Greenberg. 2014. *Crisis Cities: Disaster and Redevelopment in New York and New Orleans*. New York: Oxford University Press.

Gottschalk, Peter, and Sheldon Danziger. 2005. "Inequality of Wage Rates, Earnings, and Family Income in the United States, 1975–2002." *Review of Income and Wealth* 55(2): 231–54.

Graif, Corina. 2016. "(Un)natural Disaster: Vulnerability, Long-Distance Displacement, and the Extended Geography of Neighborhood Distress and Attainment after Katrina." *Population and Environment* 37(3): 288–318.

Green, Rodney D., Marie Kouassi, and Belinda Mambo. 2013. "Housing, Race, and Recovery from Hurricane Katrina." *Review of Black Political Economy* 40(2): 145–63.

Grube, Laura E., Rosemarie Fike, and Virgil Henry Storr. 2018. "Navigating Disaster: An Empirical Study of Federal Assistance Following Hurricane Sandy." *Eastern Economic Journal* 44(1): 576–93.

Hacker, Jacob S. 2006. *The Great Risk Shift: The New Economic Insecurity and the Decline of the American Dream.* New York: Oxford University Press.

———. 2012. "The Middle Class at Risk." In *Broke: How Debt Bankrupts the Middle Class,* edited by Katherine Porter. Stanford, Calif.: Stanford University Press.

Halpern-Meekin, Sarah, Kathryn Edin, Laura Tach, and Jennifer Sykes. 2015. *It's Not Like I'm Poor: How Working Families Make Ends Meet in a Post-Welfare World.* Oakland: University of California Press.

Hamilton-Webb, Alice, Louise Manning, Rhiannon Naylor, and John Conway. 2017. "The Relationship between Risk Experience and Risk Response: A Study of Farmers and Climate Change." *Journal of Risk Research* 20(11): 1379–93.

Hancock, Ange-Marie. 2004. *The Politics of Disgust: The Public Identity of the Welfare Queen.* New York: New York University Press.

Haney, Timothy J. 2018. "Paradise Found? The Emergence of Social Capital, Place Attachment, and Civic Engagement after Disaster." *International Journal of Mass Emergencies and Disasters* 36(2): 97–119.

———. 2019. "Move Out or Dig In? Risk Awareness and Mobility Plans in Disaster-Affected Communities." *Journal of Contingency and Crisis Management* 27(3): 467–88.

———. 2021. "Development, Responsibility, and the Creation of Urban Hazard Risk." *City & Community* 21(1): 21–41. DOI: https://doi.org/10.1177/15356841211046265.

Harris, Cheryl I. 1993. "Whiteness as Property." *Harvard Law Review* 106(8): 1707–91.

Harris, Dianne. 2013. *Little White Houses: How the Postwar Home Constructed Race in America.* Minneapolis: University of Minnesota Press.

Hart, Chloe Grace. 2021. "Trajectory Guarding: Managing Unwanted, Ambiguously Sexual Interactions at Work." *American Sociological Review* 86(2): 256–78.

Hartman, Chester, and Gregory T. Squires. 2006. *There Is No Such Thing as a Natural Disaster: Race, Class, and Hurricane Katrina.* New York: Routledge.

Harvey, Hope, Kelley Fong, Kathryn Edin, and Stefanie DeLuca. 2020. "Forever Homes and Temporary Stops: Housing Search Logics and Residential Selection." *Social Forces* 98(4): 1498–1523.

Hasenfeld, Yeheskel, and Jane A. Rafferty. 1989. "The Determinants of Public Attitudes toward the Welfare State." *Social Forces* 67(4): 1027–48.

Hawley, Amos H. 1986. *Human Ecology: A Theoretical Essay.* Chicago: University of Chicago Press.

Hayden, Dolores. 1984. *Redesigning the American Dream: The Future of Housing, Work, and Family Life.* New York: W. W. Norton.

Henry, Jacques. 2013. "Return or Relocate? An Inductive Analysis of Decision-Making in a Disaster." *Disasters* 37(2): 293–316.

Hernández, Maricarmen. 2021. "Putting Out Fires: The Varying Temporalities of Disasters." *Poetics* (September). DOI: https://doi.org/10.1016/j.poetic.2021.101613.

Hertel, Florian R., and Fabian T. Pfeffer. 2020. "The Land of Opportunity? Trends in Social Mobility and Education in the United States." In *Education and Intergenerational Social Mobility in Europe and the United States,* edited by Richard Breen and Walter Muller. Stanford, Calif.: Stanford University Press.

Hess, Frederick M., and David L. Leal. 2001. "Quality, Race, and the Urban Education Marketplace." *Urban Affairs Review* 37(2): 249–66.

Hipp, John R., and Amrita Singh. 2014. "Changing Neighborhood Determinants of Housing Price Trends in Southern California, 1960–2009." *City & Community* 13(3): 254–74.

Ho, Ming-Chou, Daigee Shaw, Shuyeu Lin, and Yao-Chu Chiu. 2008. "How Do Disaster Characteristics Influence Risk Perception?" *Risk Analysis* 28(3): 635–43.

Hodson, Randy, Rachel E. Dwyer, and Lisa A. Neilson. 2014. "Credit Card Blues: The Middle Class and the Hidden Costs of Easy Credit." *Sociological Quarterly* 55(2): 315–40.

Holliday, Amy L., and Rachel E. Dwyer. 2009. "Suburban Neighborhood Poverty in U.S. Metropolitan Areas in 2000." *City & Community* 8(2): 155–76.

Holme, Jennifer J. 2002. "Buying Homes, Buying Schools: School Choice and the Social Construction of School Quality." *Harvard Educational Review* 70(2): 177–206.

Hoppe, Kimberly A., Nervana Metwali, Sarah S. Perry, Tom Hart, Pamela A. Kostle, and Peter T. Thorne. 2012. "Assessment of Airborne Exposures and Health in Flooded Homes Undergoing Renovation." *Indoor Air* 22(6): 446–56.

Horowitz, Andy. 2020. *Katrina: A History, 1915–2015.* Cambridge, Mass.: Harvard University Press.

Howell, Junia, and James R. Elliott. 2019. "Damages Done: The Longitudinal Impacts of Natural Hazards on Wealth Inequality in the United States." *Social Problems* 66(3): 448–67.

Howell, Junia, and Elizabeth Korver-Glenn. 2018. "Neighborhoods, Race, and the Twenty-First-Century Housing Appraisal Industry." *Sociology of Race and Ethnicity* 4(4): 473–90.

———. 2020. "The Increasing Effect of Neighborhood Racial Composition on Housing Values, 1980–2015." *Social Problems* 68(4): 1051–71.

Hung, Hung-Chih. 2009. "The Attitude towards Flood Insurance Purchase When Respondents' Preferences Are Uncertain: A Fuzzy Approach." *Journal of Risk Research* 12(2): 239–58.

Hunter, Lori M., Jessie K. Luna, and Rachel M. Norton. 2015. "Environmental Dimensions of Migration." *Annual Review of Sociology* 41: 377–97.

Hurlbert, Jeanne S., John J. Beggs, and Valerie A. Haines. 2001. "Social Networks and Social Capital in Extreme Environments." In *Social Capital: Theory and Research*, edited by Nan Lin, Karen Cook, and Ronald S. Burt. New York: Aldine De Gruyter.

Ihlanfeldt, Keith, and Tom Mayock. 2009. "Price Discrimination in the Housing Market." *Journal of Urban Economics* 66(2): 125–40.

Intergovernmental Panel on Climate Change (IPCC). 2021. *Climate Change 2021: The Physical Science Basis: Contribution of Working Group I to the Sixth Assessment Report of the Intergovernmental Panel on Climate Change*, edited by V. Masson-Delmotte, P. Zhai, A. Pirani, S. L. Connors, C. Péan, S. Berger, N. Caud, Y. Chen, L. Goldfarb, M. I. Gomis, M. Huang, K. Leitzell, E. Lonnoy, J.B.R. Matthews, T. K. Maycock, T. Waterfield, O. Yelekçi, R. Yu, and B. Zhou. Cambridge: Cambridge University Press. DOI: https://doi.org/10.1017/9781009157896.

Jackson, Kenneth T. 1985. *Crabgrass Frontier: The Suburbanization of the United States*. New York: Oxford University Press.

Jerolmack, Colin. 2021. *Up to Heaven and Down to Hell: Fracking, Freedom, and Community in an American Town*. Princeton, N.J.: Princeton University Press.

Jerolmack, Colin, and Shamus Khan. 2014. "Talk Is Cheap: Ethnography and the Attitudinal Fallacy." *Sociological Methods & Research* 43(2): 178–209.

Kalleberg, Arne L. 2011. *Good Jobs, Bad Jobs: The Rise of Polarized and Precarious Employment Systems in the United States, 1970s to 2000s*. New York: Russell Sage Foundation.

———. 2018. *Precarious Lives: Job Insecurity and Well-Being in Rich Democracies*. Medford, Mass.: Polity Press.

Kamel, Nabil M. O., and Anastasia Loukaitou-Sideris. 2004. "Residential Assistance and Recovery Following the Northridge Earthquake." *Urban Studies* 41(3): 533–62.

Kasperson, Roger E., Ortwin Renn, Paul Slovic, Halina S. Brown, Jacque Emel, Robert Goble, Jeanne X. Kasperson, and Samuel Ratick. 1988. "The Social Amplification of Risk: A Conceptual Framework." *Risk Analysis* 8(2): 177–87.

Katz, Michael B. 1989. *The Undeserving Poor: From the War on Poverty to the War on Welfare*. New York: Oxford University Press.

Katznelson, Ira. 2005. *When Affirmative Action Was White: An Untold History of Racial Inequality in Twentieth-Century America*. New York: W. W. Norton.

Kellens, Wim, Teun Terpstra, and Philippe de Maeyer. 2013. "Perception and Communication of Flood Risks: A Systematic Review of Empirical Research." *Risk Analysis* 33(1): 24–49.

Kennedy, Merrit. 2018. "Harvey the 'Most Significant Tropical Cyclone Rainfall Event in U.S. History.'" *NPR*, January 25. https://www.npr.org/sections/thetwo-way/2018/01/25/580689546/harvey-the-most-significant-tropical-cyclone-rainfall-event-in-u-s-history.

Kenny, Lorraine Delia. 2000. *Daughters of Suburbia: Growing up White, Middle Class, and Female*. Brunswick, N.J.: Rutgers University Press.

Kenworthy, Lane. 2013. "Has Rising Inequality Reduced Middle-Class Income Growth?" In *Income Inequality: Economic Disparities and the Middle Class in Affluent Countries*, edited by Janet C. Gornick and Markus Jäntti. Stanford, Calif.: Stanford University Press.

Khan, Shuhab D. 2005. "Urban Development and Flooding in Houston, Texas: Inferences from Remote Sensing Data Using Neural Network Technique." *Environmental Geology* 47(8): 1120–27.

Kick, Edward L., James C. Fraser, Gregory M. Fulkerson, Laura A. McKinney, and Daniel H. De Vries. 2011. "Repetitive Flood Victims and Acceptance of FEMA Mitigation Offers: An Analysis with Community-System Policy Implications." *Disasters* 35(3): 510–39.

Killewald, Alexandra, and Brielle Bryan. 2016. "Does Your Home Make You Wealthy?" *RSF: The Russell Sage Foundation Journal of the Social Sciences* 2(6): 110–28. DOI: https://doi.org/10.7758/RSF.2016.2.6.06.

———. 2018. "Falling Behind: The Role of Inter- and Intragenerational Processes in Widening Racial and Ethnic Wealth Gaps through Early and Middle Adulthood." *Social Forces* 97(2): 705–40.

Kim, Sunwoong. 2003. "Long-Term Appreciation of Owner-Occupied Single-Family House Prices in Milwaukee Neighborhoods." *Urban Geography* 24(3): 212–31.

Kimbro, Rachel. 2021. *In Too Deep: Class and Mothering in a Flooded Community*. Oakland: University of California Press.

Kimelberg, Shelley M. 2014. "Middle-Class Parents, Risk, and Urban Public Schools." In *Choosing Homes, Choosing Schools*, edited by Annette Lareau and Kimberly Goyette. New York: Russell Sage Foundation.

Kirp, David L., John P. Dwyer, and Larry A. Rosenthal. 1995. *Our Town: Race, Housing, and the Soul of Suburbia*. New Brunswick, N.J.: Rutgers University Press.

Klineberg, Stephen L. 2020. *Prophetic City: Houston on the Cusp of a Changing America*. New York: Avid Reader Press.

Klinenberg, Eric. 2002. *Heat Wave: A Social Autopsy of Disaster in Chicago*. Chicago: University of Chicago Press.

———. 2018. *Palaces for the People: How Social Infrastructure Can Help Fight Inequality, Polarization, and the Decline of Civic Life*. New York: Crown.

Klinenberg, Eric, Malcolm Araos, and Liz Koslov. 2020. "Sociology and the Climate Crisis." *Annual Review of Sociology* 46: 649–69.

Kneebone, Elizabeth, and Alan Berube. 2013. *Confronting Suburban Poverty in America*. Washington, D.C.: Brookings Institution Press.

Kochhar, Rakesh. 2018. "The American Middle Class Is Stable in Size, but Losing Ground Financially to Upper-Income Families." Washington, D.C.: Pew Research Center (September 6). https://www.pewresearch.org/fact-tank/2018/09/06/the-american-middle-class-is-stable-in-size-but-losing-ground-financially-to-upper-income-families/.

Kohler-Hausmann, Issa. 2018. *Misdemeanorland: Criminal Courts and Social Control in an Age of Broken Windows Policing.* Princeton, N.J.: Princeton University Press.

Korver-Glenn, Elizabeth. 2021. *Race Brokers: Housing Markets and Segregation in 21st-Century Urban America.* New York: Oxford University Press.

Koslov, Liz. 2016. "The Case for Retreat." *Public Culture* 28(2): 359–87.

——. 2019. "How Maps Make Time: Temporal Conflicts of Life in the Flood Zone." *City* 23(4/5): 658–72.

Koslov, Liz, Alexis Merdjanoff, Elana Salukshana, and Eric Klinenberg. 2021. "When Rebuilding No Longer Means Recovery: The Stress of Staying Put after Hurricane Sandy." *Climatic Change* 165(3): 59.

Kousky, Carolyn. 2018. "Financing Flood Losses: A Discussion of the National Flood Insurance Program." *Risk Management and Insurance Review* 21(1): 11–32.

Krivo, Lauren J., and Robert I. Kaufman. 2004. "Housing and Wealth Inequality: Racial-Ethnic Differences in Home Equity in the United States." *Demography* 41(3): 585–605.

Krysan, Maria, and Michael Bader. 2007. "Perceiving the Metropolis: Seeing the City through a Prism of Race." *Social Forces* 86(2): 699–733.

Krysan, Maria, Mick P. Couper, Reynolds Farley, and Tyrone A. Forman. 2009. "Does Race Matter in Neighborhood Preferences? Results from a Video Experiment." *American Journal of Sociology* 115(2): 527–59.

Krysan, Maria, and Kyle Crowder. 2017. *Cycle of Segregation: Social Processes and Residential Stratification.* New York: Russell Sage Foundation.

Kuk, John, Ariela Schachter, Jacob William Faber, and Max Besbris. 2021. "The Covid-19 Pandemic and the Rental Market: Evidence from Craigslist." *American Behavioral Scientist* 65(12): 1623–48.

Kull, Melissa A., Rebekah Levine Coley, and Alicia Doyle Lynch. 2016. "The Roles of Instability and Housing in Low-Income Families' Residential Mobility." *Journal of Family and Economic Issues* 37(September): 422–34. DOI: https://doi.org/10.1007/s10834-015-9465-0.

Kus, Basak. 2015. "Sociology of Debt: States, Credit Markets, and Indebted Citizens." *Sociology Compass* 9(3): 212–23.

Lacy, Karyn. 2007. *Blue-Chip Black: Race, Class, and Status in the New Black Middle Class.* Berkeley: University of California Press.

——. 2016. "The New Sociology of the Suburbs: A Research Agenda for Analysis of Emerging Trends." *Annual Review of Sociology* 42: 369–84.

Lakoff, Andrew, and Eric Klinenberg. 2010. "Of Risk and Pork: Urban Security and the Politics of Objectivity." *Theory and Society* 39(5): 503–25.

Lamont, Michèle. 1992. *Money, Morals, and Manners: The Culture of the French and the American Upper-Middle Class.* Chicago: University of Chicago Press.

——. 2000. *The Dignity of Working Men: Morality and the Boundaries of Race, Class, and Immigration.* Cambridge, Mass.: Harvard University Press.

Lamont, Michèle, and Ann Swidler. 2014. "Methodological Pluralism and the Possibilities and Limits of Interviewing." *Qualitative Sociology* 37(April 8): 153–71. DOI: https://doi.org/10.1007/s11133-014-9274-z.

Landry, Bart, and Kris Marsh. 2011. "The Evolution of the New Black Middle Class." *Annual Review of Sociology* 37: 373–94.

Lareau, Annette. 2003. *Unequal Childhoods: Class, Race, and Family Life.* Berkeley: University of California Press.

———. 2014. "Schools, Housing, and the Reproduction of Inequality." In *Choosing Homes, Choosing Schools*, edited by Annette Lareau and Kimberly Goyette. New York: Russell Sage Foundation.

Larsen, Tom. 2017. "Hurricane Harvey: Identifying the Insurance Gap." CoreLogic, September 9. https://www.corelogic.com/intelligence/hurricane-harvey-identifying-the-insurance-gap/.

Lave, Tamara R., and Lester B. Lave. 1991. "Public Perception of the Risks of Floods: Implications for Communication." *Risk Analysis* 11(2): 255–67.

Lawrence, Judy, Dorothee Quade, and Julia Becker. 2014. "Integrating the Effects of Flood Experience on Risk Perception with Responses to Changing Climate Risk." *Natural Hazards* 74(3): 1773–94.

Leicht, Kevin T. 2012. "Borrowing to the Brink: Consumer Debt in America." In *Broke: How Debt Bankrupts the Middle Class*, edited by Katherine Porter. Stanford, Calif.: Stanford University Press.

Levin, Matt. 2015. "How Hurricane Rita Anxiety Led to the Worst Gridlock in Houston History." *Houston Chronicle*, September 22. https://www.chron.com/news/houston-texas/houston/article/Hurricane-Rita-anxiety-leads-to-hellish-fatal-6521994.php.

Lewis-McCoy, R. L'Heureux. 2014. *Inequality in the Promised Land: Race, Resources, and Suburban Schooling.* Stanford, Calif.: Stanford University Press.

Li, Jingyuan, and Craig E. Landry. 2018. "Flood Risk, Local Hazard Mitigation, and the Community Rating System of the National Flood Insurance Program." *Land Economics* 98(2): 175–98.

Lindsay, Bruce R. 2010. *Federal Evacuation Policy: Issues for Congress.* Washington, D.C.: Congressional Research Service.

Link, Bruce G., and Jo C. Phelan. 2001. "Conceptualizing Stigma." *Annual Review of Sociology* 27: 363–85.

Lipsitz, George. 2011. *How Racism Takes Place.* Philadelphia: Temple University Press.

Lipsky, Michael. 1980. *Street-Level Bureaucracy: Dilemmas of the Individual in Public Service.* New York: Russell Sage Foundation.

Liu, Sida, and Mustafa Emirbayer. 2016. "Field and Ecology." *Sociological Theory* 34(1): 62–79.

Logan, John R., and Harvey L. Molotch. 1987. *Urban Fortunes: The Political Economy of Place.* Berkeley: University of California Press.

Long, Alecia P. 2007. "Poverty Is the New Prostitution: Race, Poverty, and Public Housing in Post-Katrina New Orleans." *Journal of American History* 94(3): 795–803.

Loughran, Kevin, and James R. Elliott. 2019. "Residential Buyouts as Environmental Mobility: Examining Where Homeowners Move to Illuminate Social Inequities in Climate Adaptation." *Population and Environment* 41(1): 52–70.

Loughran, Kevin, James R. Elliott, and S. Wright Kennedy. 2019. "Urban Ecology in the Time of Climate Change: Houston, Flooding, and the Case of Federal Buyouts." *Social Currents* 6(2): 121–40.

Lowe, Sarah R., Jean E. Rhodes and Arielle A. J. Scogilo. 2012. "Changes in Marital and Partner Relationships in the Aftermath of Hurricane Katrina: An Analysis of Low-Income Mothers." *Psychology of Women Quarterly* 36(3): 286–300.

Lu, Max. 1999. "Do People Move When They Say They Will? Inconsistencies in Individual Migration Behavior." *Population and Environment* 20(5): 467–88.

Luken, Paul C., and Suzanne Vaughan. 2005. "'. . . Be a Genuine Homemaker in Your Own Home': Gender and Familial Relations in State Housing Practices, 1917–1922." *Social Forces* 83(4): 1603–25.

Mach, Katharine J., and A. R. Siders. 2021. "Reframing Strategic, Managed Retreat for Transformative Climate Adaptation." *Science* 372(6548): 1294–99.

Macpherson, David A., and G. Stacy Sirmans. 2001. "Neighborhood Diversity and House-Price Appreciation." *Journal of Real Estate Finance and Economics* 22(January): 81–97. DOI: https://doi.org/10.1023/A:1007831410843.

Madden, David, and Peter Marcuse. 2016. *In Defense of Housing: The Politics of Crisis.* Brooklyn: Verso.

Major, Brenda, and Laurie T. O'Brien. 2005. "The Social Psychology of Stigma." *Annual Review of Psychology* 55(February 4): 393–421. DOI: https://doi.org/10.1146/annurev.psych.56.091103.070137.

Marshall, Josh. 2019. "As Life Rebuilds around Brio Superfund Site, Former Residents Still Reeling from Toxic Past." *KHOU-11*, January 18. https://www.khou.com/article/news/investigations/as-life-rebuilds-around-brio-superfund-site-former-residents-still-reeling-from-toxic-past/285-d4a0dc8d-4ec3-4840-8ed2-8222845eca42.

Massey, Douglas S. 1996. "The Age of Extremes: Concentrated Affluence and Poverty in the Twenty-First Century." *Demography* 33(4): 395–412.

Massey, Douglas S., and Nancy A. Denton. 1993. *American Apartheid: Segregation and the Making of the Underclass.* Cambridge, Mass.: Harvard University Press.

Massey, Douglas S., and Jonathan Tannen. 2018. "Suburbanization and Segregation in the United States: 1970–2010." *Ethnic and Racial Studies* 41(9): 1594–1611.

Mayer, Arno J. 1975. "The Lower Middle Class as a Historical Problem." *Journal of Modern History* 47(3): 409–36.

Mayorga-Gallo, Sarah. 2014. *Behind the White Picket Fence: Power and Privilege in a Multiethnic Neighborhood.* Chapel Hill: University of North Carolina Press.

McCabe, Barbara Coyle. 2005. "The Rules Are Different Here: An Institutional Comparison of Cities and Homeowners Associations." *Administration & Society* 37(4): 404–25.

———. 2011. "Homeowners Associations as Private Governments: What We Know, What We Don't Know, and Why It Matters." *Public Administration Review* 71(4): 535–42.

McCabe, Brian J. 2016. *No Place Like Home: Wealth, Community, and the Politics of Homeownership.* New York: Oxford University Press.

McCarthy, Michael A. 2017. *Dismantling Solidarity: Capitalist Politics and American Pensions since the New Deal.* Ithaca, N.Y.: Cornell University Press.

McCloud, Laura, and Rachel E. Dwyer. 2011. "The Fragile American: Hardship and Financial Troubles in the 21st Century." *Sociological Quarterly* 52(1): 13–35.

McGinnis, Edith B. 1947. *The Promised Land: A Narrative Featuring the Life History and Adventures of Frank J. Brown, Pioneer, Buffalo Hunter, Indian Fighter, and Founder of the Quaker Settlement of Friendswood.* Boerne, Tex.: Toepperwein Publishing Co.

McKenzie, Roderick D. 1924. "The Ecological Approach to the Study of the Human Community." *American Journal of Sociology* 30(3): 287–301.

McKernan, Signe-Mary, and Caroline Ratcliffe. 2005. "Events That Trigger Poverty Entries and Exits." *Social Science Quarterly* 86(s1): 1146–69.

McPherson, Miller, Lynn Smith-Lovin, and James M. Cook. 2001. "Birds of a Feather: Homophily in Social Networks." *Annual Review of Sociology* 27: 415–44.

Mead, George Herbert. 1932. *The Philosophy of the Present.* Chicago: University of Chicago Press.

Mears, Ashley. 2017. "Puzzling in Sociology: On Doing and Undoing Theoretical Puzzles." *Sociological Theory* 35(2): 138–46.

Merdjanoff, Alexis. 2013. "There's No Place Like Home: Examining the Emotional Consequences of Hurricane Katrina on the Displaced Residents of New Orleans." *Social Science Research* 42(5): 1222–35.

Merdjanoff, Alexis, David M. Abramson, Yoon Soon Park, and Rachel Piltch-Loeb. 2022. "Disasters, Displacement, and Housing Instability: Estimating Time to Stable Housing 13 Years after Hurricane Katrina." *Weather, Climate, and Society.* DOI: https://doi.org/10.1175/WCAS-D-21-0057.1.

Merton, Robert K. 1968. "The Matthew Effect in Science." *Science* 159(3810): 56–63.

Meyer, Michelle A. 2017. "Social Capital in Disaster Research." In *Handbook of Disaster Research,* edited by Havidán Rodríguez, William Donner, and Joseph E. Trainor. Cham, Switzerland: Springer.

Michel-Kerjan, Erwann O. 2010. "Catastrophe Economics: The National Flood Insurance Program." *Journal of Economic Perspectives* 24(4): 165–86.

Michel-Kerjan, Erwann O., and Carolyn Kousky. 2010. "Come Rain or Shine: Evidence on Flood Insurance Purchases in Florida." *Journal of Risk and Insurance* 77(2): 369–97.

Mileti, Dennis. 1999. *Disasters by Design: A Reassessment of Natural Hazards in the United States.* Washington, D.C.: National Academies Press.

Miller, Kimberly (PalmBeachPost.com). 2018. "Irma Forced Mass Evacuations; Officials Urge Staying Home Next Time." *Atlanta Journal-Constitution*, April 3. https://www.ajc.com/news/national/irma-forced-mass-evacuations-officials -urge-staying-home-next-time/src1jIXEdzec5hcy1TGPGK/.

Mische, Ann. 2009. "Projects and Possibilities: Researching Futures in Action." *Sociological Forum* 24(3): 694–704.

Mishel, Lawrence, and Heidi Shierholz. 2013a. "A Decade of Flat Wages: The Key Barrier to Shared Prosperity and a Rising Middle Class." Washington, D.C.: Economic Policy Institute (August 21). https://www.epi.org/publication /a-decade-of-flat-wages-the-key-barrier-to-shared-prosperity-and-a-rising -middle-class/.

———. 2013b. "A Lost Decade, Not a Burst Bubble: The Declining Living Standards of Middle-Class Households in the U.S. and Britain." In *The Squeezed Middle: The Pressure on Ordinary Workers in America and Britain,* edited by Sophia Parker. Chicago: Policy Press.

Mol, Jantsje M., W. J. Wouter Botzen, Julia E. Blasch, and Hans de Moel. 2020. "Insights into Flood Risk Misperceptions of Homeowners in the Dutch River Delta." *Risk Analysis* 40(7): 1450–68.

Morrice, Stephanie. 2013. "Heartache and Hurricane Katrina: Recognising the Influence of Emotion in Post-Disaster Return Decisions." *Area* 45(1): 33–39.

Morrow, Betty Hearn. 1997. "Stretching the Bonds: The Families of Andrew." In *Hurricane Andrew: Ethnicity, Gender, and the Sociology of Disaster,* edited by Walter Gillis Peacock, Betty Hearn Morrow, and Hugh Gladwin. London: Routledge.

Morrow-Jones, Hazel A., and Charles R. Morrow-Jones. 1991. "Mobility Due to Natural Disaster: Theoretical Considerations and Preliminary Analyses." *Disasters* 15(2): 126–32.

Moye, Richard, and Melvin Thomas. 2018. "Race and Housing Values: What Happens When Whites Don't All Move Out?" *City & Community* 17(1): 109–33.

Murphy, Alexandra K. 2010. "The Symbolic Dilemmas of Suburban Poverty: Challenges and Opportunities Posed by Variations in the Contours of Suburban Poverty." *Sociological Forum* 25(3): 541–69.

———. 2012. "'Litterers': How Objects of Physical Disorder Are Used to Construct Subjects of Social Disorder in a Suburb." *Annals of the American Academy of Political and Social Science* 642(1): 210–27.

Myers, Caitlin Knowles. 2004. "Discrimination and Neighborhood Effects: Understanding Racial Differences in U.S. Housing Prices." *Journal of Urban Economics* 56(2): 279–302.

National Oceanic and Atmospheric Administration (NOAA). 2017. "Hurricane Harvey." NOAA, August 24. https://www.nhc.noaa.gov/archive/2017/al09 /al092017.discus.017.shtml.

——. 2021. "Record-Breaking Atlantic Hurricane Season Draws to an End." NOAA, June 10. https://www.noaa.gov/media-release/record-breaking-atlantic-hurricane-season-draws-to-end.

National Oceanic and Atmospheric Administration. National Centers for Environmental Information (NCEI). 2022a. "U.S. Billion-Dollar Weather and Climate Disasters." DOI: https://doi.org/10.25921/stkw-7w73.

——. 2022b. "Costliest U.S. Tropical Cyclones." https://www.ncdc.noaa.gov/billions/dcmi.pdf.

Nau, Michael, and Matthew Soener. 2019. "Income Precarity and the Financial Crisis." *Socio-Economic Review* 17(3): 523–44.

Neckerman, Kathryn M., and Florencia Torche. 2007. "Inequality: Causes and Consequences." *Annual Review of Sociology* 33: 335–57.

Newman, Katherine. 1988. *Falling from Grace: The Experience of Downward Mobility in the American Middle Class.* New York: Free Press.

Nigg, Joanne M., John Barnshaw, and Manuel R. Torres. 2006. "Hurricane Katrina and the Flooding of New Orleans: Emergent Issues in Sheltering and Temporary Housing." *Annals of the American Academy of Political and Social Science* 604(March): 113–28.

Oliver, Melvin L., and Thomas M. Shapiro. 2006. *Black Wealth/White Wealth: A New Perspective on Racial Inequality,* 2nd ed. New York: Routledge.

Oliver-Smith, Anthony. 1999. "The Brotherhood of Pain: Theoretical and Applied Perspectives on Post-Disaster Solidarity." In *The Angry Earth: Disaster in Anthropological Perspective,* edited by Anthony Oliver-Smith and Susanna M. Hoffman. New York: Routledge.

Omi, Michael, and Howard Winant. 1986. *Racial Formation in the United States.* New York: Routledge.

Ortega, Francesc, and Süleyman Taspinar. 2018. "Rising Sea Level and Sinking Property Values: Hurricane Sandy and New York's Housing Market." *Journal of Urban Economics* 106(July): 81–100. DOI: https://doi.org/10.1016/j.jue.2018.06.005.

Owens, Lindsay. 2014. "Intrinsically Advantageous? Reexamining the Production of Class Advantage in the Case of Home Mortgage Modification." *Social Forces* 93(3): 1185–1209.

Pais, Jeremy F., and James R. Elliott. 2008. "Places as Recovery Machines: Vulnerability and Neighborhood Change after Major Hurricanes." *Social Forces* 86(4): 1415–53.

Parisi, Domenico, Daniel T. Lichter, and Michael C. Taquino. 2015. "The Buffering Hypothesis: Growing Diversity and Declining Black-White Segregation in America's Cities, Suburbs, and Small Towns?" *Sociological Science* 2(8): 125–57.

Park, Robert E. 1936. "Human Ecology." *American Journal of Sociology* 42: 1–15.

Park, Robert E., and Ernest W. Burgess. 1969. *Introduction to the Science of Sociology.* Chicago: University of Chicago Press. (Originally published in 1921.)

Patricola, Christina M., and Michael F. Wehner. 2018. "Anthropogenic Influences on Major Tropical Cyclone Events." *Nature* 563(7731): 339–46.

Pattillo, Mary. 2005. "Black Middle-Class Neighborhoods." *Annual Review of Sociology* 31: 305–29.

——. 2007. *Black on the Block: The Politics of Race and Class in the City.* Chicago: University of Chicago Press.

——. 2013. "Housing: Right versus Commodity." *Annual Review of Sociology* 39: 509–31.

Pattillo-McCoy, Mary. 1999. *Black Picket Fences: Privilege and Peril among the Black Middle Class.* Chicago: University of Chicago Press.

Pescosolido, Bernice A., and Jack K. Martin. 2015. "The Stigma Complex." *Annual Review of Sociology* 41: 87–116.

Pierre, John K., and Gail S. Stephenson. 2008. "After Katrina: A Critical Look at FEMA's Failure to Provide Housing for Victims of Natural Disasters." *Louisiana Law Review* 68(2): 443–93.

Phinney, Robin. 2013. "Exploring Residential Mobility among Low-Income Families." *Social Service Review* 87(4): 780–815.

Piven, Frances Fox, and Richard A. Cloward. 1971. *Regulating the Poor: The Functions of Public Welfare.* New York: Vintage.

Platt, Rutherford H. 1999. *Disasters and Democracy: The Politics of Extreme Natural Events.* Washington D.C.: Island Press.

Poulshock, S. Walter, and Elias S. Cohen. 1975. "The Elderly in the Aftermath of Disaster." *The Gerontologist* 15(4): 357–61.

Pralle, Sarah. 2019. "Drawing Lines: FEMA and the Politics of Mapping Flood Zones." *Climatic Change* 152(January): 227–37. DOI: https://doi.org/10.1007/s10584-018-2287-y.

Prasad, Monica. 2012. *The Land of Too Much: American Abundance and the Paradox of Poverty.* Cambridge, Mass.: Harvard University Press.

Preston, Benjamin L. 2013. "Local Path Dependence of U.S. Socioeconomic Exposure to Climate Extremes and the Vulnerability Commitment." *Global Environmental Change* 23(4): 719–32.

Quadagno, Jill. 1994. *The Color of Welfare: How Racism Undermined the War on Poverty.* New York: Oxford University Press.

Quarantelli, Enrico L. 1999. *The Disaster Recovery Process: What We Know and Do Not Know from Research.* Wilmington: Disaster Research Center, University of Delaware.

Quillian, Lincoln, John J. Lee, and Brandon Honoré. 2020. "Racial Discrimination in the U.S. Housing and Mortgage Lending Markets: A Quantitative Review of Trends, 1976–2016." *Race and Social Problems* 12(1): 13–28.

Quinn, Katherine, Lisa Bowleg, Julia Dickson-Gomez. 2019. "'The Fear of Being Black Plus the Fear of Being Gay': The Effects of Intersectional Stigma on PrEP Use among Young Black Gay, Bisexual, and Other Men Who Have Sex with Men." *Social Science & Medicine* 232(July): 86–93. DOI: https://doi.org/10.1016/j.socscimed.2019.04.042.

Rainwater, Lee. 1982. "Stigma in Income-Tested Programs." In *Income-Test Transfer Programs: The Case for and Against,* edited by Irwin Garfinkel. New York: Academic Press.

Raker, Ethan. 2020. "Natural Hazards, Disasters, and Demographic Change: The Case of Severe Tornadoes in the United States, 1980–2010." *Demography* 57(2): 653–74.

Ratcliffe, Caroline, William Congdon, Daniel Teles, Alexandra Stanczyk, and Carlos Martín. 2020. "From Bad to Worse: Natural Disasters and Financial Health." *Journal of Housing Research* 29(suppl. 1): S25–S53.

Reese, Ellen. 2005. *Backlash against Welfare Mothers: Past and Present.* Berkeley: University of California Press.

Reeves, Richard V. 2018. *Dream Hoarders: How the American Upper Middle Class Is Leaving Everyone Else in the Dust, Why That Is a Problem, and What to Do about It.* Washington, D.C.: Brookings Institution Press.

Reeves, Richard V., Katherine Guyot, and Eleanor Krause. 2018. "Defining the Middle Class: Cash, Credentials, or Culture?" Washington, D.C.: Brookings Institution (May 7). https://www.brookings.edu/research/defining-the-middle -class-cash-credentials-or-culture/.

Reid, Megan. 2013a. "Social Policy, 'Deservingness,' and Sociotemporal Marginalization: Katrina Survivors and FEMA." *Sociological Forum* 28(4): 742–63.

———. 2013b. "Disasters and Social Inequalities." *Sociology Compass* 7(11): 984–97.

Reinke, Kelly. 2022. "Marshall Fire Victims Worry They Won't Be Able to Afford to Rebuild Their Homes." *9News,* February 15. https://www.9news.com/article /news/local/wildfire/marshall-fire/marshall-fire-victims-afford-to-rebuild -homes/73-bcddf049-d552-4a60-a161-8d99ea795a1b.

Rhodes, Anna, and Max Besbris. 2021. "Best Laid Plans: How the Middle Class Make Residential Mobility Decisions Post-Disaster." *Social Problems* (July 17). DOI: https://doi.org/10.1093/socpro/spab026.

Rhodes, Anna, and Stefanie DeLuca. 2014. "Residential Mobility and School Choice among Poor Families." In *Choosing Homes, Choosing Schools,* edited by Annette Lareau and Kimberly Goyette. New York: Russell Sage Foundation.

Riad, Jasmin K., and Fran H. Norris. 1996. "The Influence of Relocation on the Environmental, Social, and Psychological Stress Experienced by Disaster Victims." *Environment and Behavior* 28(2): 163–82.

Rice, Whitney S., Carmen H. Logie, Tessa M. Napoles, Melonie Walcott, Abigail W. Batchelder, Mirjam-Colette Kempf, Gina M. Wingood, Deborah J. Konkle-Parker, Bulent Turan, Tracey E. Wilson, Mallory O. Johnson, Sheri D. Weiser, and Janet M. Turan. 2018. "Perceptions of Intersectional Stigma among Diverse Women Living with HIV in the United States." *Social Science & Medicine* 208(July): 9–17.

Risser, Mark D., and Michael F. Wehner. 2017. "Attributable Human-Induced Changes in the Likelihood and Magnitude of the Observed Extreme Precipitation during Hurricane Harvey." *Geophysical Research Letters* 44(24): 12457–64.

Robinson, John N., III. 2021. "Surviving Capitalism: Affordability as a Racial 'Wage' in Contemporary Housing Markets." *Social Problems* 68(2): 321–39.

Rogers-Dillon, Robin. 1995. "The Dynamics of Welfare Stigma." *Qualitative Sociology* 18(December): 439. DOI: https://doi.org/10.1007/BF02404490.

Rosen, Eva. 2017. "Horizontal Immobility: How Narratives of Neighborhood Violence Shape Housing Decisions." *American Sociological Review* 82(1): 270–96.

Rosenblatt, Peter, and Stefanie DeLuca. 2012. "'We Don't Live Outside, We Live in Here': Neighborhood and Residential Mobility Decisions among Low-Income Families." *City & Community* 11(3): 254–84.

Rosenfeld, Jake. 2014. *What Unions No Longer Do.* Cambridge, Mass.: Harvard University Press.

Rothstein, Bo. 1998. *Just Institutions Matter: The Moral and Political Logic of the Universal Welfare State.* New York: Cambridge University Press.

Rothstein, Richard. 2017. *The Color of Law: The Forgotten History of How Our Government Segregated America.* New York: W. W. Norton.

Samenow, Jason. 2017. "Forecasts for Harvey Were Excellent but Show Where Predictions Can Improve." *Washington Post,* August 28. https://www.washington post.com/news/capital-weather-gang/wp/2017/08/28/forecasts-for-harvey -were-excellent-but-show-where-predictions-can-improve/.

Saporito, Salvatore. 2003. "Private Choices, Public Consequences: Magnet School Choice and Segregation by Race and Poverty." *Social Problems* 50(2): 181–203.

Savitt, Amanda. 2017. "Insurance as a Tool for Hazard Risk Management? An Evaluation of the Literature." *Natural Hazards* 86(2): 583–99.

Schachter, Ariela, and Max Besbris. 2017. "Immigration and Neighborhood Change: Methodological Possibilities for Future Research." *City & Community* 16(3): 244–51.

Schachter, Daniel L., Donna Rose Addis, and Randy L. Buckner. 2007. "Remembering the Past to Imagine the Future: The Prospective Brain." *Nature Reviews Neuroscience* 8(9): 657–61.

Schade, Christian, Howard Kunreuther, and Philipp Koellinger. 2012. "Protecting against Low-Probability Disasters: The Role of Worry." *Behavioral Decision Making* 25(5): 534–43.

Schram, Sanford F., Joe Soss, Richard C. Fording, and Linda Houser. 2009. "Deciding to Discipline: Race, Choice, and Punishment at the Frontlines of Welfare Reform." *American Sociological Review* 74(3): 398–422.

Schwartz, Barry. 1975. *Queuing and Waiting: Studies in the Social Organization of Access and Delay.* Chicago: University of Chicago Press.

Sewell, William H., Jr. 1996. "Historical Events as Transformations of Structures: Inventing Revolution at the Bastille." *Theory and Society* 25(6): 841–81.

Sharkey, Patrick. 2012. "Residential Mobility and the Reproduction of Unequal Neighborhoods." *Cityscape* 14(3): 9–31.

———. 2013. *Stuck in Place: Urban Neighborhoods and the End of Progress toward Racial Equality.* Chicago: University of Chicago Press.

———. 2014. "Spatial Segmentation and the Black Middle Class." *American Journal of Sociology* 119(4): 903–45.

Shapiro, Thomas. 2017. *Toxic Inequality: How America's Wealth Gap Destroys Mobility, Deepens the Racial Divide, and Threatens Our Future.* New York: Basic Books.

Sherman, Jennifer. 2006. "Coping with Rural Poverty: Economic Survival and Moral Capital in Rural America." *Social Forces* 85(2): 891–913.

———. 2009. *Those Who Work, Those Who Don't: Poverty, Morality, and Family in Rural America.* Minneapolis: University of Minnesota Press.

———. 2013. "Surviving the Great Recession: Growing Need and the Stigmatized Safety Net." *Social Problems* 60(4): 409–32.

———. 2021. *Dividing Paradise: Rural Inequality and the Diminishing American Dream.* Oakland: University of California Press.

Siegrest, Michael, and Heinz Gutscher. 2008. "Natural Hazard and Motivation for Mitigation Behavior: People Cannot Predict the Affect Evoked by a Severe Flood." *Risk Analysis* 28(3): 771–78.

Sierminska, Eva, Timothy M. Smeeding, and S. Allegrezza. 2013. "The Distribution of Assets and Debt." In *Economic Disparities and the Middle Class in Affluent Countries,* edited by Janet C. Gornick and Markus Jäntti. Stanford, Calif.: Stanford University Press.

Skobba, Kimberly, and Edward G. Goetz. 2013. "Mobility Decisions of Very Low-Income Households." *Cityscape* 15(2): 155–71.

Small, Mario Luis. 2009a. "How Many Cases Do I Need? On Science and the Logic of Case Selection in Field-Based Research." *Ethnography* 10(1): 5–38.

———. 2009b. *Unanticipated Gains: Origins of Network Inequality in Everyday Life.* New York: Oxford University Press.

———. 2017. *Someone to Talk To.* New York: Oxford University Press.

Small, Mario Luis, and Monica McDermott. 2006. "The Presence of Organizational Resources in Poor Urban Neighborhoods: An Analysis of Average and Contextual Effects." *Social Forces* 84(3): 1697–1724.

Small Business Administration (SBA). 2017. "SBA Disaster Loan Program: Frequently Asked Questions." Washington, D.C.: SBA (August 31). https://www.sba.gov/sites/default/files/articles/sba-disaster-loans-faq.pdf.

———. 2018. "Inspection of SBA's Initial Disaster Assistance Response to Hurricane Harvey." Washington, D.C.: SBA (January 19). https://www.sba.gov/sites/default/files/2019-07/SBA_OIG_Report_18-10.pdf.

Smiley, Kevin T., Junia Howell, and James R. Elliott. 2018. "Disasters, Local Organizations, and Poverty in the USA, 1998 to 2015." *Population and Environment* 40(December): 115–35. DOI: https://doi.org/10.1007/s11111-018-0304-8.

Smith, Kevin B., and Kenneth J. Meier. 1995. "Public Choice in Education: Markets and the Demand for Quality Education." *Public Research Quarterly* 48(3): 461–78.

Smith, Stanley K. 1996. "Demography of Disaster: Population Estimates after Hurricane Andrew." *Population Research and Policy Review* 15(December): 459–77. DOI: https://doi.org/10.1007/BF00125865.

Spilerman, Seymour. 2000. "Wealth and Stratification Processes." *Annual Review of Sociology* 26: 497–524.

Sobel, Adam H., Suzana J. Camargo, Timothy M. Hall, Chia-Ying Lee, Michael K. Tippett, and Allison A. Wing. 2016. "Human Influence on Tropical Cyclone Intensity." *Science* 353(6296): 242–46.

Sullivan, Esther. 2018. *Manufactured Insecurity: Mobile Home Parks and Americans' Tenuous Right to Place.* Oakland: University of California Press.

Sullivan, Teresa A., Elizabeth Warren, and Jay Lawrence Westbrook. 2000. *The Fragile Middle Class: Americans in Debt.* New Haven, Conn.: Yale University Press.

Sykes, Jenifer, Katrin Kriz, Kathryn Edin, and Sarah Halpern-Meekin. 2015. "Dignity and Dreams: What the Earned Income Tax Credit (EITC) Means to Low-Income Families." *American Sociological Review* 80(2): 243–67.

Tach, Laura. 2014. "Diversity, Inequality, and Microsegregation: Dynamics of Inclusion and Exclusion in a Racially and Economically Diverse Community." *Cityscape* 16(3): 13–46.

Tavory, Iddo, and Nina Eliasoph. 2013. "Coordinating Future: Toward a Theory of Anticipation." *American Journal of Sociology* 118(4): 908–42.

Tavory, Iddo, and Stefan Timmermans. 2012. "Theory Construction in Qualitative Research: From Grounded Theory to Abductive Analysis." *Sociological Theory* 30(3): 167–86.

———. 2014. *Abductive Analysis.* Chicago: University of Chicago Press.

Tavory, Iddo, and Robin Wagner-Pacifici. 2021. "Climate Change as an Event." *Poetics* (August). DOI: https://doi.org/10.1016/j.poetic.2021.101600.

Taylor, Dorceta E. 2014. *Toxic Communities: Environmental Racism, Industrial Pollution, and Residential Mobility.* New York: New York University Press.

Taylor, Keeanga-Yamahtta. 2019. *Race for Profit: How Banks and the Real Estate Industry Undermined Black Homeownership.* Chapel Hill: University of North Carolina Press.

Terpstra, Teun, and Michael K. Lindell. 2012. "Citizens' Perceptions of Flood Hazard Adjustments: An Application of the Protective Action Decision Model." *Environmental Behavior* 45(8): 993–1018.

Thiede, Brian C., and David L. Brown. 2013. "Hurricane Katrina: Who Stayed and Why?" *Population Research and Policy Review* 32(6): 803–24.

Thomas, Melvin E., Richard Moye, Loren Henderson, and Hayward Derrick Horton. 2018. "Separate and Unequal: The Impact of Socioeconomic Status,

Segregation, and the Great Recession on Racial Disparities in Housing Values." *Sociology of Race and Ethnicity* 4(2): 229–44.

Thompson, Rebecca R., Dana Rose Garfin, and Roxane Cohen Silver. 2017. "Evacuation from Natural Disaster: A Systematic Review of the Literature." *Risk Analysis* 37(4): 812–39.

Tierney, Kathleen J. 1999. "Toward a Critical Sociology of Risk." *Sociological Forum* 14(2): 215–42.

———. 2007. "From the Margins to the Mainstream? Disaster Research at the Crossroads." *Annual Review of Sociology* 33: 503–25.

———. 2014. *The Social Roots of Risk: Producing Disasters, Supporting Resilience.* Stanford, Calif.: Stanford University Press.

———. 2019. *Disasters: A Sociological Approach.* Cambridge: Polity Press.

Tighe, J. Rosie. 2012. "How Race and Class Stereotyping Shapes Attitudes toward Affordable Housing." *Housing Studies* 27(7): 962–83.

Tilly, Charles. 1998. *Durable Inequality.* Berkeley: University of California Press.

Torche, Florencia. 2011. "Is a College Degree Still the Great Equalizer? Intergenerational Mobility across Levels of Schooling in the United States." *American Journal of Sociology* 117(3): 763–807.

Tormala, Zakary L. 2016. "The Role of Certainty (and Uncertainty) in Attitudes and Persuasion." *Current Opinion in Psychology* 10(10): 6–11.

Townsend, Nicholas W. 2002. *The Package Deal: Marriage, Work, and Fatherhood in Men's Lives.* Philadelphia: Temple University Press.

Tulloch, John, and Deborah Lupton. 2003. *Risk and Everyday Life.* London: Sage Publications.

U.S. Census Bureau. 2017. "Tigerline Shapefiles: Places." Washington: U.S. Department of Commerce. Accessed December 6, 2021. https://www.census.gov/cgi-bin/geo/shapefiles/index.php?year=2017&layergroup=Places.

———. 2018. "Median Household Income, 2014–2018 American Community Survey 5-year Estimates." Social Explorer. Accessed December 6, 2021. https://www.socialexplorer.com/tables/ACS2018_5yr/.

———. 2019a. "Median Household Income, 2015–2019 American Community Survey 5-year Estimates." Social Explorer. Accessed December 6, 2021. https://www.socialexplorer.com/tables/ACS2019_5yr/.

———. 2019b. "Non-Hispanic White Population, 2015–2019 American Community Survey 5-year Estimates." Social Explorer. Accessed December 6, 2021. https://www.socialexplorer.com/tables/ACS2019_5yr/.

Van der Linden, Sander. 2015. "The Social-Psychological Determinants of Climate Change Risk Perceptions: Towards a Comprehensive Model." *Journal of Environmental Psychology* 41(March): 112–24. DOI: https://doi.org/10.1016/j.jenvp.2014.11.012.

Van Holm, Eric Joseph, and Christopher K. Wyczalkowski. 2019. "Gentrification in the Wake of a Hurricane: New Orleans after Katrina." *Urban Studies* 56(13): 2763–78.

Wachinger, Gisela, Ortwin Renn, Chloe Begg, and Christian Kuhlicke. 2013. "The Risk Perception Paradox—Implications for Governance and Communication of Natural Hazards." *Risk Analysis* 33(6): 1049–65.

Wacquant, Loïc. 2009. *Punishing the Poor: The Neoliberal Government of Social Insecurity.* Durham, N.C.: Duke University Press.

Wagner-Pacifici, Robin. 2017. *What Is an Event?* Chicago: University of Chicago Press.

Warikoo, Natasha. 2020. "Addressing Emotional Health while Protecting Status: Asian American and White Parents in Suburban America." *American Journal of Sociology* 126(3): 545–76.

Warren, Elizabeth, and Deborah Thorne. 2012. "A Vulnerable Middle Class: Bankruptcy and Class Status." In *Broke: How Debt Bankrupts the Middle Class,* edited by Katherine Porter. Stanford, Calif.: Stanford University Press.

Watkins-Hayes, Celeste. 2019. *Remaking a Life: How Women Living with HIV/AIDS Confront Inequality.* Chicago: University of Chicago Press.

Waters, Mary C. 2016. "Life after Hurricane Katrina: The Resilience in Survivors of Katrina (RISK) Project." *Sociological Forum* 31(S1): 750–69.

Weber, Lynn, and Lori Peek. 2012. *Displaced: Life in the Katrina Diaspora.* Austin: University of Texas Press.

Weick, Karl E. 1995. *Sensemaking in Organizations.* Thousand Oaks, Calif.: Sage Publications.

Weininger, Elliot B. 2014. "School Choice in an Urban Setting." In *Choosing Homes, Choosing Schools,* edited by Annette Lareau and Kimberly Goyette. New York: Russell Sage Foundation.

Whitmarsh, Lorraine. 2008. "Are Flood Victims More Concerned about Climate Change than Other People? The Role of Direct Experience in Risk Perception and Behavioural Response." *Journal of Risk Research* 11(3): 351–74.

———. 2011. "Scepticism and Uncertainty about Climate Change: Dimensions, Determinants, and Change over Time." *Global Environmental Change* 21(2): 690–700.

Wiedemann, Andreas. 2021. *Indebted Societies: Credit and Welfare in Rich Democracies.* New York: Cambridge University Press.

Wilkinson, Iain. 2001. "Social Theories of Risk Perception: At Once Indispensable and Insufficient." *Current Sociology* 49(1): 1–22.

Winger, Alan R. 1969. "Trade-Offs in Housing." *Land Economics* 45(4): 413–17.

Wisman, Jon D. 2013. "Wage Stagnation, Rising Inequality, and the Financial Crisis of 2008." *Cambridge Journal of Economics* 37(4): 921–45.

Wright, James D., Peter H. Rossi, Sonia R. Wright, and Eleanor Weber-Burdin. 1979. *After the Clean-up: Long-Range Effects of Natural Disasters.* Beverly Hills, Calif.: Sage Publications.

Wrinkle, Robert D., Joseph Stewart Jr., and J. L. Polinard. 1999. "Public School Quality, Private Schools, and Race." *American Journal of Political Science* 43(4): 1248–53.

Wuthnow, Robert. 2013. *Small-Town America: Finding Community, Shaping the Future*. Princeton, N.J.: Princeton University Press.

——. 2017. *American Misfits and the Making of Middle-Class Respectability*. Princeton, N.J.: Princeton University Press.

Zaloom, Caitlin. 2019. *Indebted: How Families Make College Work at Any Cost*. Princeton, N.J.: Princeton University Press.

Zavisca, Jane R., and Theodore P. Gerber. 2016. "The Socioeconomic, Demographic, and Political Effects of Housing in Comparative Perspective." *Annual Review of Sociology* 42: 347–67.

Zelizer, Viviana A. 1994. *The Social Meaning of Money: Pin Money, Paychecks, Poor Relief, and Other Currencies*. New York: Basic Books.

——. 2012. "How I Became a Relational Economic Sociologist and What Does That Mean?" *Politics & Society* 40(2): 145–74.

Zhang, Fuqing, et al. 2007. "An In-Person Survey Investigating Public Perceptions of and Responses to Hurricane Rita Forecasts along the Texas Coast." *Weather and Forecasting* 22(6): 1177–90.

Zhang, Lei. 2016. "Flood Hazards Impact on Neighborhood House Prices: A Spatial Quantile Regression Analysis." *Regional Science and Urban Economics* 60(C): 12–19.

Zhang, Yang, and Walter Gillis Peacock. 2009. "Planning for Housing Recovery? Lessons Learned from Hurricane Andrew." *Journal of the American Planning Association* 76(1): 5–24.

Index

Boldface numbers refer to figures and tables.

developments in flood-prone areas,
5, 125, 129–132, 135, 150; mucking
out after, 17, 86, 97, 175n75; toxic
water and, 51, 57; warning systems
for, 128–129. *See also* flood insurance;
floodplain maps; flood risk
assessment; Hurricane Harvey
Friendswood, Texas, 19–21, 24–40;
appeal of, 16, 21, 27–31, 34–35, 39–40,
177n12; blue-collar residents of, 35–38;
community volunteers for disaster
recovery, 86–90; conservative political
views in, 130–133; development into
middle-class suburb, 31–35; flood risk
mitigation efforts of, 126, 134–138;
growth of, 30; home values following
Hurricane Harvey, 32–37, 39–40;
housing characteristics of, 25–27;
overview, 13–16, **14**, 174–175nn69–74;
racial makeup of, 15, 24–25, **26**, 31–32;
research site selection and, 12–13,
157–158; social infrastructure of,
53–55, 179n17; socioeconomic
diversity in, 15–16, 26–28, **26**, 34,
177n9; white-collar residents of, 38–40

GoFundMe, 120
government post-disaster aid, 78,
79, 80–85, 182n10. *See also* Federal
Emergency Management Agency;
Small Business Administration
gratitude and face-saving, 105, 185n10
guilt and help-seeking behavior, 57,
90–92

Halpern-Meekin, Sarah, 166
Hazard Mitigation Grant Program of
FEMA, 134, 151, 174n58
help-seeking behaviors. *See* local
ecology of aid
Hispanic people, 10, 25
homeowners' associations (HOAs),
25–26, 115

homeownership: cultural ideals and,
24, 176n1; disaster aid eligibility
and, 10; increased costs of, 8, 27–28,
31, 178n20; racism and, 24, 176n2,
177n13, 178n22; risk assessment
responsibility and, 48; wealth and,
27–28, 34, 40
home repairs after Hurricane Harvey:
completed by homeowners, 2,
98–103, 106–107, 119; contractor
issues and, 72, 100, 108–110, 115–116;
fully recovered, 98–104; inequality
in completion rates, 97–98; major
repairs remaining, 112–123; mostly
recovered, 104–112
home values: equity as insurance,
178n21; financial stability and,
6, 8; floodplain maps and, 125;
following Hurricane Harvey, 32–37,
39–40, 68–69, 75–76, 96, 100–101;
neighborhood characteristics
and, 21, 39–40; racial makeup of
neighborhoods and, 27, 40, 177n13;
wealth and, 9, 27–28, 177n13
housing developments in flood-prone
areas, 5, 125, 129–132, 135, 150
Houston, Texas: growth of, 5, 125, 150;
housing characteristics in, 26; map,
14; median household income of,
15, 26, **27**; racial and socioeconomic
characteristics of, **26**, 25–26, 177n9.
See also Friendswood, Texas;
Hurricane Harvey
human ecology framework, 182n6
Hurricane Florence (2018), 11
Hurricane Harvey (2017), 21, 41–61;
characteristics of, 41–42; flooding
caused by, **45**, 48–50; flood insurance
and, 11, 44–48; as freak storm
unlikely to reoccur, 125, 127–128,
131, 144; past storms compared,
42–44; rescue and evacuation, 50–53;

for, 59, 180nn21–24; flood insurance coverage rates and, 11, 185n12; Friendswood and, 31–35; government aid, lack of experience with, 79, 82; long-term planning and stability, 63–64, 181nn11–12; Matthew effect and, 10, 96, 146; privilege and acceptance of risk, 142, 187–188 nn24–25; social capital and infrastructure of neighborhoods, 9–10, 53–55, 179n17

Mileti, Dennis, 5

mortgage forbearances, 180n23

mucking out wet homes, 17, 86, 97, 175n75

National Flood Insurance Program (NFIP), 11, 150, 173–174nn58–59, 185n7

National Hurricane Center (NHC), 41

National Oceanic and Atmospheric Administration (NOAA), 4

National Weather Service, 134

new construction in flood-prone areas, 5, 125, 129–132, 135, 150

Pattillo, Mary, 5, 7

Pew Research Center, 5

poverty: association with race and, 7–8, 182–183n13, 183n19; disaster recovery loan eligibility and, 83; in Friendswood vs. Houston, 177n9; inequality in disaster recovery and, 96; relocating after disasters and, 64; residential segregation and disaster severity, 184n1; social networks and, 184n30; stigma of, 7, 79, 81, 93, 182–183n13, 183n19, 183n25; waiting for government assistance and, 183n19. See also residential segregation; welfare

privilege, 40, 142, 187–188nn24–25. See also White people

race and racism: disaster policy inequality and, 10; environmental racism and, 5, 64; home values and racial makeup of neighborhoods, 27, 40, 177n13; housing financing disadvantages and, 24, 177n13, 178n22; Hurricane Katrina and, 173n54; inequality in disaster recovery and, 96, 185n8; poverty associations with, 7–8, 182–183n13, 183n19; racial hierarchy and, 176n6, 178n18; rule-breaking during emergencies and, 54; school quality perceptions and, 178n19; social networks and support, 180n22, 184n30; wealth gap and, 172n43. See also residential segregation

Raker, Ethan, 173n55

real estate values after disasters, 32–37, 39, 68–69, 75–76, 96, 100–101

Red Cross, 54, 56

Reeves, Richard, 6

Reid, Megan, 183n19

relocating after disasters, 63, 65–70, 74–75, 180n4

rental assistance, 59, 81–82

renters: disaster policy and, 10; flood insurance for, 139; relocating after disasters, 65–68, 74–75

residential plans and post-disaster decisions, 22–23, 62–77; certainty vs. uncertainty on risk of future storms, 130–134, 135–136, 144, 187nn17–18; contingent future plans, 141–143, 187–188nn24–25; financial circumstances and, 69–70, 73–76, 114–116; middle class and, 62–65, 181nn11–12; relocating and, 65–70; returning and, 70–73; vulnerable places and, 72–73, 96–97, 122–123, 149–152